"Furio Cerutti has written a wide-ranging and profound analysis of the nature, the purpose and the morality of politics. In a time of post-truth, fake news, and rising populism across the West he reminds us that the art of government must fail if it does not respect scientific knowledge, and that while it is prudence rather than theoretical knowledge which leads to good choices in politics, clear concepts and rational argumentation are still essential aids. A compelling read."
—*Professor Andrew Gamble, Emeritus Professor of Politics, University of Cambridge*

"The wager on which *Conceptualizing Politics* rests is that by focusing on the concepts fundamental to politics one can break through the complexity ordinarily associated with that subject. On that score this book is an extraordinary success. Recommended not only to those who wish to be introduced to politics but also to those who want to deepen their knowledge of the subject."
—*David M. Rasmussen, Professor, Boston College; Editor-in-Chief, Philosophy and Social Criticism*

CONCEPTUALIZING POLITICS

Politics is hugely complex. Some try to reduce its complexity by examining it through an ideological worldview, a one-size-fits-all prescriptive formula or a quantitative examination of as many 'facts' as possible. Yet politics cannot be adequately handled as if it were made of cells and particles: ideological views are oversimplifying and sometimes dangerous. Politics is not simply a moral matter, nor political philosophy a subdivision of moral philosophy. This book is devised as a basic conceptual lexicon for all those who want to understand what politics is, how it works and how it changes or fails to change. Key concepts such as power, conflict, legitimacy and order are clearly defined and their interplay in the state, interstate and global level explored. Principles such as liberty, equality, justice and solidarity are discussed in the context of the political choices confronting us.

This compact and systematic introduction to the categories needed to grasp the fundamentals of politics will appeal to readers who want to gain a firmer grasp on the workings of politics, as well as to scholars and students of philosophy, political science and history.

Furio Cerutti is professor emeritus of political philosophy at the University of Florence. Ten years of his academic career were spent at the Universities of Heidelberg and Frankfurt am Main and later at Harvard (Law School and later Center for European Studies). He has also been a visiting professor at China Foreign Affairs University, Beijing; London School of Economics; Université de Paris 8; Scuola superiore Sant'Anna, Pisa; Stanford University in Florence.

Cerutti's main two research topics are the theory of politics after modernity (*Global Challenges for Leviathan: A Political Philosophy of Nuclear Weapons and Global Warming*, 2007; 全球治理: 挑战与趋势 [*Global Governance: Challenges and Trends*], 2014) and the theory of political identity and legitimacy, with a focus on the question of European identity (*The Search for a European Identity: Values, Policies and Legitimacy of the European Union*, 2008; *Debating Political Identity and Legitimacy in the European Union*, 2011, both coedited and published by Routledge in the Garnet book series). He is now working on the present significance of the 'future' in political debate and decision making.

CONCEPTUALIZING POLITICS

An Introduction to Political Philosophy

Furio Cerutti

LONDON AND NEW YORK

First published 2017
by Routledge
2 Park Square, Milton Park, Abingdon, Oxon OX14 4RN

and by Routledge
711 Third Avenue, New York, NY 10017

Routledge is an imprint of the Taylor & Francis Group, an informa business

© 2017 Furio Cerutti

The right of Furio Cerutti to be identified as author of this work has been asserted by him in accordance with sections 77 and 78 of the Copyright, Designs and Patents Act 1988.

All rights reserved. No part of this book may be reprinted or reproduced or utilised in any form or by any electronic, mechanical, or other means, now known or hereafter invented, including photocopying and recording, or in any information storage or retrieval system, without permission in writing from the publishers.

Trademark notice: Product or corporate names may be trademarks or registered trademarks, and are used only for identification and explanation without intent to infringe.

British Library Cataloguing-in-Publication Data
A catalogue record for this book is available from the British Library

Library of Congress Cataloging-in-Publication Data
Names: Cerutti, Furio, author.
Title: Conceptualizing politics : an introduction to political philosophy / Furio Cerutti.
Description: Abingdon, Oxon ; New York, NY : Routledge, [2017] | Includes bibliographical references and index.
Identifiers: LCCN 2016046339 | ISBN 9781472475688 (hbk) | ISBN 9781472475718 (pbk) | ISBN 9781315614946 (ebk)
Subjects: LCSH: Political science. | Political science—Philosophy.
Classification: LCC JA71 .C399 2017 | DDC 320.01—dc23
LC record available at https://lccn.loc.gov/2016046339

ISBN: 9781472475688 (hbk)
ISBN: 9781472475718 (pbk)
ISBN: 9781315614946 (ebk)

Typeset in Bembo
by Apex CoVantage, LLC

CONTENTS

List of figures   x
Preface   xi
Acknowledgements   xvii

PART I
What is politics?   1

1 Politics and power   3
   1 A first definition of politics 4
   2 Power and political power 9
   3 Operating areas, instruments and modus operandi *of political power 11*
   4 Political power and the others 13
   5 Objections and consequences 14
   6 Politics and power, a fatal connection? 17

2 The subjective side of politics: legitimacy, identity, obligation   24
   1 Legitimacy and legitimation 25
   2 Political identity 28
   3 Political obligation 33

   Excursus 1: What is political philosophy?   36

PART II
How politics works   45

3 Order, institutions, models   47
   1 What does order mean in politics? 47
   2 Rules, institutions and the regulation of fear 49
   3 Historic models of political order 52

4 The state   57
   1 The state and sovereignty 57
   2 The rise of the modern state in Europe 59
   3 State and society 64
   4 State and nation 67
   5 The state and the law 70
   6 State and values 72

5 Government and democracy   79
   1 Democracy one and two 81
   2 From representation to national democracy 83
   3 Democratic government 86
   4 How is democracy possible? Does it have alternatives? 95
   5 Democracy and capitalism 98

PART III
World politics and the future of politics   105

6 The states: power, peace and war in anarchical society   107
   1 The anarchical international society 108
   2 War 112
   3 Restraints to war, or peace? 115
   4 The pacification of Europe 120

7 The globalised world: a challenge to politics   126

   Part I: Globalisation and global governance   127
   1 What is globalisation? 127
   2 Globalisation and politics 128
   3 Global governance? 131

   Part II: Global/lethal challenges: politics after modernity   134
   4 The two present challenges 135
   5 What to do with future generations? 140

6 Politics after modernity: another definition 143
  7 Global troubles for democracy 145

  Excursus 2: Politics and death   151

PART IV
Ethics and politics   **157**

  8 Liberty, equality and rights   159
    1 Concepts of liberty 159
    2 Equality and egalitarianism 163
    3 Rights 168
    4 Rights: universal or not? 170

  9 Justice and solidarity   175
    1 Versions of justice 176
    2 Distributive justice 177
    3 Solidarity 181

  10 Ethics, philosophy and politics   187
    1 Ethics and politics 187
    2 Which ethics for politicians? 190
    3 For and against ideal theory 193
    4 Critical Theory 195

    Epilogue: what drives people to politics   201

Index   206

FIGURES

1.1	Reconstruction of the western pediment of the Parthenon, Athens (Source: Courtesy of the photographer Telemahos Efthimiadis, Athens)	8
3.1	Persepolis (Source: Photograph taken at the archaeological site of Persepolis by Renata Carloni and Furio Cerutti, December 2014)	49
5.1	NHS scene at the London 2012 Olympic Opening Ceremony (Source: Released by Agenzia Contrasto, Rome on behalf of the copyright owner, NYTCREDIT: Doug Mills/ *The New York Times.* © *The New York Times*)	94
7.1	Levels of greenhouse gases (Source: Courtesy of the Intergovernmental Panel on Climate Change, Geneva. It reproduces Figure SPM.1 from *Climate Change 2007: The Physical Science Basis. Working Group I Contribution to the Fourth Assessment Report of the Intergovernmental Panel on Climate Change* [Solomon, S., D. Qin, M. Manning, Z. Chen, M. Marquis, K. B. Averyt, M. Tignor and H. L. Miller (eds.)]. Cambridge and New York: Cambridge University Press 2007)	139
9.1	*Fraternité* (Source: Courtesy of the Gallica Collection, Bibliothèque nationale de France, Paris, Département Estampes et photographie, RESERVE QB-370 (45)-FT. More information at http://catalogue.bnf.fr/ark:/12148/cb40255796v)	183

PREFACE

This book is devised as a basic tool for all those who, faced with politics, want first of all to understand it – to understand what politics is, how it works and how it changes or fails to change. In the Western tradition since the ancients (Aristotle and Cicero much more than Plato) and down to Immanuel Kant and John Rawls, this endeavour to understand politics has been pursued by creating and refining concepts capable of identifying its basic structures, constraints and normative alternatives. Concepts, or more exactly, categories, are the protagonists of this book; they require an attitude of abstract thinking capable of providing us with some orientation in the wide sea of events, processes, conflicting claims. As Max Weber and Norberto Bobbio knew, sticking to conceptual clarity and using an atlas of this region of human life make the best starting point for an unbiased inquiry into what politics is as well as into the possibility and the limits of change and reform – an inquiry that should accompany any attempt at giving politics and policy making one or another direction according to one's own preferences. Politics as a tentatively rational activity needs a clear picture of its own architecture in order to keep illusion, self-delusion and ideological confusion away from itself – not an easy business indeed.

Concepts, however, are intended here not so much as they develop in the history of political ideas, which will appear on the stage only briefly and only where strictly necessary, but rather as forms of reflection ('conceptualization') on things, that is on processes taking place – primarily in our time – in the polities and the societies associated with them. Very much unlike in works aimed at devising ideal polities, in this book history, political science and anthropology will therefore play a role in the description of the stuff – political experiences of groups, peoples and humankind – that we are trying to adequately conceptualize. Yet notwithstanding all cross-fertilisation with other disciplines, in particular history, this book's approach to politics remains highly philosophical. It tries – hence the title – to put the world of politics in concepts. The final result is expected to be a conceptual lexicon of politics.

As to normative categories, besides giving an account of the general debate on them, they will be introduced mainly in the specific configuration in which they arise from new evolutionary achievements and challenges (the uncertain future of liberal democracy; globalisation malaise; lethal threats such as the existence of nuclear weapons and the worsening of climate change). The search for an overarching formula of justice or freedom has in its generality little significance for the real politics addressing and afflicting real human beings. In the same line of thinking, fictional examples of moral dilemmas or behavioural prescriptions regarding the insulated individual – so frequent in writings somehow influenced by the analytic tradition – will not be discussed here, since people act in politics as associated individuals, or as citizens congregated in groups, movements, parties, nations under political or social rather than moral premises.

Is this a book just for philosophers? Hardly so. For readers with some background in philosophy and political science it will obviously be an easier read; but a good level of general culture and an ability to follow a formal, though not mathematized argument is indeed sufficient. What is then the point of reading this book? The following, I would think: if you want to achieve some unconventional understanding or practical orientation in front of the questions you feel to be confronted with while watching the news or going to the polls, a measure of abstract and overarching, hence philosophical, reconsideration of the issues at stake is a necessary help.

This textbook has the ambition to be possibly readable to not only a Western readership. I am fully aware that my underlying knowledge of the history and politics of non-European peoples does not match this ambition often enough; on the other hand a truly worldwide view on politics and history is still a fledgling. Besides, this book does not conceal its strong, though critically reconsidered roots in Western, especially European, culture and politics. Politics, and the thinking of it, does not exist without what I understand as political identity. Yet this is not irreconcilable, I like to think, with the scholarly attitude to give representation to all the relevant notions and opinions out of not just of tolerance, but curiosity as well. These used to be leading virtues of European modernity on its sunny side and should not stop before the multifarious and puzzling life-forms of politics.

★ ★ ★

What follows is a summary of the book, presented in a narrative style.

Politics in its reality allocates resources and settles conflicts by the use of a type of power that is guaranteed by force, but in order to achieve acceptance and stability, political power must be able to legitimate itself, drawing on the values and principles that lie at the core of political group identity. Only legitimate power can generate a sense of political obligation and keep the polity together, thus allowing for peaceful conflict resolution and prevention – on the other hand, sooner or later the resource operated by political power is bound to generate new conflicts (Part I).

Politics, whatever the actors' goals, generates on the whole some kind of order, which is underpinned by institutions. In political philosophy, several models of order – descriptive accounts of the origins of the polity and/or prescriptive designs of the 'best polity' – can be (and are here summarily) identified. With all of this in mind, the core political institution, the state, can be now defined, also in its relationship to society, the nation, the law and more in general to values. How can the state be ruled? This is the thorny subject matter of the chapter on government and democracy; on the latter a demythologizing view is proposed (Part II).

Next step: the state, and in particular the modern state, since the Peace of Westphalia of 1648 cannot be understood without widening our vision to the states or the international system. War, peace and the widening web of international institutions – what can be called the 'anarchical society' – are described, especially with an eye on the European Union as an example of non-imperial pacification. The evolution of war towards nuclear war makes it, at the same time, unavailable as a Clausewitzian instrument of politics and suicidal for humankind and its civilisation. This is seen as the original global (and lethal) challenge, which can only be addressed if politics will be able to go beyond its classical definition mentioned above and will also (a problematic coexistence of different tasks!) become able to take care of the global commons and the survival of civilisation – this is the turn from modern to post-modern politics (nothing to do with the postmodernists' views!). The specific features of the second global challenge – climate change – are discussed with regard to our attitude towards future generations (Part III).

In the end (Part IV), the relationship between morality and politics is examined, along with the main categories of normative political philosophy: liberty, equality, justice and – unlike in other accounts – solidarity. The main positions and the open problems in these fields – including those concerning human and fundamental rights – will be presented, along with the difficulties raised by any temptation to see moral and political philosophy as identical. A brief look at Critical Theory concludes this Part. But the volume also contains an Epilogue recapitulating all that drives us to political action as well as two Excurses: the first deals with the nature and limits of political philosophy, the second, with the philosophically significant relationship of politics and death.

Lastly, this book does not contain a chapter on gender because I prefer giving this fundamental and transversal issue the appropriate relevance wherever it comes into an interplay with other political categories.

How to use this textbook

Beyond the philosophical reflections that are the main content of this book, the hints at world history and world politics, the stuff from which my political philosophy is drawn, require enough space in and of themselves so that any additional content would overburden the volume and make it thicker in pages than I wanted. This is why the reader will not find here what can be easily retrieved on the Internet, from the description of events (such as battles, peace treaties, revolutions and parliamentary votes) to the biographies of notable protagonists (only the year of birth and death is indicated for a preliminary orientation; living persons' names carry no such indication). This notwithstanding, to put some flesh around conceptual definitions, I have sometimes cited historical or economic or sociological facts that may not be immediately present to the mind of non-European readers.

The References at the end of each chapter contain the sources of the texts quoted in that chapter, which are kept at a minimum. Additionally, each chapter, as well this introductory note, is complemented with the indication of Further readings, in case the reader wants to learn more about certain topics. For ease of access, whenever possible, the e-version of books and articles is cited instead of the hard copy. Wherever it is important to know the year of composition or first publication of a book, this year is quoted, while the publication year of the edition actually used comes at the end of the entry.

Titles are quoted in their original language, followed by the English translation (italicised if corresponding to a published edition). Only on two or three occasions was it necessary to refer to a work lacking an English translation. I have introduced concepts based on ancient Greek and Latin using these languages, as well as in sporadic cases Arabic, Chinese and Russian words.

There is, in my view, a twin rationale for doing so. First, the triumph of English as *lingua franca*, a blessing for international understanding and scientific communication, should not lead to erasing the use of all other languages. It is as curious as it is lamentable that the love for diversity, celebrated with some pomp everywhere in Western societies, must stop at the language barrier, beyond which all is homogenised in English as if Babel had never existed or were still a divine punishment to be finally remedied. The other reason is that giving up all linguistic multiplicity and all erudition with the alleged aim of making a book or a discipline accessible to everybody makes them intellectually poorer, while a less standardised linguistic sensitivity remains open only to students of the very best and exclusive universities around the world. In some measure, it would amount to a hidden contribution to even more inequality.

In any case, the tiny opening made to *linguistic diversity* in this book is a signal and an offer to those who accept this stimulation, and an act of respect towards readers of mother tongues other than English. But do not make any mistake: the book can be fully read and completely understood in English only.

Conventional wisdom holds that political philosophy, as a purely conceptual exercise, is foreign to visual elements. In the case of a textbook, this is not necessarily true, but my wish to use *images* to complement the conceptual communication of the book's contents has been to a large extent frustrated by complicated copyright concerns. The reader will thus find only a few illustrations printed in this volume; for the remaining chapters I have sometimes indicated web links leading to the images I intended to show. The reader will choose whether or not to make use of them.

★ ★ ★

My MOOC (massive open online course) *Political Philosophy: An Introduction*, recorded in the Palagio di Parte Guelfa in Florence in 2013–14, is still available

(2016) on the <iversity.org> platform, Berlin. It follows to a good extent the same road map as this textbook, but does not overlap with it.

Inspiration for this approach to political philosophy, which has been influencing my teaching for the past twenty-five years, came originally from the articles written in the 1970s by Norberto Bobbio for the *Enciclopedia Einaudi* and later translated by Peter Kennealy into English. In 1989, they were published by Polity Press, Oxford under the infelicitous, then fashionable title *Democracy and Dictatorship: The Nature and Limits of State Power;* in it the subtitle is the true title, better corresponding to the original *Stato, governo, società*. I still recommend this book as a whole and will quote from it (Bobbio 1989) in the Further Readings.

General reference

There are two main reference works for philosophy in general online, which also contain entries regarding political philosophy, though our field is not their main focus:

1. *The Stanford Encyclopedia of Philosophy*, available at http://plato.stanford.edu/
2. *The Internet Encyclopedia of Philosophy*, available at www.iep.utm.edu/

As far as *Wikipedia* is concerned, it can and should be obviously widely used, provided the readers are able to distinguish well-carved and complete entries from those still in need of some or much additional work.

For a more analytical orientation tour in our field, two handbooks are useful:

Estlund, David (2012) *The Oxford Handbook of Political Philosophy*, Oxford: Oxford University Press.
Gaus, Gerald and Fred D'Agostino, eds. (2013) *The Routledge Companion to Social and Political Philosophy*, London: Routledge.

Whoever wishes to know more on a scholarly key about a number of categories, in particular normative in character, addressed in this book can make use of

Besussi, Antonella, ed. (2012) *A Companion to Political Philosophy*, Farnham: Ashgate.

Given this book's theoretical rather than historical approach, an indispensable complement to it is a history of political philosophy. For a preliminary orientation see:

Klosko, George, ed. (2011) *The Oxford Handbook of the History of Political Philosophy*, Oxford: Oxford University Press.

Not to forget is a classical work, whose chapters deal each with a major thinker:

Strauss, Leo and Joseph Cropsey, eds. (1987) *History of Political Philosophy*, 3rd edition, Chicago: The University of Chicago Press.

Since one thing is how philosophers of the past conceived of politics and polity, and quite a different thing how these effectively developed, equally important would be a worldwide comparative *history of political institutions*, which does not, however, exist. For Europe, two now classical research works can be cited:

Rokkan, Stein (1999) *State Formation, Nation-Building, and Mass Politics in Europe*, edited by Peter Flora *et al.*, Oxford: Oxford University Press.
Tilly, Charles, ed. (1975) *The Formation of National States in Western Europe*, Princeton: Princeton University Press.

ACKNOWLEDGEMENTS

My students of the some twenty-five years in which I gave an introductory course at the University of Florence and, later, at the international Ph.D. School, Scuola Superiore Sant'Anna, Pisa, along with the followers – primarily from India and Pakistan – of my MOOC since 2013, deserve my gratitude for the many questions raised and remarks made, from which I was able to learn a lot.

A number of colleagues and friends were so kind as to read one or more of the chapters: Stefano Burzo, Ian Carter, Dimitri D'Andrea, Anna Loretoni, Sonia Lucarelli, Rodolfo Ragionieri, Bernardino Regazzoni, Enno Rudolph, Vivien Schmidt, Mario Telò. Their criticism and their suggestions have been invaluable and have greatly improved the text. Any mistakes or omissions remain my own.

I also remain grateful to Kirstin Howgate, then at Ashgate, my original publisher before the merger with Routledge, for accepting to publish this book.

Aura Frangioni, the last student who graduated at Florence under my guidance before my retirement, has been my research assistant in the preparation of this volume. I also owe her some philosophical remark on the text. My English has been edited by Molly A. (Flynn) Tanş, a Ph.D. student at Trinity College, Dublin. I am very grateful to both ladies not only for the work they have done, but also for the kindness and friendship with which it was done.

It was a joy to write this book under the loving watch of my wife Renata Carloni, who also gave me some helpful pieces of advice. The book is dedicated to her.

PART I
What is politics?

1
POLITICS AND POWER

What is politics?

This book begins questioning the very notion it is dedicated to, because with a philosophical approach, notions are not left in the unclear state in which they are used in common parlance. This shall be our method all throughout the book. But in the case of politics, a preliminary clarification is required even more so, given the array of meanings and nuances this word comes surrounded with. In the last decades the century-old endeavour to define politics according to a core goal such as the pursuit of the common good or the reconciliation of interests has mostly been abandoned, as scholars of politics have got to acknowledge that – given the irreducible plurality of conflicting aims that political actors pursue – no common language about politics could materialise, no convergence on questions such as: who is entitled to define what the common good is? is reconciliation of interests truly possible and, what is more, is it to everyone's advantage instead of one party's?

Rather than insisting on a teleological approach,[1] scholars of politics have increasingly seen it as characterised by the items this human activity makes use of (power, influence, force) or results in (making collective decisions). This turn away from goal-setting has thus been looking for an encompassing formula capable of describing what kind of actions and phenomena take place under the heading 'politics', whatever aims, ideals or projects actors may strive for. Real individual and collective actors remain obviously highly teleological: they all pursue their own particular goals and uphold their particular (even if they are universalistic in content)[2] values, thereby colliding or striving to form coalitions. Time and again they come to some (never perpetual) agreement as to the *framework of rules* under which to realise one's own interests and life plans in an ordered and peaceful way. This is what the polity or πολις/*polis* is about, as we shall see in the following chapters.

Against this background political philosophy is an attempt to understand the structures that originate from the games actors play with and against each other, the rules they set up willingly or unwillingly, and the principles under which they try to justify and coordinate their actions. Only on the basis of this complex understanding does it make sense for political philosophy to evaluate general goals such as justice, or the models of society such as democracy that actors mean to pursue in their political life. Without this frame of reference, mere normative indications as to how best shape the polity must remain futile. The political philosophy the reader will become acquainted with in these pages is rather different from what is meant by this expression in today's mainstream literature.

1. A first definition of politics

On these premises I am now introducing the first, classical definition of politics: it is *the social activity in which scarce and unequally distributed resources are allocated among conflicting parties by an authority whose legitimate power is guaranteed by force.*

No doubt this is a highly conceptual and squared-off description of a multi-faceted phenomenon. It follows the pattern used over sixty years ago by David Easton (1953). It is not the only image of politics to be found in this volume: recent developments, which shall not be anticipated here, have created the necessity to add a second definition, to be formulated in Chapter 7, Part II. Now, the best way to make good use of it is in the disassembling of its singular components, which we will comment upon separately: 1. activity, 2. resources, 3. conflict, 4. power and force, 5. legitimacy/authority. Components 1–4 are explained in this chapter, while the fifth one requires a separate and much larger discussion, which will be undertaken in Chapter 2.

★ ★ ★

1. Politics is one of the activities human beings perform socially, possessing features that make it a very *special* social activity – working them out and preventing politics from being merged with society and social activity at large will be a principal care of this book. Politics remains in some respect what used to be in old times dubbed 'the art of government', that is, an eminent practical issue, and all attempts made in the time of positivism at establishing a 'scientific politics' could not but fail. To put it with the ancients, it is not theoretical knowledge (σοφία/ *sophia*), but prudence (φρόνησις/*phronesis*) that leads us to good choices in politics. *Sophia*, in the meaning of clear, non-illusionary concepts and a habit of rational argumentation, can however be a great help in making the right choices in awareness of the consequences. This is why the insufficient ability or willingness of sectors of today's politics to take good note of what science has to say about the world that we have to govern, be it economic insights or warnings concerning new technologies. The 'art of government' must fail if it does not respect scientific knowledge, as we shall see in the chapter on global/lethal challenges.
2. The *resources* involved in political struggle can be material (territory, energy sources, precious metals, financial capital) or positional/relational; in this case they only exist in the actors' relationships and beliefs, as it was once the case with glory and honour and is nowadays with prestige, status and credibility.[3]

To be politically relevant, resources must be scarce[4] or unequally distributed or both (relative scarcity is the most frequent case), thus generating conflicts among particular actors, each striving to redress the inequalities in her/his/its favour,[5] or in the best case in favour of the majority. Were actors altruistic and not interested in a different distribution of resources, there would be no politics. 'If men were angels, no government would be necessary', as James Madison (1751–1836) put it in *The Federalist* No. 51 (Hamilton et al. 1788, 266).

3. Scarce and unequally distributed resources lead to *conflict*, but the typology of conflict goes beyond those around resources. First and foremost we have to elucidate what we mean by conflict. Unlike in International Relations[6] or the media's language, in political philosophy as well as in theoretical sociology conflict does not mean armed conflict or war, and is rather seen as a general structure of social and political interaction. This meaning goes as far back as Heraclitus of Ephesus (BCE 535–475), who in his Fragment 53 wrote that 'πόλεμος/*polemos* (strife, conflict, war) is both father of all and king of all'. For a conceptual definition of conflict we turn to Max Weber's (1864–1920) formula for struggle, but also modify it slightly: *it is the social relationship in which an actor strives to affirm her/his/its own preferences against other actors' resistance.*[7]

Let us remark that here as everywhere in philosophical definitions we abstain from overburdening the definition with any anthropological reference to the actor's 'will' (as Weber still did) or 'interest' that may lie behind her/his/its preferences; that the actor has preferences of whatever origin is all we need to know in order to examine their affirmation being rejected or resisted by other actors. To be minimalistic is a good premise for essential and elegant definitions.

The definition we have just given comprises all possible sorts of conflict, as defined by the use of violent or non-violent *means* (bargaining, arguments, persuasion, blackmail) or by the type of settlement (military victory, electoral success, favourable legal sentence, arbitration, agreement without manifest losers as in win-win games). More substantial is, however, the typology of conflict according to its field or source: conflict of interest, identity conflict, ideological conflict.[8]

Conflict of interest revolves around the acquisition of a larger slice of material or positional resources by actors that remain separated even if they may, in certain cases, coalesce. Self-interest remains their leading or exclusive driving force; among the participants in a coalition, no sense of a shared identity arises. As long as one has a clear mind about the interest s/he or it pursues, the prevailing course of action is led by either strategic or instrumental rationality: this means searching for the most efficient ways to achieve the outcome envisioned, in other words, for the best means in order to get to the goal indicated by self-interest. These means can include manipulating or coercing men and women, treating them in a strategic attitude; here 'strategic' (closely connected to 'instrumental') has nothing to do with the military and means employing whatever or whoever you may deem useful as a means for achieving a goal that is not itself an object of deliberation.

It is a still widespread reductionism of alleged Marxist origin to see the conflict of interest as the paramount or exclusive type of conflict, as if the others were its mere derivatives. They are not, and to think so precludes an articulate understanding of political behaviour. 'Identity conflict' has a very different nature, which is better understandable if we talk more properly of a *conflict for the recognition of one's own political identity*. What political identity is will be explained in a later chapter; it is sufficient for now to think of it as the sense of belonging that keeps the members of a political group together.

Political identity can refer to a new or renewed (the former fascist countries, but also France after 1945) nation, a party, a social movement (industrial workers in the nineteenth century) or a cultural and political movement (feminism in the second half of the twentieth century). The recognition they look for is two-sided: it comes from the prospective members of the new actor, whom the initiators try to involve and convince, and from external players (the former imperial or colonial power, the existing members of the political system, international institutions). The new identity is not pre-existent to the struggle for recognition, and ripens only in the course of it – often in the fractured shape of opposing factions, as happened with national liberation movements. To make this visible, one only needs to replay the evolution of his country's or her party's identity. Identity formation and struggle for recognition are self-standing processes of cultural and political nature, deeply rooted in human anthropology, and in as much they accompany political life everywhere. By no means can they be reduced to their pathological developments such as nationalism or religious fanaticism and easily dismissed, as they represent a major moment in what in the second chapter of this Part I shall call 'the subjective side of politics'.

There are obviously intersections between identity formation processes on the one hand and coalitions based on rationalised self-interest on the other. A new group striving to assert its identity may sometimes coincide with a coalition of people interested in gaining more wealth against formerly privileged groups. But the overlapping is never so broad and frequent as to allow for the assumption of a systematic coincidence; what is more, the drivers in identity struggles are essentially different from the materialistic and calculating mentality that dominates conflict of interest.

Ideological conflict comes closer to identity conflict, but should not be mistaken for it. At stake here is not the consolidation of a new collective actor and its recognition by other players, but rather its self-identification by a unifying and defining conception of humankind's or a nation's destiny – what in German is called *Weltanschauung* or conception of the world. *Weltanschauungen* are mostly exclusive and universalistic ideologies; they include all the possible faithful and deny the rights of all others. Soviet Communism in the Cold War was the paramount example,[9] though some versions of Western ideology did not display a higher degree of inclusiveness. Throughout history monotheistic religions have time and again played the role of expansive and truth-touting ideologies; the recent emergence of fundamentalist and murderous positions in the Islamic world is witness to the fact that ideological conflict has not ended with the Cold War.

The three types of conflict are, in Max Weber's words, 'ideal types', in the sense that they design conceptual models that only rarely come up in reality in their pure form and unmixed with each other. Concrete conflicts are often a mix of two or more types, in which, however, one type is prevailing and defining. This can be said of the archetypical conflict that opposes *men to women*, though often we should speak of sheer oppression and exploitation rather than conflict, because the element of resistance is weak or absent. Beyond all anthropological, socio-economic and religious aspects, this conflict also heeds direct political moments, as in the long-lasting exclusion of women from electoral franchise (even in Switzerland until 1971) and in the war against women (exclusion from education in Taliban-ruled Afghanistan until 2001 and in Taliban-infiltrated areas of Pakistan, later kidnapping, raping, enslavement of women and young girls in Africa and the Middle East after 2011) waged by Islamist[10] terror groups since the end of the twentieth century. In light of these events, the ideological conflict pursued by an extreme version of Islam with its moderate versions and with liberal cultures comes together with the defence of the economic, social and political privileges men enjoy in societies in which the patriarchal power structures have so far survived all attempts at cultural modernisation. The cruel and despising attitude towards women (as well as lesbian, gay, bisexual and transgender or LGBT people) displayed in this war binds together a political defence of privileges within the family and the community with pre-political, allegedly religious sense of superiority deeply rooted in a fragile and aggressive male identity, bred on violence. In this fusion the presence of both the ideological and the identity moment nourishes *fanaticism*, an attitude completely opposed to a reasonable way to manage politics and nonetheless so coessential to all conflicts in which gender, race, ethnic and religious aspects have played a role – from the persecution of heretics in the European Middle Ages through the totalitarianisms of the twentieth century to jihadism.

This differentiated account of conflict has a twofold sense. The practical sense is that whatever regime actors may choose for their polity, they must know how to come to terms with conflict in its three-tiered configuration and renounce any attempt at reducing the three types to just one, for example falling into the self-delusion that a settling of interest-based conflicts can also dissolve an identity conflict. Theoretically, the core question asks whether or not conflict is conducive to good politics, whether politics should get rid of it or coexist with it. This question sounds very normative, as if we were at this stage in the position to say what good politics is, or more in general as if the search for a 'good' model of politics were this book's leading aim, which it is not. All of this will become clear later.

Different that the models of politics people have in mind may be, one feature is likely to be common to all or nearly all of them: 'good politics' always contains a certain degree of order and regularity, which makes the life of the people somehow possible, whatever the degree of liberty, equality or happiness the regime makes room for. Daily shoot-outs or complete administrative chaos – as we shall better see in Chapter 3 – do not fulfil what the people expect from politics. But how to bring about this result? Should conflict be regarded as a threat to civil (in the sense of non-feral) order and be possibly eliminated or marginalised? Does good politics mean an order in which conflict is prevented from coming up, and conflict-less integration is the supreme aim? This is the *integrationist path* in social and political theory, prevailing in antiquity (Aristotle, BCE 384–322) and the Middle Ages (Aquinas,

FIGURE 1.1 The reconstructed west pediment of the Parthenon. In the middle is the contest, won by the goddess, between Athena and Poseidon for the patronage over the city.

1225–1274), but also in Thomas Hobbes (1588–1679), who pushed Aristotelianism out of political thought,[11] and later thinkers as different as Auguste Comte (1798–1857), Herbert Spencer (1820–1903) and the theoretical sociologist Talcott Parsons (1902–1979). Other theorists maintained that a degree of regulated conflict is vital to politics, as a safeguard for freedom and as a motor of change for the better. In his commentary on Livy, written in 1513–1519 and published in 1531, Niccolò Machiavelli (1469–1527) praised the institutionalisation of conflict between the Senate and the common people as the masterpiece of Roman politics (Machiavelli 1531, *passim*). *The Federalist* and the very Constitution of the United States regard political conflict as a constitutive element of the new polity and attempt at handling it in a system of checks-and-balances. Carl Schmitt (1888–1985) went as far as to regard the relationship between friend and enemy (whoever is 'existentially something different and alien', 1927, 27) as the very essence of politics – a hypostisation[12] of enmity that goes beyond the seminal importance of conflict.

As we will see later in more detail, democracy is by definition the regime that regards conflict and diversity as its core moment along with the rules preventing conflict from becoming murderous for the citizens' lives and freedoms and disruptive for their safety and wellbeing. Conflict becomes proceduralized, which means that shared procedures are provided to come to terms with it; procedures that facilitate a temporary solution, which is to an extent pregnant with future conflicts, to be met again by the same or modified procedures. In this sense, democracy is the culmination of the *conflictualist path*, whose philosophical background is vividly illustrated by Max Weber's picture of an irreducible 'politheism' of values. By saying 'politheism' Weber likened the plurality of conflicting values upheld in the various belief system inside a society or among cultures to the many gods and goddesses honoured in Greek and Roman mythology – as shown in both Parthenon pediments in Athens (see Figure 1.1) and celebrated in the temple called Pantheon ('all gods') in Rome.[13]

In other corners of political thinking, the alternative of conflict and integration is stretched over time: Marx and Engels saw class struggle as the motor of history and lastly emancipation, but their picture of the coming communist society is highly integrationist (plenty of wealth, full self-realisation of the individuals, the government brought down to a minimal technical function).

Procedures can, at best, provide the tracks on which conflicts unfold and are handled. What makes the characteristics of politics is that conflicts are sooner or later settled by power, the next station of our disassembled definition of politics.

2. Power and political power

While we all welcome the power of the sun to make life on earth possible or enjoy the purchasing power of our salary, when it comes to political power, many are likely to be wary of it or to loathe it from the outset. We will discuss later our attitude towards this ambiguous notion, but let us first find an agreement on what we mean by it.

For power in human and social relationships we have an overarching definition, which is in its simplicity logically elegant: power it is *the ability of actor A to make actor B (or actors B, C, D . . .) act as B would not otherwise act.* This definition is called relational because power is all-defined as a feature intrinsic to and deriving from the relationships among actors. It tells us nothing about the actors or the tools used by them, and it does without 'thick' notions such as will or interest. Power is not just actual power, as it is rather an ability – as Thomas Hobbes noted – projecting itself in the future, promising to bring us 'some future apparent Good' (Hobbes 1651, 58).

In this definition B would not act like that without A's intervention, but not necessarily because s/he or it is opposed to A's indications. For example, traffic laws and the enforcing agencies have the power to make a boy or girl who is learning to drive respect traffic rules, not however against their will or interest – on the road, driving by the rules is first of all in my own interest. Maybe we simply did not know about them, and do easily agree to submit to them; but without the power of the parliament passing the rules and the administration enforcing them, we would not drive in a regular manner;[14] on the other hand, finding on every ride an agreement on how to drive with all other traffic participants would be infeasible, time-wasting and lastly life-destroying. Political power with the same formal features (legislation+enforcement in a sovereign polity) can result either in top-down impositions ('pay more taxes', 'obey the conscription law and go to the front') or in binding central coordination, as in the case cited.

Now, the scattered presence of this second moment of coordination does not go as far as to justify Hannah Arendt's definition of power as 'to act in concert' (Arendt 1972, 143); this is a shapeless view on power and does not at all fit political power, from which the moments of verticality and asymmetry (see §6 in this chapter) cannot be removed. Even power instances in which the moment of coordination is significant cannot be seen as a 'concert' of equal voices, because in any case the coordinator possesses a better knowledge of the process than everybody else and insofar also more power.

All-inclusive (from the economy to human relationships in the family) as it is in its abstractness, the relational definition is a good basis for understanding power, though not capable of closing in on what we strive to grasp in its specificity: *political* power. We move therefore to a second definition, which indicates the instrument used by political power to assert itself, insofar as adding to the formal structure described in the first definition an element related to its content. This second instrumental or substantive[15] definition reads: *A's ability to make B act as B would not otherwise do constitutes political power if it is guaranteed in the very last instance by A being able to use or threaten force for the implementation of her/his/its preferences.* We will later see how in the entities called states, political power is endowed with the legitimate monopoly of force.

It is wrong to say that political power consists primarily or exclusively of *force*. Not even the prince of political realism, Niccolò Machiavelli, went so far, given that in Chapter XII of *Il Principe/The Prince* he wrote that state power relies on both 'good laws' and 'good armies' (Machiavelli 1532, 42). It is one thing to say that power uses or threatens force in the first place in order to impose its preferences; it is a very different thing to say that domestically or internationally political power sometimes uses force, but mostly employs other procedures to assert itself, while in any case, these other procedures are backed by A's and B's knowledge that, if they fail, force could (but will not necessarily) be in the very last instance brought to bear. B can be a tax evader, in the countries in which tax evaders can be given prison sentences, or a region on its way to unilaterally seceding from the home country, or a state caught in an irreconcilable tension with state A. Guaranteeing A's power is different from being the whole of it, while force remains in the 'horizon of expectations'[16] of the participants of a political game. More on the link between political power and force as well as on the notion of influence will be said in the following.

Instead of force we can almost interchangeably say *violence*. I do not see chances for a conceptual distinction to be established, not at all in the untenable sense that force is legitimate whereas violence is not. When we say violence we are simply putting the accent on how B perceives the effect of the physical force applied by A on her or his body. Force or violence though it be, it is nearly always – except in duels between princes, abounding in literature rather than in history – *organised* force or violence (police forces domestically; armies, navies, air forces and cyber war units internationally), as political interaction happens among collective actors such as parties or countries.

Power guaranteed by force is not the only way how actor A can change the behaviour of actor B. Going back to the relational definition, A can try to drive B to acting as B would have not otherwise acted also without relying on the guarantee of last resort provided by force and without expecting B to act in a binding way according to A's preferences. In this case we speak of *influence* rather than power, a concept that explains many an interaction in the political field and is particularly important in international relations. Influence is however a complement rather than an alternative to political power guaranteed by force, which mostly finds its culmination and stabilisation in state power, supported by the monopoly of legitimate force.

3. Operating areas, instruments and *modus operandi* of political power

After defining political power, let us now look at the essential features with which it appears and works; then at its operating areas, instruments and *modus operandi*.

First, it is mostly *institutionalised* and *legitimate*. What institutions and what legitimacy are will be examined later, but let us hold that political power, even if originated by a revolution or coup or military defeat, has the tendency to last over time, to percolate into a stable framework of rules and authority and to resonate with the preferences and the models the population, or its majority, has in mind when thinking about the polity.

Second, it includes on the side of those ruled some possible degree of *voluntary compliance* with the preferences of the power holders. This excludes that a regime mostly consisting of the use or threat of force can be sensibly regarded as a form of political power. Forced dependence on arbitrary rule should be called *domination*[17] rather than power; in the extreme case we have to do with state terrorism. In many European countries the Nazi occupation regime (1939 or later–1944 or 1945) was sheer domination by state terrorism and could not be said to be endowed with political power; so was Japanese rule in many of the occupied territories.

Compliance can be motivated by full or half-hearted convictions or else by an overall assessment that compliance is, for reasons of prudence, better than opposition or rebellion. Underlying it is some sharing of ideas and beliefs between the rulers and the ruled ones, or, in other words, a commonality of culture. Unlike in the famous, rather deterministic dictum by Karl Marx (1813–1883) and Friedrich Engels (1820–1995),[18] this phenomenon is well-taken in Antonio Gramsci's (1891–1937) notion of hegemony, seen as the ability of the ruling class or group to influence and reorient the ideas heeded by the people, who are thus inclined to consent to the existing regime.

Third, political power is *universal*, in the sense that its orders are valid against all and everybody (*erga omnes* in Roman law) within a given unity. This is another differentiation from force, which can have full sway only on those on whom it is actually applied or have to fear its imminent use.

The (legal, but also effective) universality of political power as far as exerted in the state is made possible by its pyramidal or top-down structure, which in the early modern European state was imposed after the 'intermediate bodies' (clergy, nobility, towns and guilds with special jurisdictions and feudal privileges) were deprived of any independence and brought under the central political authority.

★ ★ ★

Political power, in combination with influence, operates mainly in two areas:

- it makes substantive *decisions*, allocating goods and recognising identities, and
- it determines which issues will be taken to public debate and decision making, which will be left out or postponed: this is the *agenda-setting* power in democracies scattered among government, media and other power centres such as trade unions and industrial associations.

Agenda-setting is no less important than decision-making power, sometimes even more so, as it can prevent crucial issues such as emerging faults in a country's financial architecture or climate change from being addressed in the policy-making process. The openly political (in Parliament) agenda-setting process is obviously intertwined with the cultural background (values, worldviews) of a people and its elites. Ideas and beliefs matter in domestic as well as foreign policy more than it appears in the media.

The *instruments* of political power, as well as influence, are incentives and sanctions, or positive and negative incentives. Many things can be used as incentives in one way or another: money for politicians or their constituencies or clans, political friendship or enmity, positions to be attributed, allocation of prestige or infamy and more.

The *modus operandi* of political power, but far less of influence, are manifold, but the basic patterns are two:

- *compellence* or in extreme cases coercion: A makes B do things (or stop doing things) B would not otherwise do (or stop doing). This happens only marginally by physical force; economic or psychological pressure are often enough, as well as persuasion.

The same holds for

- *deterrence* (A makes B keep doing or omitting to do certain things B would otherwise stop or start doing). The best known case, nuclear deterrence, is just a particular, reciprocal case of deterrence, which remains a basic structure of any political interaction. In it both powers, the mightier and the less mighty, have enough nuclear power (the so-called second strike capability) as to dissuade each other from launching an attack. An incumbent office-holder, threatening her/his constituency to withdraw public funding if they do not vote for her/him and s/he gets nonetheless re-elected, also acts in a deterrent mode.

4. Political power and the others

As everybody knows, political power is intermingled with economic and cultural power and their many derivatives; the latter is also called ideological or in another profile 'soft' power (as differentiated from the 'hard' economic and military one). Domestically, as well as internationally, these several forms of power are often hardly extricable from one another. The question can be raised if one should not give up insisting on keeping these sorts of power from another and rather talk about power as one composite, multifaceted single item. I am going to argue against that, but before doing so it is advisable to specify what makes one form different from the others. The distinction is based on what constitutes the ultimate source of power in the several spheres: command over organised force for political power, ownership and/or control of the means of production for economic power, ownership and/or control over the shaping of ideas, images, beliefs and the related media (including the educational system) in the case of cultural power.

Now, the first and generic reason for keeping the various types of power from another is the superiority of distinction over conflation, which is – unfortunately not for all writers – an epistemological pillar.[19] The second one is substantive: neither economic nor ideological power can give the rulers the pervasive and binding control over everybody's behaviour that the chance of resorting to force confers upon them. Neither a financial tycoon nor an influential spiritual leader would have reason to, say, sing, 'I have attained supreme power', as the new tsar does in Act 2 of Mussorgsky's Борис Годунов/*Borís Godunóv* (1868–72). That the US or the French president would not say so either is due to her/his limits as constitutional power-holder, not to a structural limit of political power. Due to its universal, binding and physically compelling character, this power – except in failed states or where a regime is fading – has a higher efficacy than the other types, as it can penetrate the society in all its pores – schools, police stations, government offices, courts and prisons are everywhere. Economic constraints can also spread everywhere, and the power of money or of its scarcity certainly does, but they are not tied to a single source of command, a single will. On the other hand, economic (rather than cultural) power needs a legal framework in order to operate: rules that bind debtors to repay their creditors, companies to deliver their products at the time written in the contract, employers to pay workers their full salaries on payday. Only political power can write these rules into law and enforce them, thus being an indispensable complement to other powers – though an anarcho-capitalist would disagree on politics being indispensable.

Having given an analytical clarification of the relationship between political and economic power, what remains to examine is the overall assumption on politics as just a reflex of economic power relations that can be found in different (from rough to differentiated) terms in the various Marxist traditions. Marx himself oscillated between regarding government as nothing but 'a committee for managing the common affairs of the whole bourgeoisie', as he and Engels wrote in the *Communist Manifesto* (1848, 5), and opening up in his late years to the chance for political processes different from the violent revolution of the Paris *Commune* to bring about the overcoming of class society.[20] The deterministic dependence of politics on economic power was never a theoretically correct view, and cultural factors – as Max Weber[21] showed more than a hundred years ago in his studies on the 'economic ethics' of world religions – are important in shaping economic and social structures. Worldviews, beliefs and ideas are of fundamental importance in shaping the reaction of individuals and communities to economic facts and conditions.

Today no scholar of politics would deny the relevance of economic factors and constraints, and a bright scholar would peer into the interplay of political processes with the shifting of economic structures and positions. But in many situations the much-talked-about 'overwhelming power of the economy' can turn out to be the failure of politics to set up timely and innovative strategies. To be overwhelmed in this case is obsolete politics and leaderships unable to catch up; they cannot reinvent themselves in a way capable to cope with the new constraints of the economy and technology and indulge in lamentation. Some reaction to modernisation and globalisation seem to go back to this pattern.

5. Objections and consequences

The reader may at this point be disappointed by the absence in these reflections on power of some questions that are otherwise widely discussed in publications[22] and public debates regarding the very same item, such as the field on which power is exerted (preferences of the actors? or their needs or interests? declared or covert, illusionary or real?) or the conflicts (open and visible, as in the Weberian definition I have adopted above? or non-visible but possible?) that it temporarily settles. Others may miss notions introduced by Michel Foucault (1926–1984) such as biopower and governmentality, and largely used in the last decades.

My reasons for this absence, or the deflating of these and other notions like domination, are the following:

A. This is an introduction to political philosophy (in the very specific understanding of it, to be explained in Excursus 1), not to a general social theory that includes a phenomenology of life-forms in the society at large.
B. Being this is an introduction, I aim at defining and explaining the elementary *concepts* that support the structure of political interaction, while not getting involved – as far as it goes – in a debate concerned with conflicting *conceptions* of politics and society endowed with a high amount of presuppositions and value-laden assumptions.[23] To add – as suggested by Lukes – to decision making and agenda setting a third dimension of power, that is the power to prevent people from enacting the so far 'latent' conflict between the interests of those holding power and the 'real' interests of those excluded, requires a comprehensive philosophy of history and society indicating what the visible but elusive and what the hidden but 'real' interest of the people is, and what they should do in order to become aware of the latter and pursue it. Now, the philosophically most refined version of this theory remains Lukács (1923), the incunabulum of Critical or Western (as opposed to Soviet) Marxism. According to this eminent theorist (1885–1971) of Communism, the overturning of capitalism, not its reform – as social-democrats wanted to have it – was seen to be the real interest of the working class. Lukács wrote this at the dawn of Soviet Communism, and we cannot today ignore what this strategy led to in the history of the twentieth century: division of the left in Western Europe resulting in its weakening in front of Fascism, state terror with 10 million victims and economic backwardness in the Soviet Union. I shall pursue no further the question of the 'real' interest. Apart from the reasonable wish not to overburden our study of the elements of politics with philosophical disputes among various positions and ideologies, there are indeed in our time, unlike in the nineteenth century, enough open conflicts and well-articulated interests in and between our societies to make the search for 'real' but latent interests redundant.
C. Having replied to some possible objection, let us now work out some consequences deriving from our definitions. That politics lives among conflicts, their settlement by acts of power and influence and the new arising conflicts means that political processes normally end in the making of *decisions* about the conflict matter. Decision making has two sides, the *political* and the *policy* side. The former revolves around the conflicting parties, the conflict techniques

(from rational arguing to negotiating to cheating and threatening) and the crucial achievement of *consensus* in the public opinion, between parties and in the elites. In the policy corner the focus is on the issue at stake, its substantive features, the efficacy and efficiency of the solution found. As it happens, political reasons (aimed at gaining consensus or neutrality from some less privileged parties, but also at avoiding conflicts with powerful actors) do quite often lead to solutions that in technical or economic or even legal-constitutional terms are sub-optimal.

On the other hand, political processes do not always lead to a decision, as they can be suspended, delayed, with any decision postponed – or reach a deadlock. The omission to decide is a political act as much as making a decision, and it understandably changes the initial settings of the process and generates consequences of its own – mostly the search for other solutions or other partners or other tools, including resorting to force. *Time* is an essential element in both politics and policy making, as it can change the physical configuration of the issue, the coalition supporting a certain solution, the perception of the issue among those concerned.[24]

Before this section comes to an end, it is wise to make possible equivocations explicit. I shall make three examples:

- a decision can come into being through several channels, such as arbitrary acts of the powerful or, on the contrary, collective deliberation, as we shall see when talking of (deliberative) democracy in Chapter 5.
- in advanced democratic societies, social and political power comes to bear as a network of influences and impersonal constraints rather than the pyramidal command structure it used to be in an absolute or aristocratic regime.
- the settlement of a conflict is not necessarily a zero-sum game, in which the winner gets what the loser is deprived of. Well-known is the recent expression 'win-win game', at the end of which all partners gets something that meets their wishes, though someone gets more (be it simply more prestige), while the losers may exist, for example future generations, but do not appear on the stage among the actual players. This was the case with the neo-corporatist agreements between governments, employers and trade unions that were popular in Europe in the 1960–70s and could rely in some countries on heavy borrowing and expansion of public debt, which is now burdening the younger generations.

This section ends with a warning to non-Anglophone readers: do not underrate the importance of language, which mirrors different political and intellectual histories, in adding difficulty to the complexity of political affairs. In proper terms, 'power' overlaps neither with *pouvoir* (French) nor with *poder* (Spanish) or *potere* (Italian), not to speak of the confusing German couple *Herrschaft* and *Macht* or 政权(*zhengquan*/political power in Chinese). The English word is much more generic and neutral and therefore more flexible than most of its translations; the same holds for its Latin predecessor *potestas*, though 'power' and *potestas* (as well as κράτος/*kratos* in ancient Greek) also fail to overlap (in some case 'power' translates *imperium*). When using translations we should always be aware of the major or minor equivocations due to the Tower of Babel in which, despite all homogenisation in globalisation, we – to our good luck – are living.

6. Politics and power, a fatal connection?

After clarifying the main notions, it is now time for a commentary from several venture points.

First, politics, as it has been so far and will not cease to be, has been defined in this textbook according to its main tool or medium: power (complemented by influence). This *instrumentalist definition* replaces the traditional one, in which politics was defined according to its aim. There are two reasons for this shift. One is that any single teleological definition makes a largely shared image of the nature and structure of politics impossible. This is not the case with the more neutral instrumentalist approach, which leaves room for the study of later developments related to the diverse goals people have in mind when acting politically.

The other reason is that, in this book – as already noted – we are interested in finding out what politics is and how it effectively works rather than shaping it in the way every one of us regards as the most conducive to justice or happiness. Not that we deem these goals to lie outside the field of political philosophy, but we regard as vain all theoretical efforts to design the best polity ever conceived that does not take note of how human beings and their groupings really act when acting politically.

As an illustration of the shift from the teleological to the instrumentalist view on politics let us look at the notion of *common good*. Aristotle and later Aquinas identified it substantively with virtue and happiness for all beings, i.e. for the community, as defined by philosophers, while in our time we – with the exception of Neo-Aristotelians – are rather inclined to share John Rawls's procedural notion of common good as what we pursue when 'maintaining conditions and achieving objectives that are similarly to everyone's advantage' (Rawls 1999, 205) – as defined by every single actor in an individualistic rather than communitarian way.

Second: in terms of the history of political thought, our definition of politics clearly goes back to the tradition of *political realism*, which comprises Thucydides, Machiavelli, Hobbes, and more recently Carl Schmitt, Reinhold Niebuhr (1892–1971), Edward H. Carr (1892–1982), Hans Morgenthau (1904–1980) and Kenneth Waltz (1924–2013). This book's relationship to realism is however substantially qualified and modified by the attention to recent developments that have made the realist approach insufficient, as we shall see in Chapters 7 and 10; even before and even more radically, that relationship is qualified by the focus on the adjective 'legitimate' that in our definition of politics accompanies the very notion of power. I put the adjective in quotation marks because, first, the link between power and legitimacy is questioned by many and needs to be discussed, as will happen in the next chapter; and, second, this link does not hold in international politics in the same way as within the state, as we will learn in the corresponding Chapter 6.

Accepting the link of politics and power does not need to be blind to its costs and dangers. First of all, if we stick to the basic link 'no politics without power',[25] this implies that, power being an asymmetrical, vertical relationship, politics always entails a degree of *inequality* – this is a first problematic aspect of that link (granted that in most worldviews, inequality is seen as something negative that should be contained). This was very clear to the classics of contractarianism,[26] who regarded the equality reigning in the state of nature as lethal, since everybody can be killed by everybody, whereas the unequal, overwhelming power of the sovereign created by social contract can be expected to protect everybody. How much inequality is generated depends on the rules that set limits to power and regulate access to it, including the duration of office tenure. The asymmetry between rulers and ruled regards in any case not just the ability of the authority to issue commands (which may or may not come in the form of laws) and to employ force, but also in a larger amount of knowledge. Foucault insisted on the link *pouvoir-savoir*/power-knowledge, but even aside from the pre-democratic examples he researched, this asymmetry holds in democracies too, in which a superior degree of knowledge remains an asset of the elite and the executive, not just in the field of intelligence.

On the other end, one (a person, a party, a country) *must* seek power, accepting the built-in inequality and other unpleasant features of politics, if one is serious with the goals s/he wants to achieve and the principles s/he proclaims – however tough or benevolent these goals and principles may be. There are certainly other paths on which one can try to achieve them, for example cultural reform, religious appeal, personal example; however, if collective goods are to be gained and evils to be avoided in a reasonable time and in an effective manner, politics remains the most promising way to go, to organise human society instead of abandoning it to chaos or to destructive conflict or indulging in lamentations and wishful thinking. Though politics may look disgusting to citizens, it remains a terribly serious business, whose cancellation overnight would only set out an even more violent and unequal world. Is it also a sombre business, poor in ideas and ideals, and must it be? This question will be answered at the end of Chapter 2 and later in Part IV of the volume.

Having this in mind, all demonization of politics as being such a dirty business is vain, because it suggests that we would be better off without politics; often it is also counterproductive, as it makes distinguishing honest from corrupt politicians impossible. Almost one hundred years ago, in *Politik als Beruf/Politics as a Profession* Max Weber discussed in a vivid and stringent way the moral dilemmas in which one is involved when trying to balance effectiveness of action and the price to pay when engaging in politics (cf. Chapter 10, §2). The attention for these prices used to be a recurrent *topos* in world literature from *Bhagavad Gita* (with regard to war, third century BCE or later) to Sophocles's *Antigone* (piety vs. reason of state, BCE 441), from Shakespeare (1564–1616) (particularly in *Macbeth, Julius Caesar* and *Richard III*) to Racine's (1639–1699) *Britannicus*; later, in the last two centuries of Western literature, the attention shifted for several reasons to dramas that may mirror politics and society but play in the individual soul as in Fyodor Dostoyevsky (1821–1881) and Thomas Mann (*Doktor Faustus* in particular, written 1943–1947). In political literature, in the hundred years since Weber's speech, the sensitivity for the moral and intellectual troubles one has to reckon with when engaging in politics has only grown thinner.[27]

As we have seen, a degree of political inequality between who is in government and who is not is a preliminary unavoidable price we have to pay when accepting politics as the fundamental tool aimed at governing human society. The true problem is another one altogether: how much inequality and what kind of inequality? Should *political inequality* between those in government and the citizens be allowed to reinforce the existing social and cultural inequality, as it used to happen in Western countries during the *ancien régime* and began to change only with mass democracy and the welfare state? We will come back to inequality when addressing problems of normative political philosophy. As to the amount of specifically political inequality, the asymmetry between rulers and ruled ones has decreased in the wake of democratisation; on the other hand, the state as impersonal machine has nowadays a controlling power over individuals it could not dream of in the time of the old monarchies.

There is a second price that comes with political power. A power position is and has always been the outcome of a competition among persons and parties, a costly activity that requires money and a staff serving the leader – be it the *clientes* of a senator in ancient Rome, the courtiers of a medieval king or the secretaries and counsels of a present-day politician. In modernity, the personal staff and 'war machine' of a politician has become separated from the state bureaucracy. Now, gathering more consensus than the competitors and prevailing over them in a conflict is the essential function of politics as different from policy, which aims at the efficient solution of the problems faced by a community. But gaining consensus requires much more (costly) things than good arguments. Through this activity private *money* gains an illegitimate sway over political decisions, far from any transparency; or public monies are diverted to fund a leader or party. On the one hand, this is an endemic phenomenon, co-essential to politics, and promises to eradicate it altogether should be seen with some scepticism. On the other hand, it must be monitored and contained, as it represents a danger not just for democratic politics, but for politics in general, since it threatens to substitute the logic of political processes with the logic of short-term economic advantages.

It represents a danger also because the acquisition of tools for the competition can become self-referential and degenerate: this is egregiously known as seeking more *power for the sake of power*, more and more regardless of the goal or the view one wanted to assert in political conflict, and more and more for self-aggrandizement. The current populist view that sees this as the very essence of politics tackles a built-in danger and misses the real target, which is not to delegitimise politics altogether but to invent and reinvent checks and counter-poisons.

★ ★ ★

Let us finally highlight the philosophical implications of the theory of political power illustrated so far. Its premise, still very much in the contractarian tradition, is that the self-rule of human beings on the basis of perfect equality must fail, thus making the establishment of an unequal political power necessary in order to save them from self-inflicted lethal wounds. This view does not only rely on the fictional state of nature of the contract theorists, but also on the recurrent experience with failed states and the resulting 'one man, one rifle' (rather than one vote) equality (Lebanon in the mid 1980s, Somalia in the 1990s and later, Libya after 2011). Self-government is only possible in an established state with central power, rule of law and representative government.

There is another reason for the inevitability of political power. Governing a political community is a complex business requiring knowledge, skills and experience. With modernisation and later globalisation, complexity and the related requirements for government have only surged and become a professional activity (it can be learned, but not overnight, since it requires an increasing competence in issue-related policy making, well beyond political manoeuvring). Not everybody can fulfil its requirements – perhaps not even most of the professional politicians in charge do – and, what is more, not everybody has interest or vocation for this activity. Binding involvement in politics for everybody would result in a nightmare for the most. Entrusting politics to the institutional power structure and its officials therefore represents for all others an 'unburdening' or relief,[28] which makes them free to pursue their own inclinations. The picture of a community in which everybody goes daily or weekly to the agorà (maybe the electronic one) and engages in deliberation over state affairs with all other fellow citizens is an idyll dreamt of by philosophers or literati unaware of how real citizens live in a mass democracy. In any case, it is less the intensity of citizens' participation but rather the quality of the politicians and bureaucrats to which the daily management of the state is delegated that makes the difference.

The view underlying the previous considerations is a moderate *anthropological pessimism:* human beings are not really capable of successfully practising in their associated life the self-rule some have theorised and praised. Or at least not in the form of a power-less community, in which everybody is an equal decision-maker on all daily common affairs. The idea of a radical e-democracy in which everybody participates on a daily basis in government is only the last and least felicitous version of this idea, according to which government is not a difficult art that needs to be learned and everybody is at any time a fully informed and rational actor – two hardly credible premises (more in Chapter 5 with respect to direct democracy).

The alternative to a power-free egalitarianism in politics is obviously not submission, but rather the effort to keep power painstakingly under control and to minimise this necessary evil down to the size that is indispensable to its organising, protecting and relieving functions. To ask political power to prove its legitimacy is, as we shall soon see, the fundamental question that cannot only contain it, but also help it fulfil the task it has been created for.

Notes

1 From Greek τέλος/*telos* or goal: based on the indication of goals.
2 Justice or freedom for all is a universalistic claim, but upholding it within a plurality of opinions remains the particular value or belief of its supporters.

3   In the Falklands (Spanish: Malvinas) War of 1982 between the United Kingdom and the Argentinian dictatorship, these relational resources were as much at stake as the possession of territory.
4   For positional goods such as prestige, scarcity results from their intrinsically competitive nature. Scarcity can be both absolute (absolute lack of a resource) or relative (the resource is unavailable to a group or area because of the way it is distributed). The threshold under which a resource is perceived as scarce and can ignite conflicts depends on the evolutionary stage of the society.
5   The actor can be a man or a woman, but also a group or institution, therefore in alphabetic order 'her/his/its'.
6   The scholarly convention has it that this notion, if capitalised (IR), refers to the discipline, while in lowercase the real thing is meant.
7   Cf. Weber 1922, Chapter 1, §9.
8   This triad was formulated by the sociologist Alessandro Pizzorno (cf. Pizzorno 1993).
9   Properly speaking, the monopolistic pretence of the Communist Party of the Soviet Union began with the revolution of October 1917 and was reinforced around 1923 by Stalin's (1878–1953) theory of 'socialism in one country' and only attenuated when the Popular Front's strategy was launched in 1935 at the Seventh Comintern Congress.
10 I uphold the distinction between Islamic (adjective of Islam) and Islamist (adjective of Islamism, a totalitarian and extremist version of political Islam).
11 Against Aristotle, Hobbes acknowledged conflict as the basic fact of life, but sought safety from it in the highly integrationist architecture of the covenant leading to the establishment of Leviathan.
12 To hypostasize something means to attribute the nature of a substance (ὑπόστασις) to elements that are rather accidental or changeable. I shall not enter a discussion of Schmitt's notion of 'the political', being unable – unlike others – to perceive it as a major and still influential turn in the thinking about politics.
13 Weber 1919 is the main source for his conception of politheism.
14 *Regula* means rule in Latin.
15 Substantive is what is related to the content as different from the form or method or procedure; substantial is what is essential and not accidental (or secondary, occasional) to an entity.
16 I borrow this expression from Koselleck 1979.
17 In today's political philosophy, particularly in so-called republicanism, the meaning of domination is much debated and not unequivocally defined in the sense I have described. In my usage 'domination' is just one species of illegitimate power, not a concept alternative to power.
18 'The ideas of the ruling class are in every epoch the ruling ideas, i.e. the class which is the ruling material force of society, is at the same time its ruling intellectual force' (Marx and Engels 1845, 67).
19 See Excursus 1.
20 Marx recanted the exemplary importance he previously gave to the *Commune* in a letter to the Dutch socialist Domela Nieuwenhuis, available at www.marxists.org/archive/marx/works/1881/letters/81_02_22.htm.
21 The complete relevant writings are now available in the volumes I, 18–21 of the new *Max Weber Gesamtausgabe*, published between 1989 and 2016 in Tübingen by Mohr Siebeck. Partial English translations are *The Protestant Ethic and the Spirit of Capitalism*, translated by T. Parsons (New York: Norton 2009), and the sections on the religion of China (Glencoe, IL: Free Press, 1951) and on ancient Judaism (also Free Press, 1952).
22 The most illuminating among them still is Lukes 2005, notwithstanding my disagreement expressed below on one of its positions.
23 For this distinction cf. Rawls 1999, 5–9.

22 What is politics?

24 On time and the future being elements of the upcoming reshuffling of the concept of politics see Chapter 7, Part II.
25 Better known is Weber's quote from *The Profession and Vocation of Politics:* 'Anyone engaged in politics is striving for power' (Weber 1919, 311).
26 Thomas Hobbes, John Locke (1632–1704), Jean Jacques Rousseau (1712–1778), Immanuel Kant (1724–1804).
27 A broader look at how 'dark' politics is mirrored in the arts should include film and TV, from Eisenstein's *Ivan the Terrible* I–II (1944–1958) to *All the President's Men*, from *Frost/Nixon* to *House of Cards*.
28 The term (originally *Entlastung*) was introduced by the German social philosopher Arnold Gehlen (1904–1976) to mark the role of social institutions for human life.

References

Arendt, Hannah (1972) *On Violence*, in *Crises of the Republic*, San Diego: Harcourt Brace, 103–184.
Easton, David (1953) *The Political System*, New York: Knopf.
Foucault, Michel (1976) *Il faut défendre la société: Cours au Collège de France* (1975–1976)/*Society Must Be Defended: Lectures at the Collège de France, 1975–76*, available at http://rebels-library.org/files/foucault_society_must_be_defended.pdf
Hamilton, Alexander, John Jay, James Madison and John Jay (1788) *The Federalist Papers*, London: Dent, 1992.
Heraclitus of Ephesus, Fragment 53, available at https://en.wikisource.org/wiki/Fragments_of_Heraclitus#Fragment_53
Hobbes, Thomas (1651) *Leviathan*, Oxford: Oxford University Press, 1998.
Koselleck, Reinhart (1979) *Vergangene Zukunft: Zur Semantik geschichtlicher Zeiten*/*Futures Past: On the Semantics of Historical Time*, New York: Columbia University Press, 2005.
Lukács, Georg (1923) *History and Class Consciousness*, Cambridge: MIT Press, 1971
Lukes, Steven (2005) *Power: A Radical View*, 2nd edition, New York: Palgrave.
Machiavelli, Niccolò (1531) *Discorsi sopra la prima deca di Tito Livio*/*Discourses on Livy*, New York: Oxford University Press, 2003.
Machiavelli, Niccolò (1532) *Il Principe*/*The Prince*, edited by Quentin Skinner and Russell Price, New York: Cambridge University Press, 1988.
Marx, Karl and Friedrich Engels (1845) *Deutsche Ideologie*/*The German Ideology Including Theses on Feuerbach and Introduction to the Critique of Political Economy*, Amherst, NY: Prometheus Books, 1998.
Marx, Karl and Friedrich Engels (1848) *Manifest der kommunistischen Partei*/*The Communist Manifesto*, Oxford: Oxford University Press, 1992, available at www.marxists.org/archive/marx/works/1848/communist-manifesto/ch01.htm
Pizzorno, Alessandro (1993) Come pensare il conflitto/How to Conceive Conflict, in *Le radici della politica assoluta e altri saggi*/*The Roots of Absolute Politics and Other Essays*, Milano: Feltrinelli, 187–203.
Rawls, John (1999) *A Theory of Justice*, revised edition, Cambridge: Harvard University Press.
Schmitt, Carl (1927) *Der Begriff des Politischen*/*The Concept of the Political*. Chicago: University of Chicago Press, 2007.
Weber, Max (1919) *Wissenschaft als Beruf*/*Science as a Vocation*, in Hans Gerth and Charles Wright Mills, eds., *From Max Weber: Essays in Sociology*, New York: Routledge, 2009, 77–128 (this is the classical translation; a more recent one is in: Weber, Max (2004) *The Vocational Lectures*, Indianapolis: Hackett, 1–31.).

Weber, Max (1922) *Wirtschaft und Gesellschaft/On Law in Economy and Society*, translated by Edward Shils and Max Rheinstein, New York: Simon and Schuster, 1967.

Further readings

Alternative conceptions of political philosophy are illustrated in the several articles of:

Klosko, George, ed. (2011) *The Oxford Handbook of the History of Political Philosophy*, Oxford: Oxford University Press, Part I, *Approaches*, 11–74.

2
THE SUBJECTIVE SIDE OF POLITICS
Legitimacy, identity, obligation

What is the subjective side of politics?

In coining this expression, I want to highlight that politics is not only what it sometimes appears to be to the reader of newspapers or political science analyses – a certain amount of commands issued by the authority (of which laws are but a particular type), policies, statements, parliamentary or administrative procedures and the like. We are interested here in what binds actors, individuals and groups to this 'objective' side of politics, and will work out the fundamental categories of the subjective side.

We will start with *legitimacy*, seeing in it the resource that represents the essential complement to power, and have a look at how this resource can become actual *legitimation* of polities and policies – a process in which *political identity* plays an important role. In this process, legitimacy as a claim raised by a ruling instance (Weber's *Legitimitätsanspruch*) turns out to only exist as a belief heeded by the ruled *(Legitimitätsglauben)*. Lastly, the legitimacy granted to institutions and policies provides the matter by which the *obligation* of the ruled to obey is nourished. Once again, the international arena will require a specific discussion of the question of legitimacy.

Before we start, a warning to the reader: legitimacy and its family of related notions are even more complicated a matter than power. S/he who desires notions with one stable and unequivocal meaning will be disappointed. Philosophy is the mental activity that can provide clearly differentiated definitions of the same word, thus reproducing but also conceptualizing a complex reality. Studying legitimacy is, from the outset, marked by ambivalence, as we can follow an analytical as well as a normative path: on the first path we want to learn under what conditions a regime can effectively be seen as legitimate by the ruled, on the second we debate what a regime should look like in order to be seen as legitimate. In this chapter, we will go down the first path, while the second will be visited in the normative chapters (8–10) at the end of the volume.

1. Legitimacy and legitimation

The legitimacy of a regime or an institution or a policy is what makes the involved actors *believe that it ought to be obeyed* or implemented, even if they did not actually participate in its making (they were members of neither the US Congress nor the German Bundestag nor the Standing Committee of the Central Committee of the Communist Party of China).

This is a first, clear-cut definition, based on the behaviour of those affected, something that can be ascertained by empirical methods (voting, opinion polls). As such, it has some advantages. On the other hand, since this behavioural definition identifies legitimacy with consensus and regards it as matter-of-fact, it provides no clues as to why people believe in legitimacy and how this belief came into being and had the opportunity to evolve. The second definition opens up exactly these aspects and can be called Weberian in acknowledgement of the scholar whose work inspired it: legitimacy is here regarded as *a resource to which political power can resort, consisting in the chance to successfully activate meta-conventional and non-daily reasons that provide a justification for power itself.*

By *resource*, we mean something residing as a potential belief in the minds of the citizens, which can be under certain conditions made explicit, thus leading them to obey the authority's commands. They will do so if these commands can be credibly reconnected to ultimate sources or reasons or motives that go well beyond our daily business: in pre-modern or early modern times it was God's will,[1] the cosmic order of nature (a belief dismissed by Galilean-Newtonian physics) or the sanctity of tradition. The people's will came later, in the wake of the American and the French Revolutions, and is now the overwhelming source of legitimacy, at least in rhetoric. What the paramount content of the people's will is varies across space and time: the protection of the rights to life, liberty and the pursuit of happiness (according to the US Declaration of Independence of 1776), the establishment of virtue (Maximilien Robespierre in the French Revolution), the abolition of class domination (Russian Revolution of 1917), respecting and protecting the dignity of the human being (*Grundgesetz*/Basic Law of the German Federal Republic, Art.1, 1949). Over long periods in history, the decisive content or paramount value against which institutions and policies are measured is subject to change: responsibility for future generations with regard to climate change and control over lethal technologies, such as nuclear weapons, may become in the decades ahead a leading parameter in assessing the legitimacy of global governance.[2]

In this light, and more generally speaking, legitimacy appears as the conformity of a regime or institution or policy to some (well-defined or fuzzy) *model or ideal of good governance* the people have in mind, based as it is on one of those deep-lying reasons (or a combination of some of them). This is not yet actual legitimation, but it makes it possible if other, substantive conditions are satisfied.

Though we are not going to devise any typology of those models, we cannot but recall Weber's own, as developed in Chapter 3 ('The Types of Legitimate

Domination') of *Economy and Society*, Part 1.³ His typology has not yet been declared obsolete after a hundred years, even if it looks nowadays insufficient, particularly with regards to politics in the globalised world; besides, it refers to social power in general, not specifically to the political one. It is based on the belief of legitimacy and has three tiers:

- in the traditional type, people believe the leadership to be legitimate due to its roots in the sanctity of a long tradition,
- in the rational power type, people believe in the legality of statute or case law (*scil*. as different from natural law) and of the acts of the bureaucracy implementing it, and
- in that of charismatic power, the followers believe in the exceptional qualities of a leader, be it a warlord or a party leader in a democracy.

These are 'pure' types, which rarely come up unmixed in the political reality, even if in their combinations one type usually prevails. The combination of charismatic and legal-bureaucratic aspects in leaders of democratic parties and governments, which Weber originally described, has not lost its fascination in our times – in spite of some inflationary use of 'charismatic leader' in the media.

Needless to say, in politics the second version of legitimacy, which I have dubbed Weberian, has almost nothing to do with the legal declination of the word (according to law, lawful). A further clarification: in old times, the legitimacy of a regime referred to the entitlement of the ruler to rule, while its legality had to do with the effective way to exert power by respecting or breaking the laws. Another example, in which both terms come up, is revolutionary power, which can be legitimate though lawless in the sense of the former regime. More importantly, political legitimacy is also different from consensus and cannot be gauged by votes or opinion polls. Were *legitimacy* and *consensus* merged, there would be conceptual tools left neither for the understanding of change in legitimacy patterns, due to new challenges or new alternatives; nor for the deficit of legitimacy that can stay hidden in electoral consensus, because voters see no viable alternative or, especially in authoritarian regimes, fear reprisals in the event that they act against the sitting leadership. Plebiscitary and authoritarian democracy, which in its best days had a lot of consensus, would result to be the best form of democracy. These are all considerations that justify keeping our notion of legitimacy on two levels, behavioural and deep-sitting or Weberian. In order to better understand these ambiguous situations, we now turn to explaining the notion of legitimation.

We understand legitimacy as a resource, in other words as a chance that, thanks to its constitutive characteristics, a political regime can be recognised by citizens as corresponding to their models of good governance. This chance is realised, if ever, in a process called *legitimation*: not a once-for-all event, but a process winding through the daily and yearly vicissitudes of the polity. This is a process in which the regime does not simply confirm its claim to correspond to principles and ideals, but also proves itself capable of providing the ruled with *substantive goods* or *basic performances* that the citizens cannot do without, right-wing or left-wing that the regime and their beliefs may be:

- internal and external minimum security: not to be robbed as soon as one leaves home, not to be invaded by whatever neighbouring country.
- minimum wellbeing, not only as non-starvation, but related to the average amount of basic wealth that a socio-economic system can bring about (political power must create the framework conditions under which the society can do so). The avoidance of striking, destabilising inequalities also has to do with this performance.
- minimum legality, avoidance of arbitrariness on the side of the rulers, otherwise the society cannot work and feed its members.

This is not the end of the story. A fourth condition, or rather a meta-condition, is also necessary and crucial for legitimation: political identity – it will come up in the next section. Only if these three plus one conditions are present can a regime or a policy suggesting conformity to a chosen model of governance be actually legitimised by the ruled, thus attaining the stability a leader or a government needs in order to implement their projects. Legitimacy as a requirement is a permanent thorn into an existing regime, not only as normative request not to belie its own principles and promises, but also as a stimulus to readapt itself to changing conditions (new technologies, demographic change, upcoming or declining foreign powers), while still sticking to its own standards.

In all of this, it is important not to blur the distinction between Weberian legitimacy and the substantive conditions (3+1) for legitimation: they are not on the same level and cannot be traded for one another. This is the mistake contained in the widespread (in political science) formula 'input and output legitimacy', which was first introduced some twenty years ago by the distinguished German scholar Fritz Scharpf with regard to the European Union (Scharpf 1999). In the case of input legitimacy policy decisions are legitimate if and in as much as they reflect the will of the people, thus realising 'government of the people'; while output legitimacy is measured by the degree in which they further common welfare. The trouble for the European Union (a second-order polity not supported by the direct will of the people and – so Scharpf – primarily relying on output legitimacy) began since it struggled to further generate prosperity for the member countries, the performance that in Scharpf's view used to replace its thin input legitimacy. Leaving aside the unprecedented case of the EU, my point is that good socio-economic performances cannot be assumed to substitute – except for brief periods – a lacking citizens' belief that the polity embodies their image of good governance, even less so for a weak political identity. Over the long haul, 'government for the people', paternalism or an efficient colonial administration have not proven able to replace self-rule; using the same word – legitimacy – for legitimacy proper and for what are only its substantive conditions is what is misleading in the input/output legitimacy formula.

It is perhaps now the time to be more explicit about the function or, in common language, the *use of legitimacy* and legitimation. It is not a nice and lofty, but optional addition to the features of political power we have seen in Chapter 1, not something that we require from power in order to satisfy our ethical needs. This book rejects the old realist tenet, according to which the power that holds the monopoly of force is as such legitimate. Political philosophy is interested in what makes a regime capable of lasting over time, thus leaving its mark over a country and building or reforming its institutions (see the next chapter) with a view on their effects in a medium-long term period. Being legitimate and also in a position to preserve its legitimation is an essential element in order for a regime to be stable and provide effective government to a polity. It is what makes political power really universal and different from a rule relying on force and intimidation. This varies according to the culture and the history of the polity in case, which rules out that only full democratic regimes are legitimate, because legitimacy is a category as old as the polity, born well before democracy was – though in our days democratic power has the highest chance to be felt as legitimate.

2. Political identity

No polity can be perceived as legitimate if its members do not feel enough identity among themselves and with the polity, even if they find their idea of good government implemented and the substantive conditions for legitimation are satisfied. The same holds, only with readapted wording, for the legitimation of policies.

To understand this we have to first get rid of the conventional wisdom about identity in politics. In its elementary definition, which we will soon meet, it is not the same thing as racism, sectarianism, 'politics of identity', exclusive communitarianism or the Francophone *communautarisme ethnique*. These are all pathological forms of political identity, not its core; mistaking them for the core deprives political philosophy of an important tool for the understanding of how polities stay together or dissolve.

Let us understand *political identity* as the set of values, principles, memories and symbols that a political group (movement, party, nation state, alliance or federation) recognises as its own, in other words, what makes it possible for them to say 'we'. More important than identity (the set) is self-identification, that is the process in which a group absorbs into its conscience those elements received from previous generations or a recent act of foundation, but also transforms them. Identity is neither pure path dependency, a burden from the past one cannot get rid of, nor something any generation can rebuild from scratch after a revolution – elements of the *longue durée* have resurfaced in post-revolutionary France or post-Maoist China years after those violent cleavages.

Samuel Huntington's view – 'We know who we are only when we know who we are against' (Huntington 1996, 221) – is wrong, as it always happens with simplistic *pars pro toto* arguments, in which a part or pathological case is taken as if the entire thing were at stake. There are, obviously, political identities relying on opposition and exclusion, for example in extreme nationalism or Islamist fundamentalism, but in the more frequent and more fundamental cases, people define themselves according to positive and non-exclusionary patterns, though the moment of 'being themselves and not someone else' remains seminal. In a conceptual metaphor, political identity conjoins *mirror-identity* and *wall-identity*. Under the first, someone from the group (a new or re-founded party, a new or rebuilt nation state) determines in intellectual and constitutional debates and later in high political acts what its leading values and goals are; this conversation of the group members with themselves is the founding act of self-identification. Yet groups are situated in space, time and history, and their identity cannot be diffuse if it is to give consistency to the group itself; this explains why it also contains a moment of distinction from other groups – the fledgling and limited humankind identity being an exception (see Chapter 7). This wall can be open and allow for encounters and exploration between the groups, but it can also transform distinction into separation or exclusion or enmity – there are various kinds of walls.⁴ To name an illustration, the USA Declaration of Independence, drafted by Thomas Jefferson, contains a classical instance of balance between mirror (the 'truths' or values regarded as self-evident) and wall (the motives for separating from Britain).

Bearing the connection between legitimacy and identity in mind, three aspects now need to be clarified. First, the relevant identity is the political, neither the *cultural* nor the *social* one. The belief that the first cannot stand without being merged with the second and the third is based on an unjustified generalisation of national identity, which is not a timeless or definitive model, but only the most relevant example of political identity in modern history after the French Revolution. It was characterised by the forced neutralisation of local cultures and traditions in a centralised statehood, in which political and cultural identity were forced to coincide; a passage post-national and regional identities such as the fledgling European one are far from requesting. To name another striking example, the peoples who are now members of the European Union share with Russia an encompassing European cultural identity including Pushkin and Goethe, Tolstoy and Stendhal, Mussorgsky and Verdi, whereas the same cannot be said of their political traditions, autocratic as they are in Russia and liberal-democratic in most of the EU member states.

Similarly, homogeneous social structures are not associated with the same political identity wherever the groups sharing them are kept separated by ethnic, cultural or institutional factors; nor do necessarily citizens sharing the same political identity also live in the same social structures. For example, as far as the EU member states have been able to develop their quasi-polity and the related identity, this happened in a continent in which up to four different versions of the 'European social model' have been identified by sociologists. Post-national identities are not national identities writ large; besides, even within nation states, social and political identities do not always overlap, as the North-South divide shows.

If political, cultural and social identities fail to overlap, they do not belong to different planets either. For political identity to develop, a measure of homogeneity in the *political* culture of the group is necessary, which can occur in the framework of different general (religious, philosophical, literary, legal) cultures. For example, tenets of a liberal-democratic culture are shared by groups having very different cultures in the background: Christian, Jewish, Islamic, Buddhist, agnostic, atheist, not to name other divides such as common law/civil law. Nonetheless sudden mass migrations from ethnic, cultural and political (mostly Islamic) areas, whose values and traditions with regard to politics and religion, gender equality, the role of tribal and family ties are difficult to reconcile with Western political culture, can shake the stability of European countries, if not enough time (generations) is allowed and not enough smart policies implemented for the integration of the migrants into the social and political culture of the host country – granted this is feasible and cleavages can be neutralised. The policies implemented thus far, or rather omitted, have been disastrous even if time enough was given, as the troubles with second generation immigrants prove; although more felicitous examples such as the Turks living in Germany since the Sixties should not be forgotten. Yet, persistent cleavages in the worldviews of populations living together in the same economic country system can create huge obstacles to the process of reciprocal *recognition as fellow citizens* among diverse persons and communities that is parallel to their recognition of the same political values and principles as fundamental for the polity. Celebrating 'multiculturalism' while omitting the problems of political integration has been neither a remedy nor a policy that prevents disasters. If all or most of the groups constituting a community insist on asserting each its own 'politics of identity', regardless of the broader identity based on the same model of generalised cooperation and respect, the polity, whose traded or reformed institutions are the ultimate guarantee for all citizens and all guests, is threatened by disunion and paralysis, if not collapse. For the ethnic version of this path, in recent European history a frightening example is constituted by the dissolution of Yugoslavia in the 1990s.

Still, a corollary to these fundamental elements of political identity must be named, though it consists of a question rather than an assertion. Where do values and principles, wrapped in symbols and memories, come from when shaping the mind of the citizens? The answer suggested in these pages has been: from the value systems of one's own civilisation as modified and reinterpreted through the historical experience of a specific group, for example a nation. But what could happen if those value systems are losing their directing force or are dismissed and find no equivalent? This is the preoccupation expressed on several occasions by conservative thinkers with regards to the modern dismissal of the sturdy religion-backed beliefs of medieval or early-modern times. Is a secularised or even relativistic worldview capable of providing enough motivation to the people for respecting each other and observing the law of the polity? A sharp formulation was given in the 1970s to this preoccupation by the German law philosopher Ernst-Wolfgang Böckenförde, who asked:

> The liberal, secularized state lives by prerequisites which it cannot guarantee itself. This is the great adventure it has undertaken for freedom's sake. As a liberal state it can only endure if the freedom it bestows on its citizens takes some regulation from the interior, both from a moral substance of the individuals and a certain homogeneity of society at large. On the other hand, it

cannot by itself procure these interior forces of regulation, that is not with its own means such as legal compulsion and authoritative decree.

(Böckenförde 1976, 60)

This so-called Böckenförde dilemma is quoted here to document a problem, not to prove that secular or, as others prefer to say, republican conceptions of the human being and the state cannot nourish peaceful coexistence and cooperation; that is what they did in liberal-democratic and social states over the past century – notwithstanding the dark times that in particular Europe went through between the World Wars. Yet it seems to be wise to keep our attention focused on the problem in times in which globalisation and globalisation malaise are putting so many elements of world order and domestic cohesion in distress.

Second, political identities are not merely a photograph of what the members of a group (polity, party, movement) believe to be as a result of preceding developments, but also an image of what the group wishes or feels the duty to become – particularly in the case of parties. In other words, political identities contain a moment of self-adopted normativity.

Third, and very importantly, identities are not pure argumentative or logical constructs, and need *symbols* in order to find cohesion and collective expression. Symbols are not just flags and national anthems, but also inspiring documents (the Constitution, if inspiring at all) or images, often related to one's own past (in Europe for example the Auschwitz gate or the Berlin Wall torn down by Eastern and Western citizens in November 1989, both as symbols of Europeans' 'never again' pledge). It is a matter of fact that people still are accustomed to thinking of themselves, their families and countries in historical terms, in spite of the attempts made by analytical philosophers to eradicate any historical dimension from political discourse. As a result, political identities contain not just beliefs in values and shared goals, but also some narrative of the group's evolution – be it the memory of past wars or past misery or past glory – and often find symbolical expression in building and monuments, such as the Gate of Heavenly Peace in Beijing's Tian An Men with Mao Zedong's (1893–1976) portrait hanging outside it or the Vietnam Veterans Memorial in Washington, DC. This, however, should not be misunderstood in the sense that political identities are fully a-logical or even irrational formations – something residing in the guts. Political symbolism is a-logical, but not outright irrational *tout court*, while irrationalism prevails in identities in which the mirror-identity coincides with the most divisive version of the wall-moment, because the group is kept together by hatred for others and has no other value to lay at its foundation. Political identities are, indeed, a complex mix of diverse moments, with a general but variable structure that requires careful analysis of each single case – as it is often the case with the concrete life of categories. Could we perhaps do better dropping the latter and concentrating on the single cases? This is an illusion, because we would then miss the deeper mechanisms that, in our case, make identity an indispensable notion, if one wants to see its core structure, whose variations explain the possibility of change – say, of how a conservative identity can open up to progressive positions or a liberal one adopt elements of authoritarianism. Categories and awareness of their variations under modified conditions help understand change and, even more importantly, being perceptive to its first signals – in political life a precious skill.

As a corollary to what we have learned about identity and symbols, let us tackle the delicate issue of myth. Symbol and *myth* are no namesake, and using them interchangeably reveals confusion. Symbols are a basic medium in human communication as well as in the very way by which we grasp the world and put order to our thoughts, figures being the best known example; we have just learned what symbols are for political identity. Symbols also play a role in *foundational narratives*, that is the account a community gives itself of its own origins (as a part of its mirror-identity) and the rest of the world. In liberal regimes, these narratives are subject to argument and revision in the framework of conversation of the community with itself and its partners – think of how the USA modified its own narrative after the success of the Civil Rights movement, and how Germany and Italy did the same after the fall of the Fascist dictatorships. On the contrary, foundational narratives of mythical character (the *mythes d'origine* so much talked about in Franche and Québec) are untouched by this critical chance and so is the Manichaeic 'us vs. them' pattern that defines them. They are not capable of revision and stand or fall as a whole, and so did in 1945 the nationalist and Fascist myths used by Mussolini (1883–1945) and Hitler (1889–1945) to galvanise the masses. Sticking to this conceptual difference does not preclude from our vision the cases in which foundational narratives based on an argumentative view on history can assume mythical traits, or more exactly, risk to become 'legends', particularly when they become part of patriotic rituals and mass ideologies – as it sometimes happened to the narrative of the Resistance in the countries once occupied by the Third Reich. The drive to merge symbol and myth, foundational narrative and origin myth is a postmodernist fashion, inspired by a Schelling-like predilection – as his counterpart Hegel (1770–1831) sarcastically put it – for 'the grey night, in which all cows are grey' (Hegel 1807, 9).[5]

On the other hand, symbols should not be seen as tools used by the powerful in order to induce allegiance among the people, as suggested by older classics of political science (Lasswell 1935; Edelman 1976). The notion of politics as an exclusively rational, goal-oriented business, which astutely employs a-logical elements as *instrumenta regni* or tools of domination, is naive reductionism of a multifaceted activity, though instances of such an instrumentalism can be found throughout history. Another warning regards the notion of *symbolic policy*, which indicates token acts that only do so, as if important issues were effectively managed by the rulers, while only the symbolic appearance of it is enacted. This use of the word symbol is possible, but remains reserved to this very specific feature, which by no means should be mistaken for the entire complex of political symbolism.

A last warning is not to mistake political identity for a namesake of *citizenship*, a category not belonging to the subjective side of politics, as it rather describes in 'objective' legal and sociological terms the rights of the members of the polity. Only as far as the possession of, or the struggle for, these rights are perceived by the citizens and become an element of their political identity does citizenship enter the field we have been examining.

3. Political obligation

By political obligation we understand the obligation that members of the polity (subjects or citizens that they may be called) perceive and enact when obeying the commands issued by the political authority. It is not safe to say 'obeying the law' because laws are only the most common, but not the only form taken by the will of the political authority (proclamations or decrees were in pre-modern times more common and still exist). They do so because they regard the issuing authority as legitimate, which makes political obligation the twin category of legitimacy. This nexus is valid only within the polity, that is a stable and cohesive association shaped by legal norms – as already Cicero (BCE 106–43) defined the *res publica* or commonwealth (*De Re Publica* I, 25, 39). In a chaotic and lawless situation, neither legitimacy nor political obligation makes sense. These twin categories lie at the ground of the very existence of the polity: without sense of obligation on the part of its members, there would be no polity, no order – as we shall soon see – and permanent civil strife, disunion, lack of cooperation would make everybody's life a nightmare, as proved by the reality of failed states. Yet only those who acknowledge some legitimacy of the ruling instances are ready to act according to the laws as well as to sanction those who do not – once again legitimacy turns out to be an indispensable element of a functioning and stable power structure. Beyond being a constitutive element of political power, the nexus legitimacy-obligation is also an important limit to it.

Political obligation is not to be mistaken for the moral or legal one. Unlike the latter, it does not entail coercive sanctions for those who infringe upon it and may abstain from doing so because they are convinced the regime is legitimate, not just for fear of being fined or landing in prison. Unlike moral obligation, political obligation is a matter of behaviour, not of the intimate belief in the rightness or sanctity of a polity or policy; nor needs to be re-examined in every situation, since belief in legitimacy and sense of obligation are subject to stabilisation as permanent beliefs, until new upsetting questions and conditions arise. This is only one of the many occasions on which acting politically reveals its difference from thinking morally, which makes the simplistic replacement of political reasoning by moral argument – as often the case with normativist thinkers – miss the specificity of politics.

★ ★ ★

At the end of our journey through power and legitimacy we are finally able to answer the question already raised in Chapter 1: is politics entirely a sombre matter of conflicts, scarcity, power, force, in which the actors' self-interest shapes all that happens? Is there no place for *ideas and ideals*?

This has been an immensely controversial question in the history of philosophy, and we cannot possibly recapitulate centuries of debate. I shall limit myself to one possible answer, which has evolutionary character and reorders elements already illustrated on our journey; something more will be said in the Epilogue to this volume.

34 What is politics?

While politics, or more generally any regulation of human community life since its inception, has never severed its roots lying in the conflict for material and positional resources, it has soon generated debates on conflicting patterns of distribution and corresponding models of good governance, which we have seen to be an essential component of power's legitimation. To begin with, these patterns and models display, even if rarely in a conceptualized language, the significant link between political power and religion, especially monotheism – a link we cannot unfortunately explore in a systematic way. This happened already in ancient texts such as the Behistun inscription near Kermanshah (Iran), in which Darius I the Great, king of Persia from BCE 522–486, celebrated the feats of his reign and acknowledged the support given to him by Ahuramazda, the supreme deity of Zoroastrianism; that link was loosed or severed only in recent centuries, but sometimes strongly reinstated, as in Iran since 1989. In Western civilisation philosophy, religion and law (meaning both the institutionalisation of the rules regulating conflicts and the inquiry into their foundation) focused more and more on the principles underlying the political order already in existence or the one hoped for, in a particular culture or country.[6]

More will become clear after reading Chapter 3 and the last three 'normative' chapters of the volume, but here we are already watching the development in which ideas and ideals, or the passions ideas can ignite in the human mind, arise from the activity dedicated to finding acceptable general representations of how conflicts should be regulated or prevented. On this path, even dying for one's own ideas becomes possible: Socrates (BCE 470–399), the first major Greek philosopher, accepts the death penalty to which the Athenian jury has unjustly sentenced him for 'corrupting the youth with his ideas' and rejects all proposals of escaping from prison out of loyalty to his *polis*.

From Socrates or the idealised (by William Shakespeare) figures of Brutus and Cassius to our present, a not-so-thin red line of men and women who suffered and died on behalf of their political ideas intersects the history of politics. We do not need to change or give up its original definition in order to grasp the concept that organising our conflict-laden communal life in one way or another can be perceived as a task in its own right, capable of justifying the sacrifice of something or even our entire life, in order not to give up the values and the vision that we attach to that task – prosaic that ordinary political life may be.[7]

Notes

1 Nowadays, only the Holy See or rather Vatican City State, the Islamic Republic of Iran, Art. 2 of the Constitution, and the Kingdom of Saudi Arabia, Art.1, 9 and 11, make explicit reference to this source.
2 Cf. Chapter 7 and Cerutti 2011.
3 Available at https://archive.org/stream/MaxWeberEconomyAndSociety/MaxWeberEconomyAndSociety_djvu.txt, 112–301.
4 A petrified image of (racist) wall-identity is in the known photograph of the two segregated water-fountains for white and coloured, see https://pro.magnumphotos.com/C.aspx?VP3=

SearchResult&VBID=2K1HZOL1TCEO7N&SMLS=1&RW=1600&RH=775#/SearchResult&VBID=2K1HZO6G1TLFV6&SMLS=1&RW=1600&RH=775.
5 Friedrich W.I. Schelling (1775–1854) was, along with Hegel and Johann Gottlieb Fichte (1762–1814), one of the main thinkers of philosophical idealism.
6 It would be of the highest interest to compare these Western, but also Islamic developments, with what has happened in other civilisations and religions.
7 Democracy, notwithstanding all its prosaic aspects to be examined in Chapter 5, is one of such ideas. An eminent example was given on 11 September 1973 by President Salvador Allende of Chile, who died in the armed defence of the democratic institutions of his country against the military coup backed by the USA. See the iconic photo taken at the presidential palace shortly before Allende took his life while rejecting any offer to go into exile at https://iconicphotos.files.wordpress.com/2009/08/017.jpg?w=700&h=468.

References

Böckenförde, Ernst-Wolfgang (1976) *Staat, Gesellschaft, Freiheit/State, Society, and Liberty*, New York: Berg, 1991, English passage available at https://en.wikipedia.org/wiki/Böckenförde_dilemma

Cerutti, Furio (2011) 'The Deeper Roots of Legitimacy and Its Future', in James Brassett and Eleni Tsingou, eds., *Global Governance and Legitimacy*, Special Issue, 'Review of International Political Economy', 18(1), 121–130.

Cicero (54 BCE) *De Re Publica*, e-book available at www.thelatinlibrary.com/cicero/repub.shtml

Edelman, Murray (1976) *The Symbolic Uses of Politics*, Champaign: University of Illinois Press.

Hegel, Georg Wilhelm Friedrich (1807) *Phänomenologie des Geistes/Phenomenology of Spirit*, translated by A.V. Miller, Oxford: Oxford University Press, 1977.

Huntington, Samuel (1996) *The Clash of Civilizations and the Remaking of World Order*, New York: Simon & Schuster.

Lasswell, Harold (1935) *World Politics and Personal Insecurity*, New York: McGraw-Hill.

Scharpf, Fritz (1999) *Governing in Europe*, Oxford: Oxford University Press.

Further readings

On democratic legitimacy, an innovative book is:

Rosanvallon, Pierre (2011) *Légitimité démocratique/Democratic Legitimacy*, Princeton: Princeton University Press.

Two classical readings on national identity:

Anderson, Benedict (2006) *Imagined Communities*, London: Verso (first published in 1983).
Renan, Ernest (1882) *Qu'est-ce qu'une nation?/What Is a Nation?* edited by Charles Taylor, Toronto: Tapir Press, 1996.

A research volume on elements and problematic aspects of a European identity:

Cerutti, Furio and Sonia Lucarelli, eds. (2008) *The Search for a European Identity*, London: Routledge.

EXCURSUS 1
What is political philosophy?

Hegel derided those who wanted to teach the method without tackling at the same time the very thing the method should open the way to, and compared them to a scholar pretending to learn how to swim before venturing into the water (Hegel 1830, §10). Remembering Hegel's sarcasm, I have abstained from talking about the method followed in this book – more exactly about its epistemological premises – before taking the reader on a tour through a certain amount of the material. Now, past two chapters, it is presumably possible to entertain readers about the notion of political philosophy after they have had a taste of what this thing looks like.

We are talking about the epistemology[1] of political philosophy and not its methodology because our discipline, being non-empirical and non-quantitative, is not subordinate to requests to exhibit its method as empirical-analytical science is. It is also clear that, as a scholarly discipline, political philosophy does not mean the general orientation or the leading ideas inspiring in a partisan way a political actor – as it is understood in common parlance. We would here rather use the word 'ideology', though the meaning of this word is ambivalent: on the one hand, it indicates doctrines and policy indications as expression of the culture and the interests of a social or political group. On the other hand, 'ideology' can still retain the meaning, attributed to it by Marx and Engels,[2] of false conscience or false representation of a social structure or situation, due not to a mendacious manipulation by the powerful, but to the objective deformation of the real state of affairs operated by the division of intellectual and manual labour. A third use of the term – more frequently adopted in this book – calls ideological the views that result rather from an overarching (political and social) *Weltanschauung* generating strong beliefs than a philosophical or analytical examination of the topic pursued in a critical attitude.

Against the widely spread opinion that acknowledges only one type of political philosophy, nearly identical with ethics, this book sees in it the classical and articulated structure consisting of two main types: reconstructive and normative.

What I call[3] *reconstructive political philosophy* investigates (reconstructs) the – mental rather than material – conditions, the deep-lying reasons and motives (including values and principles) under which human beings construct a political community or polity, acknowledge and preserve it also in the interaction with a plurality of such formations. We have already gone down this path, defining and connecting fundamental concepts such as: conflict, power/force, legitimacy/identity, obligation; we are now about to examine how these concepts interact within the state, with other states, and at the global level. Besides, the initial definition of politics is being enriched by the continuous attention to its nature (others call it the nature of 'the political'), which will culminate in the discussion of its relationship to morality.

In this type of political philosophy, the leading research interest is *to understand* at a philosophical level what politics is rather than how it ought to be, how it works in the minds of the actors and what is possible within its present architecture or what should change in order to make certain values or goals more likely to be attained or certain problems more likely to be solved. Digging into real politics and resurfacing armed with concepts that give us some ability to understand and master it is intellectually more difficult, but also closer to the real lives of men and women than stating, refining and celebrating the supreme values and principles one thinks to be best for human coexistence.

Normative political philosophy, on the other hand, is interested in determining what the best values and principles in giving order to the polity are with respect to human nature or God's will or other worldviews, including the image of a social bond established by an assumed social contract. It is a discourse *de optima republica*, or about the best polity, to put it in the words of Cicero. Normative is also the argument against the *worst* principle, such as against the state in anarchism of its various kinds. The philosophical intention to keep freedom from serfdom or justice from injustice and to tell people how to act brings this type of political philosophy closer to ethics and moral philosophy;[4] it is a difficult balancing act to avoid that the common normative interest leads to an unlucky merger of moral and political philosophy as well as to preserve the specificity of the latter. Political philosophy is not moral philosophy and remains an autonomous discipline, even if it has robust connections to it – as we shall learn in Part IV. As a vaccine against vain attempts at absorbing politics into morals, it is appropriate to remember that

- political philosophy has to do with groups defined by interest, identity and institutions rather than with individuals engaged in an abstract search for justice, and
- values and principles are relevant to the people's real lot only in as much as actors are identified who are motivated to endorse them and to create adequate forces and coalitions.

This vaccine was rarely used in the normative political philosophy of the last twenty (at least) years, in which little thought has been given to the specificity of politics, and the development of concepts runs in a way fully unaware of and uninterested in real processes and real actors; political philosophy is often, and speechlessly, (without any epistemological justification) welded to moral philosophy in an ancillary position. I shall dub this attitude *normativism* and, in the extreme case, hyper-normativism. The result risks to be futile (no real political situation or problem is grasped and conceptualized) as well as self-celebrating, as if all that philosophy has to say about politics had been said by designing ideal models of justice or freedom and deducting from them maxims for any concrete case, regardless of other factors and categories politics consists of. An unpleasant side effect lies in the leeway this attitude gives to the bookish attitude to draw on the authority of an author or school while endlessly quibbling over her/his/its principles instead of putting them to test in the confrontation with situations and problems of political, ethical and theoretical relevance – not unlike what happened to Aristotle in the philosophical schools of the Middle Ages. John Rawls himself went the opposite way, taking more and more stock of real politics and institutions with every new publication, down to the twin track (the normative design of a covenant between states based on principles of justice paired to a strong attention to change in international relations) followed in his last book.[5] Unfortunately, many of his followers lack the same humility and the same attention to the 'thing itself'.[6]

As a practical conclusion, the readers will find in this book a version of political philosophy very different from, indeed opposed to, today's mainstream thought and may find themselves to be disoriented. Normative categories – freedom, equality, justice and solidarity – will be examined at the end of the book, after acquiring knowledge of the entire structure of politics. Wherever appropriate, normative perspectives (such as universalism in space and, unexpectedly, in time) will be argued in the appropriate chapter, being worked out from the specific challenges politics is currently confronted with, rather than asserted as general, ever-lasting principles. Normative questions surface in the middle of reconstructive paths, as most notably in the case of legitimacy; the distinction of reconstructive and normative should not – as is true for all things human – be taken as if it were true only in its absolute, hence reified version. More in general the reconstructed map of what politics is and how it works defines the terrain within which normative arguments can develop in a way that is aware of the limits, constraints, challenges political action has to do with.

Illuminating is still Bobbio's account of the three main research paths of political philosophy (Bobbio 1989, Chapter 3):

- the nature of political life or, as some prefer to say, of 'the political'
- the search for the roots of political obligation
- the inquiry *de optima republica*, or about the best possible polity.

Though redefining the field, reconstructive and normative attitudes do not exhaust it. Political philosophy can also live in works dealing with its history, whether its focus be authors, traditions, schools, concepts or ideologies (the '-isms'). Reinterpreting authors or works of the past always occurs through the lenses of the present and contributes to the self-awareness of the latter, provided the philosophical interest is not suffocated by erudition or the mere reproduction of past works. On the other hand, political philosophy as systematic thinking, reconstructive or normative that it may be, can hardly do without exhibiting its own relationship to relevant authors from its history.[7] More generally, it must be remembered – in a Weberian language – that the types of thought we are talking about are 'pure' or 'ideal' types, which help penetrate and classify the world of political philosophy, but come up rather rarely in their conceptual purity, as phenomenal reality consists here, as everywhere, of mergers, combinations, inter-penetrations – in a word, the incredible and incoercible, but also stimulating mess of which, talking to his friend, Prince Hamlet elegantly said: 'There are more things in heaven and earth, Horatio, Than are dreamt of in your philosophy.'[8]

★ ★ ★

Let us now look at the relationships political philosophy has or could develop with other disciplines.

Social philosophy is not the closest relative of political philosophy, and is even less so interchangeable with it. Epistemically, the object 'society' is different in its structure from the object 'politics'; what is more, the representation of politics as a sub-sphere of society, entirely dependent on its dynamics, is a widely spread but not firmly founded bias – it is at the same time a low-value piece of Marxist heritage and a pillar of the conventional wisdom called sociologism (the attitude that interprets whatever happens in the human being, its history and its relation to nature as an exclusively 'social' process). This is not to deny that social philosophy is an indispensable conceptualization of phenomena interesting the society at large, and in as much, illuminates the background of phenomena that can reset the stage for politics as well, such as cultural globalisation or changing forms of individualism and emotions. On the other hand, the lack of a stringent definition of its object ('society' is not as well-carved a concept as 'politics') and the overambitious aspiration to be the real-time interpreter of the *Zeitgeist* have misled some works in social philosophy to engineer brilliant metaphors of the (for example, 'liquid') state of the world rather than provide analytically documented interpretations. Moreover, the unbridled holism of these pictures does not contribute to their precision and verifiability. Lastly, a further motive for maintaining the distinction between the two disciplines, even where they can usefully cooperate, is that the normative dimension remains the exclusive business of political philosophy; this is not reversed by the fact that normative, if undeclared, statements can often be found in social philosophy as well.

The differentiation of social and political philosophy is as much a matter of epistemological clarity as it is the result of the history of politics and society, of which the latter became a sphere in itself, relatively autonomous from politics, only with the rise of the bourgeois society that in most of Europe and in North America accompanied the expansion of capitalism in early modern times – as documented also by economic liberalism (see above). More in general, politics was able to become an object of scientific knowledge as a discipline of its own only after putting an end to, or at least attenuating, its original fusion with other realms of human activity and normativity, such as religion and morality. From the first steps in this direction taken during the Renaissance even before Machiavelli[9] through Hobbes and Locke to the Enlightenment, this was the genesis of the scientific study of politics as a specific creation of modernity brought about with the decisive contribution of political realism (cf. Chapter 10).

On hearing the expression 'scientific study of politics', (empirical) political science would first come to mind for most people. Political science, with no further adjective, includes all mental efforts to come to grips with the elusive monster called politics, provided they respect basic intellectual standards, such as a clear and well-argued method including: clarity, consistency (non-contradiction), criteria of relevance for, and orderly partition of, the subject matter. In this sense, political philosophy also belongs to the large family of political science. Not so if *empirical political science* is meant, which was born in some conjunction with sociology at the turn between the nineteenth and twentieth centuries, and first flourished in the 1930s and 1940s. Its ambition was to reach, with regards to politics, the same degree of precision as physics by addressing facts instead of debating theories, making its findings verifiable by analysing facts with quantitative methods, primarily statistics. A further claim was to be able to abstain from value-laden judgements unlike ethics and political philosophy, thus respecting neutrality against all parties and all hypotheses involved in a matter of investigation; it is the attitude called by Max Weber *Wertfreiheit*/value freedom. These were positivistic premises, and in their pretences to deliver a firmly 'scientific' study of politics they must fail, according to the post-empiricist turn in the science of philosophy and in science itself (Newtonian physics relativised by first relativity, then quantum physics and later quantum mechanics, along with Heisenberg's uncertainty principle). Facts turned out to be themselves theory-dependent, thus losing the aura of being the last truth on reality; values turned out to be present even in allegedly value-free research. The related epoch-making changes in the image of science struggled to reshape the self-image of political science and were received in its epistemology rather than in the daily practise of numerous scientists, in which an unreflected confidence in the truth-bringing virtues of mathematically analysed 'facts' persists. This may be a consequence of the fascination exerted on political research by recent *economics*, itself fairly far from the broad approach of classical political economy. Along with the monopolistic preference for quantitative methods, which risk to be rough and distorting if not paired with a qualitative approach, this type of political science (for example the rational choice and its development, the public choice approach) imported from economics an image of the actor as being self-interested, rational and well-informed. This is, in many cases, not even heuristically productive of new knowledge, for example in the research upon what I have called the subjective side of politics. Once again, methods cannot be chosen or imposed regardless of the particular nature of the parcel of reality under inquiry; political identity shifts in a nation or federation require different tools from those that can help analyse the voting behaviour of a small community, a beloved object of empirical research. A further difficulty lies also with the extreme fragmentation of the research objects in political science; their relevance for the (empirically anchored) conceptualization of politics is not always easy to grasp. A case in point is policy analysis, which is hardly the royal road to the understanding of politics as sphere of complex and intertwined processes. This posture sounds like an extreme reaction to the holism of political philosophy – a holism that is on the one hand a necessary piece of its epistemic status, on the other hand something often at risk of sliding into theories of everything.

All these drawbacks are not listed here to doubt the scientific validity of empirical political science, of which several types exist, by far not entirely prejudiced by those perplexing aspects. Especially in International Relations[10] and International Political Economy, sound empirical research is being accompanied by a permanent interest in the understanding of processes and trends.

What is more generally the actual relationship between political philosophy, in the broad version illustrated in this Excursus, and political science? Political philosophy is bound by its statute neither to refer to methodically analysed facts, used as empirical evidence for its statements, not to abstain from discussing and choosing values. Besides, diverging developments as those sketched above have made its dialogue with political science uneasy. Nonetheless philosophers, since they also refer to alleged factual truths, do good whenever they check their assertions about a certain subject against those analytically researched by their empirical cousins. 'Facts' are differently constructed according to the epistemology of the two disciplines, and a direct comparison is often naive. Yet contacts and exchanges are – most of the time and indirectly – stimulating and can prevent both partners from falling all too easily and as naive victims to empirical-analytical or philosophical blunders. It must, however, be said that in recent years the attention of the two disciplines for one another has not been significant; on both sides, the tendency to closure and self-sufficiency prevails.

Beyond political philosophy and political science, a third party or gender *(tertium genus)* has struggled to be identified: *political theory*. This label has been seen for a long time as a namesake for political philosophy, but cannot be said to be endowed with the same relevance and autonomy as its two elder cousins. It is now recognised as a field of its own, though no broad agreement exists as to its definition, also because its nature is to live at the crossroads, defying epistemological straitjackets. It designs a theoretical view on politics that is philosophically trained, but looks at political processes using tools and results from political science. It is interested in predicting the future of political institutions, such as the state or democracy or political parties, and it does not refrain from value judgements.

Further, one transversal component of political studies (rational choice scholars as well as normativists will disagree) is *history*. First of all, as history of political events, processes and institutions, its knowledge is an indispensable source of information for political philosophy, as it reconnects categories to the real experience of societies and the effective channels of identity formation. Certainly, the old belief in *historia magistra vitae* died some two centuries ago,[11] and so did three or four decades age the notion that a philosophy of history (Hegelianism, Marxism, progressivism) can show the meaning of it and tell us where to head for. No such belief can exempt us from making ourselves our own normative choices in the middle of something like Weber's 'politheism of values' mentioned in Chapter 1. Yet along with political science, history remains an essential dimension in which the political philosopher can reconnect to the variety and diversity of human life in social and political communities. The constitutional abstractness of philosophical thinking can only be strengthened by the challenge of conceptualizing ever new processes and events, rather than being exclusively busy with a sort of secluded self-refinement. In Chapter 7 on global challenges I shall try to show what this means.

The other version of history that matters for political philosophy is the *history of political philosophy* (or thought). By introducing this field, I am way far from implying the historicist sense that today's political philosophy cannot be but the result and development of what our predecessors have thought about politics. It is now clear that this author is rather inclined to believe that political philosophy consists of conceptualizing new aspects and problems of the reality we live in, being aware of what history contributes to their explanation and also with a view towards the future – as far as this outlook can be prudently performed. Taking stock of the conceptual languages philosophers of the past have invented and refined remains, however, an indispensable passage if we want to start our reflection on the present at the highest possible level of skilled formulation and elaboration – or simply avoid blunders or refished arguments introduced as if they were fresh discoveries. We hardly expect nowadays to meet 'eternal truths' in philosophy, but with respect to the mental structures that seem to be rooted in our anthropology – language, power, fear, freedom, sense of belonging – some of our predecessors in the world cultures have enriched us with reflections that can still tackle this or other essential aspects of the matter. As far as this is the case, it makes them 'classics', and no decent philosophy can be written without going back, whenever appropriate, to the lessons of the classics, which is also a way to highlight what is new or differently shaped in the problems we are confronted with. As far as warping arbitrariness is avoided, we can feel free to pick up from the classics the illuminating elements we may need in order to highlight a specific new problem, without overstuffing our relationship with them with the study of their whole system. This textbook tries to stick to these self-imposed criteria in our brief encounters with classics.

Finally, less easy to define, but important is the contribution *anthropology* can give to political philosophy. Both versions of anthropology are involved: philosophical anthropology, the reflection on 'the nature of man' in its classical definition, and cultural anthropology. The first one, present in all major political thinkers such as Machiavelli, Hobbes and Kant, is nowadays rather a reflection on how that nature, while containing constants in the relationship to nature and other beings, is also not uninfluenced by the technical change and the related shift in our attitude towards what is outside us, the world of objects. No philosophical project can ignore this knowledge, or is condemned to assign tasks to or predict a future of an actor of whom we do not even ask if her or his traits will resemble ours. On the other, cultural anthropology can illuminate how differently political forms such as democracy can impact on populations and cultures.

This excursus must end mentioning a loophole that, for architectural reasons, will be filled in Chapter 4: it regards the relationship between politics and law, or political philosophy and jurisprudence, same or similar stuff, divergent lenses (epistemic devices) to look at it through. The essential nature of this relationship is testified among other things by the fact that up to a hundred years ago political philosophy did not exist as an academic discipline in most European university systems, while the state, power and politics were topics taught in juridical fields such as *Staatsrecht*/state law or constitutional law.

More remarks on the epistemological status of political philosophy will come in the next chapters in the framework of substantive topics, and particularly in Chapter 10.

Notes

1 A discourse (λόγος/*logos*) about science or knowledge (επιςτήμη/*episteme*).
2 In the first chapter, dedicated to Feuerbach, in particular section C, of *The German Ideology*, a manuscript written in 1845–1846 and first published in 1932 (Marx and Engels 1845).
3 The term is not of general and well-known use; my understanding of 'reconstructive' goes back to Bobbio – as explained in the first section of the chapter on the state in Bobbio (1989, 44ff.) – rather than Habermas (on his use cf. https://en.wikipedia.org/wiki/Rational_reconstruction). 'Analytical' would not be perfectly adequate and engender misunderstandings.
4 I shall abstain from the hopeless attempt to give clear definitions – dozens have been advanced, often convoluted – of these terms. In my own language use, ethics points at a rule-based behaviour of individuals and groups, while moral philosophy regards the individual as such and looks at the intention rather than the behaviour. But my use does not raise any claim of universalisation. More on this in Chapter 10.
5 *A Theory of Justice* (1999a) and *The Law of Peoples* (1999b).
6 This translates Hegel's *die Sache selbst*, meaning the substantive issue or process under investigation, whose dynamics he recommended to grasp and conceptualize instead of insisting on one's own principles and beliefs.
7 To have a glimpse of this connection, one needs only to peer into the Table of Contents and the Index of two influential works, such as Rawls's *A Theory of Justice* or Habermas's *Theorie des kommunikativen Handelns* (1981); in this latter work that relationship is more explicitly worked out.
8 *Hamlet*, 1, 5. More fitting in our case is 'our philosophy', as the text reads in the First Folio edition of Shakespeare's works (1623).
9 In 1440 the Italian scholar Lorenzo Valla, a philosopher with high philological skills, proved the document attesting the donation of territory made by the Roman emperor Constantin in the fourth century to the Church was a fake, thus destroying the legitimacy of the papacy's temporal power. His writing, however, was first published in Germany after the Reformation.
10 When capitalised these words refer to the discipline, in lower case to the real thing, the relations *inter nationes*.
11 Cf. Koselleck 1979.

References

Bobbio, Norberto (1989) *Democracy and Dictatorship*, Oxford: Polity.

Habermas, Jürgen (1981) *Theorie des kommunikativen Handelns/The Theory of Communicative Action*, vols. 1–2, Boston: Beacon Press, 1984–1987.

Hegel, Georg Wilhelm Friedrich (1830) *Enzyklopädie der philosophischen Wissenschaften im Grundrisse/Encyclopaedia of the Philosophical Sciences*, available at www.marxists.org/reference/archive/hegel/works/sl/slintro.htm

Koselleck, Reinhart (1979) Historia Magistra Vitae: The Dissolution of the Topos into the Perspective of a Modernized Historical Process, in *Vergangene Zukunft: Zur Semantik geschichtlicher Zeiten/Futures Past: On the Semantics of Historical Time*, New York: Columbia University Press, 2005.

Marx, Karl and Friedrich Engels (1845) *Die deutsche Ideologie/The German Ideology*, available at www.marxists.org/archive/marx/works/download/Marx_The_German_Ideology.pdf

Rawls, John (1999a) *A Theory of Justice*, revised edition, Cambridge: Harvard University Press.

Rawls, John (1999b) *The Law of People*, Cambridge: Harvard University Press.

Shakespeare, William (1603) *Hamlet*, 1.5.167–8, available at www.shakespeare-online.com/plays/hamletscenes.html

PART II
How politics works

We have now in our toolkit the seminal elements of politics: conflict, power (along with force), legitimacy and obligation. Let us imagine we connect these single pieces with each other, feed them into an engine and set it in motion. What comes out? What are the main results of political life, when seen in its own dynamics?

Chapter 3 will deal with its main result, political order, and look into the several models of order that have come up in the history of political thought. Chapter 4 will go down a further step on the staircase leading from abstract categories to concrete forms and focus on the paramount political institution, the state. The most widespread and ambitious form government has taken – really or nominally – in the last century or so, democracy, will draw most of our attention in Chapter 5.

3
ORDER, INSTITUTIONS, MODELS

As with power, and even more than with it, the reader is now invited to clear her or his mind of all the associations and undertones that may usually accompany our first new acquaintance in this chapter: order. The order we are going to talk about is neither the grim logo of a 'law and order' police state nor a conservative appeal to stick by the given order of affairs instead of fantasising about change. Political order (§1) has as much to do with institutions as well as with fear (§2). Actors and thinkers have conceived of it in different, manners, which we will succinctly examine in §3.

1. What does order mean in politics?

The word 'order' allows, in politics, for a two-step definition: generic and political order. In the first sense it means the *patterns of regularity* we may observe in the flow of political life, exactly like how earth scientists can recognise similar patterns in the dunes shaped by the wind in a sandy desert or like economists do with business cycles. This would not call for any theoretical attention, were it not for one fact: becoming aware of some patterns of regularity in political affairs (how a certain behaviour X developed by actor A causes corresponding reactions from actor B) makes to an extent predictable what an actor can expect when repeating X. The end of complete blindness about the future, the knowledge of what X can unleash, relieves actors of total uncertainty and the ensuing fear: the surrounding world no longer appears to be totally chaotic and unpredictable. This relief goes in the direction of what we will learn to be a major outcome of politics: the regulation of fear.

Political order also comes up as a pattern of regularity, this time, however, filled with achievements giving it a specifically political character: it promotes goals or values, it establishes rules and institutions. What goals? Primarily the preservation of life, the containment of violence, in a word security; then at a higher evolutionary stage the protection of property as well as conditions favouring a minimum wellbeing for all. Above all of this, as its meta-condition, comes the observance of pacts *(pacta sunt servanda)*. We will see that the first two goals, along with the last one, are present in the international version of political order; the reader will have also perceived the similarity between these core features of political order and the essential substantive conditions for the legitimation of political power (see above Chapter 2, §1).

It is utterly important to understand that political order only very rarely comes into being as the consistent result of the actors' intentions and goal-oriented actions – especially in international politics. This may be the case in mature liberal-democratic countries or, internationally, in the UN system in its infrequent best moments or in the build-up of the European institutions in the 1980–90s. More generally, the degree of political order achieved at any a given time in history is rather the combination of the actions taken by the actors in order to pursue their own goals, rather than shared values such as the reduction of violence or the observance of covenants; this combination is unplanned to a larger degree in international relations, and to a lesser one in domestic politics, in which the achievement of order is (also, but not exclusively) the consequence of the polity being purposely established. It is 'as if' all actors had consciously endorsed those peaceful aims, whereas we know that this is far from being true – some did; others did not. By no means can we say that a peaceful order is the goal of political actors, and depict politics as a goal-oriented or teleological activity of like-minded men and women based on good will, because the goals of several groups or countries have been particular, disparate and conflicting in world history, and still are. Against this real background, the normative posture that defines politics as aiming at a just order must sound like the vain repetition of ideal models, from Plato to Kant, if the same theory is unable or unwilling to inquire how, in which case and under what conditions particular and self-centred actors can be led to endorse universal values like peace. In other words, musing on lofty universal aims without a look at philosophical anthropology or a reflection on history risks being useless for the understanding and the re-orientation of politics.

The order that comes into being, in the way sketched here, contains a degree of peace, though often at a price, as is the case with authoritarian regimes domestically and with imperial order internationally, the *Pax Romana*[1] still being its best balanced example – but not the only one, preceded as it was by other empires such as the Persian one under the Achaemenids, the builders of Persepolis (see Figure 3.1).

This has two implications: most historical versions of political order contained moments of a sharp imbalance of power, of authoritarianism and exploitation, in short the seeds of rebellion and upheaval, that is of future *disorder* and *anarchy* (lack of a central power or authority). In this sense democracy, the regime in which everybody can to an extent have a share in government while being protected by the rule of law, has reduced those self-defeating features of political order. This shows, second, that the existence of political order is not, as such, the enemy of *freedom* and *change*. It depends on how the regime guaranteeing order is shaped, on how much flexibility and adaptation it allows for. Most writers of politics, particularly in the contractarian tradition, have insisted on the order of the polity being the true condition for the human being to be free, and debunked the presumptive freedom enjoyed in the state of nature as

FIGURE 3.1 Persepolis. The highly integrated hierarchy (dignitaries, the king's guard, tributaries carrying gifts) of the ancient Persian empire as represented on the walls of Persepolis (near Shiraz, Iran), built in the sixth century BCE and burnt down by Alexander the Great in BCE 330.

illusionary and lethal. Even Jean-Jacques Rousseau (1712–1778), who praised the freedom of man in the state of nature, maintained that obedience to a law one has imposed upon oneself by a social contract fulfils (civil) liberty (Rousseau 1762, Chapters 7–8).

2. Rules, institutions and the regulation of fear

Political order does not consist primarily of courts, law enforcement, internal revenue agencies or correction facilities, but rather of rules and sets of rules residing in the mind of the polity's member; they may or may not find embodiment in organisations and buildings. Rules are rules of behaviour, not moral rules, even if, in some cases, the former may have ties to the latter. Rules of behaviour can be informal and operational, as they just arise and find implementation in the social and political life of communities, or have legal forms. Which version of rules comes first and then finds translation into the other cannot be said to be a sequel following a stable pattern.

We call an *institution* a set of rules which

- is persistent over time
- is interconnected, does not contradict itself, contains no loopholes while regulating a whole area of our collective activity and

- is meaningful within the framework of the community's cultural and social values; in other words, they must fail if they are drafted at the drawing board and then imposed over the participants – as it often happened in colonial times. Here also lies a problem, though not an insurmountable difficulty in the legislating activity of a post-national quasi-polity like the European Union.

It is now clear that the institutions we are talking about are both formal, or legal, and informal. The former prevail in domestic politics, since states all around the world have adopted the Western tendency to juridify all existing rules, except those that cannot be made explicit or public for reasons of decency or hypocrisy. Between states 'international regimes' (see Chapter 6) can be regarded as informal or semi-formal institutions.

Institutions are a key concept in jurisprudence and sociology, why not also in political philosophy? They play indeed a role in shaping the actors' behaviour in as much as they

- define their roles, that is
- the motivations and interests that are possible within the given but also ever-changing framework of shared rules, and
- give information over my and the others' expectations and the negative and positive incentives that can be brought to bear.

In a word, institutions shape the universe of meanings actors put in their own actions and recognise in the behaviour of others. They sustain a grid of interaction that is at the core of politics, of which they are along with power structures and decision making the key component. Politics is a *power-decision-institution trinity* or triangle. For actions or processes that lie outside this realm, the use of the adjective 'political' (calling, for example, the writing of a song or the wearing of a piece of cloth, a political action) seems to be misplaced and inflationary – if we agree on using words in a binding and substantial way.

★ ★ ★

We cannot leave the explanation of order and institution without looking into an element we have so far barely mentioned: *fear*. In different versions, fear is a premise, a component, but also a product of politics. Fear is an emotion or, as writers of politics used to say, a passion;[2] passions are elements of politics whose dynamics are different from, say, that of interest or obligation.

Fear is a premise of politics in the contractarian account of it: it is the fear of being killed, maimed and robbed by others in the state of nature that drives human beings, as we shall soon see, to seek respite and protection under the powerful claws of Leviathan; in the state of civility the natural and limitless fear of death and ruin is replaced by the fear of law (*metus legis*, in Hobbes's Latin) and punishment, a pillar of peace and security.

Regardless of contract theory, we know fear to be present in a multifaceted way in our communal life: fear of war, terrorism, fear of losing one's job and savings, fear of authoritarian developments in some countries, fear of losing the election along with one's own status, but also fear of foreigners and immigrants. Fear is not like fear: we need a distinction. Fear can be a protective sentinel against real dangers that threaten our community, be it our town (in the case of an increased crime or unemployment wave) or humankind (in the case of a looming nuclear war). Without this reasonable fear, communities would be at risk, and would not prepare for lasting protection against, say, floods or cyber attacks. Let us call it *realistic fear* as to keep it from the *neurotic fear* that projects our inner sense of insecurity or panic into the faces of people with a different skin colour.[3] The history of intolerance, racism and fascist movements is full of currents of neurotic fear, which, spontaneous or artificially fostered, is crucial to the build-up of pathological political identities (wall-identities, as we have seen in the last chapter). In a way, politics consists of recognising what is reasonably worth being feared, while at the same time dismissing all incitements to fear as an instrument of bellicose and irrational mass mobilisation. Without skillfully managing fear in its twin face, a political regime can hardly stabilise itself and gain legitimation with the ruled.

Postmodernists believe no distinction makes sense and that fear is just a subjective, illogical feature, to which no reality check is relevant. This belief is similar to the refusal, mentioned in Chapter 2, to keep symbol apart from myth, thus maintaining that all foundation narrative cannot but be mythical. This is all far from real politics, in which those distinctions are held valid and broadly used by actors. In particular, there are two criteria for keeping realistic and reasonable fear separate from the neurotic one: first, in a world shaped by technology, comes the check by science and scientific institutions, which can clarify questions, such as uncertainty about Genetically Modified Organisms or the so-far insufficient preoccupation with global warming. To make good use of scientific knowledge, however, a society has to be capable of open and free public debate, in which instances of the two fears are debated and citizens can develop an informed opinion. Though this does not happen in democracies alone, it happens at best in a democratic framework; the postmodernist enthusiasm for the blurring of distinctions witnesses, among other things, a disbelief in the ability of liberal-democratic procedures to have a better relationship to the truth than other regimes. This is now endangered by the nonchalant relationship to the truth, in particular the scientific truth, shown by a new generation of populist demagogues, but also by the citizens attracted by the false claims, bizarre myths and emotionally overloaded beliefs that abound on the web.

The existence of neurotic fear – as well as the use made of it by fear-mongers and charlatans in order to bring confusion among the public and make them prone to populist and dictatorial leaders – has misled some authors to see only this side of the coin and to try to expel fear from (civilised, democratic) politics altogether. This is neither possible nor convenient because of the counter-intentional effects that come with the cancellation of an element of reality; a theoretically balanced and differentiated approach promises a better regulation of fear.

3. Historic models of political order

We have so far described the key elements and functions of political order as a somehow timeless foundation of the world's political societies throughout their history. This is the task of political philosophy (in its reconstructive version, see Excursus 1), which cannot include the history of the particular concrete and institutional configuration taken in any given epoch by the order we have described in its essential features; this is lamentable, because a comparison between our core model and its concrete versions would be very instructive. Instead, deflecting for a moment from this book's abstinence from the history of thought, we will now briefly examine a number of relevant political order models that have been so far devised by Western philosophers throughout the centuries; I regret not being able to nor having the space to extend this review to non-Western authors, among whom 孔子/Kongzi or Confucius would be the main example. A warning must be issued before we start: we should not mistake the models conceived by philosophers for the real state of affairs; we should not replace the history of institutions (on which something will be said in Chapter 4) with the history of political philosophy. There are obviously intertwinements between the two, but the philosophical models do rarely correspond to the real structures and are often a protest against them, nor have the models necessarily influenced real developments.

The Aristotelian and the contractarian model have dominated Western thought, but other positions are also important.

The Aristotelian model, which was, until Thomas Hobbes, sovereign in the Western tradition, regards the polity or *polis* as a natural development of the human being's tendency to associate with others (first as a couple, then within the family and the village); the association is organic, in the sense that the two parties, for example slave and master, need each other and are advantageous to each other on the basis of their natural dispositions. The assimilation of social forms to the living organism is present also in the idea that the whole, in particular the *polis* or political community, is superior to its parts, because it is self-sufficient. Finally, Aristotelians conceive of social forms in a teleological manner, defining them according to the good they are aspiring to – in the case of the *polis*, the ability to make good life possible (*Politics*, Book 1, 1252–53).

This view is turned upside down in Hobbes's philosophy. Human beings are, by nature, separated and hostile to each other; *bellum omnium contra omnes*/the war of all against all, dominates the state of nature. To save themselves from reciprocal destruction, they need to renounce their full lawless liberty and unite by contract under a common and superior power, the sovereign, also known as the good biblical monster Leviathan. Political order arises from conflict rather than being a feature of nature. Individuals exist without the state, which is an artificial construct rather than a natural creation and is not designed to achieve superior moral good, but only the survival and coexistence of the individuals. Full obedience is the price citizens, or rather subjects, have to pay to receive from the sovereign's absolute power protection against domestic and external threats. Hobbes's absolutist view on power extended it to the cultural realm: against heresy and rebellion, obedience includes that everybody acknowledges the basic Christian truth 'Jesus is the Christ'.[4]

Locke, Rousseau and Kant all shared the contractarian foundation of the state, but only John Locke (1632–1704) formulated a major correction in as much as he set limits to the sovereign's absolute power over individuals: government cannot infringe upon man's natural rights to life, liberty (including liberty of conscience) and property. Locke also introduced the doctrine of separation of powers that was developed shortly after him by Montesquieu (Jean-Louis de Secondat, Baron de Montesquieu, 1689–1755). Locke is traditionally seen as the founder of *liberalism*[5] (the individual's rights are to be protected against state power), both, in particular Montesquieu, as the great theorists of *constitutionalism* (sovereign power is subject to a fundamental – not necessarily written – law defining its limits and architecture). Both authors were important for Alexander Hamilton (1755–1804), James Madison and John Jay (1745–1829), the authors of *The Federalist*, the text that most influenced the development of the newly founded United States of America from confederation to federation. Between the eighteenth and ninenteenth century the people, or *demos*, took the centre of the system of government under constitutional and liberal premises, which after shifting to universal suffrage fulfilled all the requirements of what we call *democracy*, or the democratic order model, – with one exception, which was brought into the agenda late in the nineteenth century and implemented still later in the twentieth: the state's intervention aimed at making effective participation in political and social life possible to everybody by giving him or her the basic elements of education, health care and age protection. This addition of *social rights* to the previous democratic model, which is now at least seen in Europe and Canada, but more limitedly in the USA, as a component of it, had its theoretical proponents in the German social-democracy (starting with Eduard Bernstein, 1850–1932), the Fabian Society and later the liberal statesman Lord William Beveridge (1879–1963) in the UK, the theoretician of 'liberal socialism' Carlo Rosselli (1899–1937, murdered by the Fascists) in Italy; while it was first realised by President F. D. Roosevelt in the USA in the Thirties and the Labour government (1945–51) in Britain.[6] In a word, constitutional rules, individual liberties and social rights are the three major features of the democratic model, as politically institutionalised remedies to the negative side effects of capitalism (more on this in §5 of Chapter 5).

This is, however, not the entire story. In the classical political economy of the Scottish (most eminently represented by Adam Smith, 1723–1790) and English Enlightenment, the freedom of man and his or her happiness were located in industry and the market rather than in politics and its institutions; the state was seen by Smith only as the provider of external security, courts of justice and basic public works – and basic education, he added interestingly, against religious fanaticism as well as the 'torpor' created by the division of labour in the worker's mind. This was the beginning of a never-ending controversy between politics and economy, the state and the market, as to which pole of this relationship can be credited with providing the best order for the associated life of human beings. *Laissez faire* liberalism vs. political liberalism,[7] neoliberalism vs. liberalism/social democracy, Robert Nozick's (1938–2002) argument for a minimal state (minarchism) vs. John Rawls's (1921–2002) two principles of justice:[8] these are only some episodes of the controversy, which is as old as the rise of capitalism as a force capable of shaping the entire society including politics. Never before in history has the economy held such sway on the whole of human life, a phenomenon later magnified by globalisation. A further, less influential episode is anarcho-capitalism, a right-wing version of libertarianism (a communist version also exists);[9] it recommends giving back to the market all state functions, also giving up – as propounded by Murray N. Rothbard (1926–1995) – its monopoly of force. This is one of the many episodes[10] in which radical and marginalised theories, which fail to build up any significant political support, can nonetheless provide arguments and recipes of use to the struggles developing in mainstream parties (libertarian positions have popped up in the debates inside the Republican Party in the USA since Ronald Reagan).

In a very distant corner in the gallery of order models we find Georg W. F. Hegel (1770–1831) and Marx, or rather Karl Marx and Friedrich Engels. To be true, historicist thinkers who see and justify political regimes on the basis of their correspondence with a given stage of history (be it history of the Spirit/Logos or the class struggle) do not advance abstract models of polity. Hegel certainly did not; in any case, unlike his thoughts on the individual and freedom, his philosophy of the state makes him nowadays a 'dead dog'[11] even more so than he was in the 1850s, as Marx saw him with regret in this shape – and reacted by flirting ('coquetting') with Hegel's dialectics in the philosophical passages of *Capital*.[12] The 'model' devised by Marx and Engels belongs to the philosophy of history and political economy rather than political philosophy, and regards political regimes as resulting (like a 'superstructure') from the respective stage of class struggle between 'freeman and slave, patrician and plebeian, lord and serf . . . in a word, oppressor and oppressed' – as they wrote at the outset of the *Manifesto of the Communist Party* (Marx and Engels 1848, 14). The last stage – between bourgeoisie and proletariat – of this struggle was thought to lead to a revolution terminating all class oppression and introducing first an egalitarian society based on the principle that everyone gets as much as s/he contributes to society with her/his labour, later evolving into a higher stage of communism under the very different principle 'from each according to his ability, to each according to his needs!' The state as bureaucratic machinery is reduced to a minimum in the first stage and will disappear in the developed communist society, giving room – according to Engels – to a mere 'administration of things'.[13]

Of the two main traditions that developed from Marx and Engels, the socialist or social-democratic one merged somehow with progressive liberalism, giving shape and justification to the mainly European model of democracy we have seen above. The communist strain produced with Lenin (1870–1924) the model of a radically egalitarian society and cannot be separated from the disasters it produced: a party dictatorship that for a long while defended its political and ideological power and privileges by means of state terrorism (Stalinism killed more people by the millions than National Socialism) and after the initial post-revolutionary stage was never able to really boost productive forces. In North Korea, under Chinese protection, communism has even produced a dynastic monarchy or rather family dictatorship. That Soviet communism was, nonetheless, a model for decades, or at least an example ('Let's do like in Russia!'), for the revolt of oppressed people and some new regimes around the world, is telling about the force of myth and ideology in generating mass movements, as well as for the only relative and fragile availability of masses for rational information and open discussion. Worth noting is, however, the claim sometime raised by Chinese officials that their own conjunction of paternal and efficient party leadership (in fact a nationalist techno-bureaucracy) and capitalist economy (with a mix of public and private enterprise) represents an alternative to conflict-ridden Western democracy with its stagnating economy. It could be asked if this alleged model, hostile to diversity, plurality and productive conflict, has any ties with the ideal of harmony deriving from the Confucian tradition, but connections and influences are, on this general level, difficult to locate and prove.

This was a survey of the most relevant models of political order developed in Europe and later in America, which are still present today in the political and theoretical debate in a more or less influential way. In Chapter 5, §4 the question if China can be regarded as another model will be briefly addressed.

Notes

1 Or *pax augustea*, the peace that prevailed in and around the Roman empire, which included all Mediterranean regions, from BCE 31 (Octavian's victory over Marc Anthony) until at least AD 180 (death of Marcus Aurelius).
2 For example Hobbes in Part I, Chapter 13 of *Leviathan:* 'The passions that incline men to peace are fear of death; desire of such things as are necessary to commodious living, and a hope by their industry to obtain them' (Hobbes 1651, 86). More on passions and politics in the Epilogue.
3 In this matter, I rely heavily on Franz Neumann's seminal essay *Angst und Politik*/Fear and Politics, written in 1954 (Neumann 1954). Neumann, a German jurist who emigrated to the United States, was close to the Institute of Social Research, the New York site of the so-called Frankfurt School in the 1930–40s. I find translating *Angst* to mean 'anxiety', as in the published English version, distorting.
4 A follower of Hobbes in an Islamic country could easily adopt the Islamic creed or *shahada* 'There is no god but God. Muhammad is the messenger of God'.
5 All throughout this book *liberalism* is used in its original and still valid European meaning, while in America liberalism refers to the welfare state policies of the Democratic administrations since F.D. Roosevelt, who was the US president from 1933 through 1945. Still another meaning has the recent term 'neoliberalism', by which the re-energized *laissez-faire* or market-friendly policies of Ronald Reagan (Republican US president 1980–88) and Margaret Thatcher (Conservative PM of the United Kingdom 1979–1990) as well as their later followers are indicated.
6 The introduction of social insurance by German chancellor Otto von Bismarck (1815–1898) in 1889 was aimed at stabilising the Kaiser's authoritarian regime, rather than expanding democracy.
7 In the 1920s, the Italian philosopher Benedetto Croce (1866–1952) argued that the ethical and political values of liberalism can stand without *laissez faire* (*liberismo*) being an essential component of it, a view which was contested by the economist Luigi Einaudi (1874–1961).
8 This matter is examined in Chapter 9.

9 *Libertarianism* is an utterly elusive term making all attempts at a conceptual definition vain; in present language use, the association with anti-government positions, favouring full liberty for capital and private property, prevails.
10 Nearly the same thing happened with the anarchism (from the Greek world *a(n)-archia*/ leaderless, lacking or rejecting a superior power) of the nineteenth and twentieth century, which killed kings, queens and presidents and officials, but left little theoretical heritage.
11 *Toter Hund*, meaning a soulless and uninspiring remnant of the past.
12 Both quotes are from Marx's afterword to the second German edition (1873) of *Capital*, Book 1, available at https://www.marxists.org/archive/marx/works/1867-c1/p3.htm.
13 Marx, who did not love to design blueprints for the future, wrote a few essential notes about it in *Critique of the Gotha Programme* of the German Social-Democratic Party (1875); Engels's prediction is in Engels 1883, 30.

References

Aristotle (335 BCE), Τὰ πολιτικὰ/*Politics*, e-book available at www.gutenberg.org/files/6762/6762-h/6762-h.htm (Aristotle is thought to have composed his major works between 335-323 BCE)

Engels, Friedrich (1883) *Die Entwicklung des Sozialismus von der Utopie zur Wissenschaft/Socialism: Utopian and Scientific*, available at www.slp.org/pdf/marx/dev_soc.pdf

Hobbes, Thomas (1651) *Leviathan*, edited by J.C.A. Gaskin, Oxford, New York: Oxford University Press, 1998.

Marx, Karl (1875) *Kritik des Gothaer Programms/Critique of the Gotha Program*, available at www.marxists.org/archive/marx/works/1875/gotha/index.htm

Marx, Karl and Friedrich Engels (1848) *Manifest der kommunistischen Partei/Manifesto of the Communist Party*, e-book available at www.marxists.org/archive/marx/works/download/pdf/Manifesto.pdf

Neumann, Franz L. (1954) *Angst und Politik/Anxiety and Politics*, in *The Democratic and The Authoritarian State*, edited by Herbert Marcuse, Glencoe: Free Press, 1957, 270–300.

Rousseau, Jean-Jacques (1762) *Du contrat social/The Social Contract*, e-book available at www.constitution.org/jjr/socon.htm

Further readings

My understanding of political order and institutions draws on two seminal international relations books:

Bull, Hedley (1977) *The Anarchical Society: A Study of Order in World Politics*, New York: Columbia University Press.

Keohane, Robert (1989) *International Institutions and State Power*, Boulder: Westview.

To mention are also:

Fukuyama, Francis (2014) *Political Order and Political Decay*, New York: Farrar, Straus and Giroux.

Huntington, Samuel (1968) *Political Order in Changing Societies*, New Haven: Yale University Press.

4
THE STATE

The abstract categories of politics we have gone through thus far find a first concrete appearance in the institution that ever since has been central – with some exception and much flexibility – in the configurations of political order known in the history of human societies: the state. Obviously, this entity has already popped up in our reconstruction of the workings of politics, but now we will define the meaning of this elusive word, then look at how in European modernity the state emerged in the shape known all over the world; the state's relationship to society and the nation will be next, while we will end with a look into the changes and challenges that this paramount political institution is presently experiencing.

1. The state and sovereignty

> *The state is the institution exerting over a population and a territory a legitimate power that is guaranteed by its monopoly of force.*

This is, with a slight variation, the definition Max Weber formulated (Weber 1922, Part 1, Chapter 1, §17) some hundred years ago as the conceptual recapitulation of what the state had turned out to be (or rather to become) in modern history. I shall not enter the taxonomy of states or quasi-states having a population, but lacking a territory, or vice versa (in the case where the potential population is still strewn over other states). As to the monopoly, it regards not only that of military and police force,[1] since states do also own an exclusive authority in fundamental financial acts (minting currency, levying taxes) and in representing themselves towards other states (diplomacy). To illustrate all of this, one only needs to go back on the one hand to the rise of the European state, as it will happen below, and on the other hand to the reconstituting of China as a state (the People's Republic of China, founded on 1 October 1949) implied for the victorious Communist Party not just the defeat of the nationalist Kuomintang army, but also the erasure of the warlords and the local powers that had contributed to the demise of the Republic of China proclaimed in 1912.

In modernity, the state is by default sovereign: without *sovereignty* there is no or an insufficient statehood. The word translates the Latin (medieval) expressions *summa potestas*/highest power or *imperium*/supreme command, thus indicating a level of power that is not inferior to anyone else. Especially in modernity, sovereign statehood is the cornerstone of whatever version of political order may have materialised and the mother of all institutions.

Sovereignty has two faces:

- internal or domestic sovereignty, that is supreme power over all citizens or subjects, none excluded, in the entire state territory; there are no limitations to this power except by a self-imposed law. A seminal case of self-limitation is the abolition of capital punishment, by which the state gives up its claim to sovereignty over the lives of the citizens with regard to law enforcement (it does not do so in a matter of self-defence, even if it can temporarily renounce conscription: conscripted or not, citizens can still be asked to expose themselves to the hazard of killing and being killed in combat).
- external with respect of other states or actors, in the sense of a recognised claim to autonomy or to govern itself by its own statutes, held valid in the same territory and over the same population: this can be upheld even in case of temporary foreign occupation, if the occupant does not attempt to cancel the state's existence or absorb it into another state.

External sovereignty is the pre-condition to the domestic one, which is very much subject to the constraints of the international system and cannot be properly studied outside this link. Sovereignty depends very much on the *recognition* granted by other states or, since the founding of the United Nations in 1945, by the UN General Assembly. In this sense, sovereignty is an interactive legal feature that wraps the state into a web of shared rules and entanglements, thus contributing to international order by giving legal form to an emerging factual power centre. On the other hand, since sovereignty denotes independence as the ultimate shield for the free existence and wellbeing of a human group, it also means the ability and the right to wage war (see Chapter 6), whatever the wish of other states or international organisations may be.

Let us now go back to the exception and the flexibility mentioned above. Strictly speaking, in the early history of humankind and even more in pre-historic stages, attempts at establishing a rudimentary political order were made in stateless societies, such as tribes and chiefdoms. This is the exception to the universal presence of the state, which belongs however to the domain of cultural anthropology rather than that of political philosophy; while in our days the recurrent claim (in protest movements or in some corner of feminism) to be willing and able to manage common affairs without resorting to the state belongs to the tradition of radical and utopian thought. 'The political' and 'the statal' are indeed since eighty years (the rise of the welfare state) strongly intertwined more than in the time before, as the state was not yet endowed with the financial, organisational and technological tools that seem to make it omnipresent and omnipotent. Nonetheless, the two notions do overlap neither conceptually nor in fact – think for example of the political role recently played worldwide by non-governmental and other transnational organisations.

Flexibility has to be shown with regard to the use of the word 'state'. In accurate terms it can be only referred to the modern European state as it was shaped in the seventeenth and eighteenth century, and then spilled over to other continents, first of all the Americas and much later (in the twentieth century) China, and by far not only as a side effect of colonialism: Japan, which was never a colony, adopted at the end of the nineteenth century a private law code that largely reproduced the German *Bürgerliches Gesetzbuch*. It was Europe, primarily France, that 'invented' the modern state in its self-definition and organisation, both unthinkable without the fitting legal system. It was adopted elsewhere because doing so favoured the modernisation process in which more and more extra-European countries were engaging. Nonetheless, we keep using 'state' to indicate the period in Chinese history (BCE 453–221) called of the seven Warring States (or Kingdoms), or speak of the Roman state, which in fact anticipated many features of its modern cousin.

Neither the history of the word nor that of the thing itself can be told here in a way respecting its complexity. Suffice it to say that it derives from the Latin expression *status rei publicae*/the state of public matters or – in the English discourse about politics – of the commonwealth. The career that later made 'state' the key word in the lexicon of institutions started in 1513 with the first line in Machiavelli's *Principe* (1532): 'All states, all powers, that have held and hold rule over men have been and are either republics or principalities'.[2] This career was shining in countries with a powerful, omnipresent central power such as France and Spain with their empires, the Hapsburg Empire, Prussia and Russia with its huge Государственное,[3] while the Anglophone culture is likely to have been the last in reluctantly adopting it – in the mid seventeenth century Hobbes was still speaking of 'Commonwealth'.

2. The rise of the modern state in Europe

What we are going to become acquainted with in the following is the rise of the modern state, which took place in Europe and subsequently spilled over to other continents and very different peoples.

Nationes/peoples were recognised elements of the political, military and legal structure of the Roman empire and became ever more relevant with the process called in French, Italian and Spanish 'barbarian invasions' and in German in a more neutral key '*Völkerwanderungen*/people's migrations'– understandably, given that the migrating peoples were almost all Germanic. Along with other domestic and external factors, this led to the demise of the empire and the establishment of 'national', or rather ethnic, kingdoms in the western-European countries, minus the part of the Iberian peninsula which had been occupied, since AD 711, by the Umayyad

Arabs (Al-Andaluz or the Emirate of Granada, as it was later called). The Roman Empire was re-founded in the year AD 800 under the Christian aegis, as the Holy Roman Empire, by the king of Franks Charlemagne, who was crowned by Pope Leo III the new 'emperor of the Romans'. Through continuous wars of submission, Charles the Great's empire came to comprise approximately France, Germany and Italy, plus the strips of Catalonyan/Spanish territory that were taken away from Arab rule. Its claim to being universal, as well as its source of legitimacy, relied on the alleged continuation of the Roman past: it was recognised by the pope as the polity of the (western-European) Christians and gave institutional shape to the *res publica christiana*, as it was later called by emperor Friedrich II (1194–1250). This claim ended substantially with the Treaties of Westphalia (1648) and was formally cancelled as late as in 1806 by Napoleon.

In medieval Europe, the other power with universal claims was the Roman Church, although it was weakened by the separation (1054) from the Eastern Orthodox Church of Constantinople and later the Reformation, which Martin Luther started in 1517. Rome was regarded as the source of the true Christian doctrine and the supreme authority in sacramental issues,[4] as well as in the legitimation of temporal authorities, first and foremost with those of the emperor. Charlemagne also transferred territories in the Italian peninsula under direct political rule of the pope, thus creating the *temporal power* of the Church, which lasted until 1870, when Rome was taken to the pope and became the capital of the newly founded Kingdom of Italy. In spite of bitter strife between popes and emperors, disunion and wars in the empire, as well as corruption of various types and degrees in the Roman Church, on the front of legal (top-down) legitimacy, the claims of the two universal powers lasted until the dawn of modern politics in the sixteenth–seventeenth centuries. This edifice of power and recognition was reinforced, but also ossified, by the hereditary personal dependence of power holders on the next upper level of patrician bondage, up to the king and/or the emperor. This was the *feudal system*, whose structure is well-known also in very different countries and cultures as in ancient China, and elements of which survive still now in not yet fully modernised societies, in organised crime networks, but also in niches inside the democratic party power – at the local level, where territorial control relying on patronage over a traditional electorate matters. The discovery and exploitation of new territories in other continents along with the emergence of a new class, the commercial and later manufacturing bourgeoisie in the cities, undermined this structure. On the other hand, the growing autonomous power of the European territorial states (which became only in the nineteenth century the nation states we are familiar with) further degraded the emperor's claim to be entitled to universal authority. Though hardly in a fully explicit way, the Treaties of Westphalia acknowledged the independence of those states and put an end to the wars of religion between Protestant and Catholic powers that had ravaged the continent for some 120 years (1524–1648).

This was the background against which the modern state arose, with differing speed and forms in different countries. This notwithstanding, we allow ourselves a certain degree of generalisation and use for the main stages of this process the following names: state of the estates, absolutist state, constitutional state, administrative state.

Before we begin describing this process, let us hold that its initial and more powerful motor was neither social (new groups, new claims) nor cultural (in the spirit of the Renaissance and later the Enlightenment), but rather interstate power relationships and war. After the introduction of fire arms, particularly artillery, wars between large territorial states required large and costly armies, and more importantly navies, for whose provision and command the feudal system was inadequate; centralisation of the armed forces required a stable and extended taxation largely at the expenses of the emerging 'productive' classes as long as nobility and clergy, but also free cities and local communities remained under the shield of their privileges. The management of the tax system was, on the other hand, not possible without extending, rationalising and professionalising administration and bureaucracy, in their turn an additional burden for the state budget. The much contested – for example by Thomas Jefferson – public debt became unavoidable and increased.[5] Economics, particularly the science of finance, soon became an important discipline, mainly in Scotland, England and France.

Over the course of these transformations, the central power of the European states asserted itself in the military, judicial[6] and fiscal realm, as well as in terms of culture and customs; thanks to the 'soft power' of the profligate royal courts in the Baroque period, the representation of royal authority in ceremonies, music, visual arts and literature became essential to power itself and its legitimation. The external representation of the country was also monopolised by the sovereign and entrusted to an increasingly professionalised diplomatic corps. This power first allied itself with the emerging third estate, including the new commercial, industrial and professional bourgeoisie, the peasants and the urban proletariat, of which only the upper layer was able to express representatives. The feudal regime was replaced by the 'state of the estates'.[7] A layer of 'intermediate bodies' filtered the effects of the sovereign's absolute power over individuals, who were as a community represented by the estates in an assembly.[8]

Later, the new social class and its various parties turned themselves against absolutism, vindicating liberal and equal liberties for the individual, governing according to a constitution, division of powers among the legislative, the executive and the judiciary branches, as well as the protection of property against interventions of the state along with respect for free trade. *Legal egalitarianism, liberalism, constitutionalism* and *capitalism*[9] became and still remain the pillars of the modern state in the West though they were recast by the unfolding of democracy and social thought. The erection of those pillars, supported by the Enlightenment's effort to bring Reason to bear in political and social affairs, culminated in the turn away from the divine right of the princes towards the recognition of the people as the only sovereign, even if it was a people marginalising women, ethnic strangers, poor and a fortiori slaves. *Popular sovereignty* was later recast in the form we are going to see, but except in times of dictatorship or foreign rule those pillars remained as permanent features of the modern state along with its being an administrative, legal, financial and military engine[10] whose central authority can be delegated to, but not infringed upon by local (states or provinces or *Länder* of an union or federation) or corporate (one-issue authorities) agencies. This is not to deny the centrifugal and disintegrating effects on the state's authority that come from the long-term consequences of globalisation, the replacement of pyramidal with network-like structures and the general weakening of politics.

The recasting of popular sovereignty and the other pillars of the modern state resulted from two intertwined novelties, one theoretical and the other economic and social. The bourgeois nature of classical liberalism, in a word the *de facto* limitation of liberties to the male citizens whose social status gave them the cultural and financial capability to make use of them was criticised in the time between the nineteenth and twentieth century by socialist, social-Christian and left-liberal authors as well as the women's movement. The other phenomenon was the capitalist transformation of peasants, farmers, artisans and small shopkeepers into masses of industrial workers concentrated in cities and increasingly organised in clubs, unions, parties – and armies, an essential side effect of the First World War or Great War (1914–1918), which also opened new chances for women's participation in industrial, cultural and political life. All of this deeply changed the liberal state, bringing, through universal franchise, masses into political life, contesting the traded version of workers' rights and economic position in capitalism, making politics no longer the occupation of a traditional elite, but rather the profession of leaders capable of managing huge party organisations. Liberalism, as conceived of so far, and democracy seemed to be at odds, a view that later seemed to be confirmed by the fact that authoritarian or even totalitarian regimes with a corporatist ideology were able to introduce in the Thirties social protection policies for workers that liberal states had failed to practise, particularly after the Great Depression began in 1929.[11] A new turn came with the New Deal realised by Franklin Delano Roosevelt, president of the USA from 1933 through 1945, which made the state an active economic actor in an effort aimed at reviving the economy by creating jobs and establishing social security (retirement pensions and unemployment insurance).

Elsewhere, primarily in Europe, the Second World War and its aftermath gave a final bent to the history of the modern state: in the UK, Lord Beveridge's Report presented to His Majesty's Government in the middle of the war (1942), identified 'the five giant evils' of society (Want, Disease, Ignorance, Squalor and Idleness) and suggested social security policies that were later implemented by the new Labour government between 1945 and 1949. West Germany with its notion of a 'social market economy' as well as France and Italy went the same path between the Fifties and Seventies, against the resistance of conservative, business-friendly liberalism and the protest of Communist parties and unions, which aimed at scrapping capitalism altogether.

These reforms saved the liberal, constitutional and democratic state from the non-participation or open enmity of the layers of population that saw its promise of *liberté, egalité, fraternité* disavowed by Beveridge's 'giant evils', more generally by their lacking access to the resources (a decent income and housing, health care and education) that could only make allegiance to the liberal-democratic state justified and meaningful. Let us anticipate that this story – a history of the twentieth century – highlights how politics can never be severed from other realms of human life in communities, in particular not from the socio-economic condition of the governed. This is true, as we shall see, in particular for democracy as a promising procedure, and does not disavow the claim of a relative autonomy of politics, raised at the outset of our journey in Chapter 1.

It is uncertain whether the success story of the democratic state in the West (including Japan after 1945 and with remarkable differences between the several countries and continents) will be continued throughout the course of the twenty-first century, but this will occupy us later on.

What has been briefly told here is the history of the state in Europe and later North America. This is not due primarily to the circumstance that this textbook is written by an European philosopher with no particular competence in the history of the state worldwide. It has rather its grounding in the objective circumstance that the state, in its modern understanding, has been an European invention, while many institutions connected to the state spilled over to other continents where they were either imposed by colonial rule or freely adopted because they were better fit to organise communal life in societies becoming more differentiated and less traditionalistic, especially after the rise of international trade and capitalism. The extra-European spread of the state as the main format of political life was a defining feature of modernisation.

Another reason for this European primacy was that no other civilisation or empire was able to pursue a similar universal projection because either it did not have the cultural and institutional resources to do so, as in the case of the Mongol empire in the thirteenth century, or the Europeans made it impossible by rejecting subjugation by the Arabs in the battles of the eighth century (Tours, central France, 732)[12] and the Turks in the sixteenth (Lepanto or Turkish İnebahtı in the Ionian Sea, 1571) and seventeenth (Vienna 1683) century. The most arguable candidate for such a projection, China with its great culture, gave up after Admiral 郑/Zheng He's seven expeditions (1405–33) in the Indian Ocean all the way to Aden, and definitively retreated into the isolation that made it later an easier prey for European colonialism.

It is this complex history – and not colonial imposition alone – that explains why political and legal forms of organisation born in Europe were adopted worldwide. Besides the conquest of new markets and new territories, not to be underestimated is the role played by an essential and exclusive component of European cultural modernity, *curiositas*/curiosity, in the push to explore and experience other countries and populations – symbolised in medieval Europe by Ulysses's literary figure depicted in Dante's *Inferno*, Canto XXVI.[13] Without this drive, modernity, with all its evils and (not only technological, but civil) blessings, would not have been born, because it would have lacked the intellectual and symbolic motor of innovation. A mix of evils (enhanced destructiveness of warfare, oppression of liberties, top-down bureaucratic organisation of the masses) and blessings (containment of violence, establishment of the rule of law, public safety, social policy) also characterises the European primacy in the invention of the state and the spreading of its various forms. In any case, this seems to be an irreversible history: the state as it is presently all over the planet cannot be reversed, or attempts to do so end up in genocide, as in Cambodia under the Khmer Rouge (1975–1979); it can only be reformed and developed according to new challenges and theories. In countries with *failed states* or underdeveloped statehood, which results in a lower ability to organise public life, ordinary citizens live less freely, unless they are criminals, and are more needy, unless they are very wealthy or children of the very wealthy and pay no taxes since the tax system has collapsed or was never set up in the first place.[14]

3. State and society

This section's title could just as well be *Politics and Society*, but I have chosen *State* because this is the level on which the underlying topic finds its closer definition. By *society* we understand the totality of the interactions between individuals and groups either in general, as it is largely the case in the following pages, or with regard to a specific place (French society) or time (Chinese society during the Ming dynasty). Politics and the state are seen as a particular area of those relationships, which comes up more clearly in the language of system theory: politics is a sub-system of the overall social system. As I have hinted at in Chapter 1, this is all right as far as it does not translate into the mechanical picture of politics being just the mirror or side effect of what happens in society. Politics, and in particular, the state do vice versa influence *society*, as we will see later, and none of these poles is as such the independent variable in social and political history. We should also not forget that politics and society (less so for the state, because of its institutional reality) are conceptual constructs that it is unwise to reify as if they were hardware, while they live primarily in their interaction. To make a long story short, political actors, primarily the state, make formal decisions and build institutions with central power, while society, though also possessing features like power and institutions, does not.

State and society is an odd couple, born in recent centuries from the splitting of something that used to be one. The Greeks and the Romans possessed the notion of the state, as attested by Cicero's definition of it as *res publica*/commonwealth given in the book he dedicated to it.[15] In antiquity, however, the items we call state and society were not different from each other, but one; religion was a dimension of public life and the οἰκονομία/economy was conceptually confined, as in Aristotle's model, to the law (νόμος) governing the household (οἶκος) as unit of production (in a prevalently agrarian economy). Religion as a sphere separated from politics, coexisting with it but on its own principles,[16] emerged first with the spread of Christianity and the discovery of interiority, as in Augustine. We have already seen that the European Middle Ages were based on the bipolarity of worldly and spiritual society and authority, notwithstanding all their entanglements. The rise of a worldwide market economy since the sixteenth century draws the philosophers' attention to the growing importance of the new economy of trade and production, seen in its growing independence from state power. In the history of economic thought, this is mirrored in the debate between free trade supporters and physiocrats on the one side, and mercantilists on the other. With *A Natural History of Civil Society* (1767), a book welcomed in all of Europe and authored by the Scottish philosopher Adam Ferguson, a new term[17] entered the learned language and found a few decades later an echo in Hegel's political and law philosophy – though the meaning of *bürgerliche Gesellschaft* adopted by Hegel was not identical with Ferguson's, for whom 'civil' means 'civilised'. A new peak in the relevance of 'civil society' was hit in the young Marx's critique of Hegel's political philosophy,[18] written in the 1840s but not published until 1927 and influential in the years thereafter.

★ ★ ★

In the present political and theoretical use 'civil society' means two things and needs some disambiguation. In connection with its classical Scottish and primarily Hegelian meaning, which I cannot elucidate any further here, it indicates the complex of the private relations between individuals and groups, be they economic, social or cultural in character. An industrialists' club or a trade union is as much a civil society organisation as a charity or a music association, such as the Viennese *Musikverein*; a particular material or set of ideal interests are the driving force. Personal relations belong to civil society as little as state institutions; our relationship to the latter are regulated by public *law*, which checks private wishes against the public interest and acts through commands of the authorities; while those who belong to civil society, its members, are shaped by the private institution of *contract*, based on consensus, though the framework for contract law is set by the state. This is the meaning I am following in my further considerations on the relationship between civil society and the state.

Another more recent meaning, widely adopted in public debate nowadays, sees *civil society* as the sphere of those initiatives and groups that intend to uphold the public interest or better pursue the public good in social and political life outside the state. Civic initiatives, neighbourhood committees, advocacy groups, charities, associations centred on sexual orientation or ethnic issues, and NGOs are the best known components of civil society in this version. Their understanding of the social world is opposed to the impersonal logic of state administration and even to ordinary political action, in particular to party politics. Their claim to represent the people's authentic interest cannot be taken at face value, because their representativeness is not guaranteed by public procedures and their defence of particular, if morally high-ranking, interests can end up in lobbyist or self-perpetuating activities; even less so can the somehow redeeming appeal they and their theoreticians seem to see in the formula 'only civil society can heal the wrongs made by the state(s)' be taken seriously, since states cannot be reformed by evoking some morally superior agent. Yet their ability to indicate situations of inefficiency, inflicted suffering and injustice is high and should be better brought to bear in democratic processes.

Now, the relationship between politics and society has been described some sixty years ago by political scientists such as David Easton (1917–2014), Gabriel Almond (1911–2002) and Karl Deutsch (1912–1992) in systemic terms: (civil) society, with its problems and changes, is the environment in which 'demands' are given as 'input' into the political system, which is expected to provide an 'output' of answers that will interact with the environment generating 'outcomes', and subsequently new challenges and demands. The notion of a *political system* was intended to replace the state as the core actor, dismissing the legal framework in which the state used to be confined. The systemic approach is no longer dominating the scene in political science, partly because of its inner problems, partly because general theory and holistic approaches are now hardly in demand in the discipline. Yet it remains the last overarching attempt to describe the relationship of politics and society after the two preceding philosophical episodes: Hegel saw civil society as the sphere of want and self-interest, capable of some self-regulation but unable to lay out real political governance, which was the exclusive performance of the state as higher manifestation of the Spirit (*Geist*). On the contrary, the young Marx (1843), whose views were still influential in the 1960–70s, saw civil society as divided until modern times by class struggle, whose temporary winner used the repressive and bureaucratic tool of the state to consolidate its power and rule out change. The proletarian revolution was expected to tear down definitively the state and make room for society's self-rule on the basis of a full satisfaction of human needs.[19]

The difference between these three models is telling: Hegel and Marx saw society and the state as elements of a philosophy of history, which explains their past and predicts their future with normative accents; system theorists stay far away from history and normativity and only suggest a conceptual and content-free frame of reference for understanding process and change. All three versions of society are no longer able to shape political theory, and the very notion of society does not seem to play any significant role in recent research, except in very specific versions such as 'knowledge society', 'information society' and 'world society', all attempts to find names for the presumptive pivot of the universe in which we live. To elaborate on these definitions is the task of social rather than political philosophy. Yet, taking note of the bottleneck in which the notion of society has ended up should not be mistaken as an endorsement for Margaret Thatcher's, British PM from 1979 through 1990, ontological rejection of it as a space of solidarity in the name of radical individualism.[20] We should rather turn our attention to the circumstance that, at least in welfare states, state policies have penetrated society, increasingly influencing the individuals' income, status and (retreating) sense of independence. This is likely to be one of the main reasons why state and society are less distinguishable than in the times of good old liberalism. Given the high level of their intertwinement, it is illusory to see society as the dimension of private interactions capable of contesting the state's intrusion or to represent a higher moral instance against it; at least in democracies, corruption in the public administration is often matched by corruption in society.

Two other terms – community and the public sphere – come up in the context of the relationship politics has with what surrounds it or lies beneath it – spatial metaphors are inevitable in the description of social and political constructs, which we tend to see as works of architecture.

Community is seen as the web of 'organic' relationships among persons, of which the family is the paradigm, based as it is on mutual emotional bonds; the will of the community is more important than that of the single members. On the contrary, society refers to the relationships between individuals that are based on the exchange of performances, shaped by contract and aimed at individual utility. This language was established by the German sociologist Ferdinand Tönnies in his book *Gemeinschaft und Gesellschaft/ Community and Society* (1887) and remains alive in sociology; a last echo of this counterposition between two ground types of socialisation came in the 1980–90s with the debate communitarians vs. liberals, which will be further explained in Chapter 9. Its interest for political philosophy derives from its ability to conceptualize the criticism of capitalism and modernisation, including liberalism and democracy, because of the destruction they have been operating on traditional and presumptively more humane personal bonds.[21] Needless to say, in this sociological vocabulary the meaning of society is different, almost opposite to the meaning it has in the dyad state-society sketched above; the content of 'society' here is to be found in the Tönnesian version of 'community'.

The other concept, the *public sphere*,[22] denotes the dimension in which the communicative interaction between citizens, with regards to social and political affairs, takes place. It is the place in which both discourses aimed at the formation of political will and the criticism of existing policies and laws are developed in freedom and outside any interference from the state and the economic powers that be. Its classical shape first emerged in the αγωρά/agorà or gathering and marketplace of the Greek city states and the *forum* in Rome and other Roman cities. A full-fledged public sphere was reborn in the coffee houses, theatres and clubs of the bourgeois civil society, with the press and its freedom as the main channels. Universal suffrage in democracy and mass parties both enlarged and eroded liberal *Öffentlichkeit*. On the one hand, its existence and vitality remain crucial as a counter-power to state power and its administrative constraints, as well as a source of new ideas and norms in a rapidly changing world; think of the role played by public discourse in putting unprecedented issues such as the environment, climate change and the responsibility to protect on the political agenda. On the other hand, the public sphere – which includes, but is much broader a concept than public opinion – is endangered not only by the more sophisticated and tentacular presence of the state, but also by a media system that is scarcely instrumental to a free exchange of ideas among equal partners, dominated as it is by oligopolistic powers and high-professionalised players. With the exception of the high quality press, this system turns out to be a self-contained 'fourth power', as in its literary or cinematographic image, rather than a space for the formation and rejuvenation of the public sphere. It cannot yet be said whether online communication and its blogosphere represent a valid reshaping of the public sphere, nor if its drawbacks (the easier dissemination of hate speech, sectarianism, and weird beliefs) prevail over the enhancement of freedom and 'voice'.[23]

4. State and nation

We are used to thinking of the state as a nation state or even, as in American politics and journalism, to speak of states in terms of nations.[24] This is not only confusing, because actors of international politics and law are states, not nations, while states can be multinational, as the old Soviet Union or the post-national European

Union, which is not a traditional state although it is a major player in international politics. It is misleading as well, in as much as it suggests an ontological coincidence of state and nation that is stranger to what happened in history and may happen in the future. The state, especially the modern one, is the main political actor in power games, has legal clothes and more or less defined goals to uphold, but acts primarily on strategic considerations with regards to winning or losing in front of impersonal challenges or recognisable adversaries: these are the coordinates within which citizens are kept together and recognise themselves as united in statehood. The nation is a rather 'communitarian' artefact, its internal bonds are of ethnic and/or cultural character, that is referred to philosophy, religion, language, tradition, life-forms; its existence is value-based rather than strategic, emotional and not merely argumentative.[25] The Romans spoke of *natio*, which comes from the same root as *nascere* (to be born) and does not overlap with the modern notion of nation, while they dubbed Rome itself *civitas* or *patria* (commonwealth or homeland). Later in the Middle Ages, things went into flux, and later Jeremy Bentham (1748–1832) first used the term 'international law' to denote what was theretofore known as the 'law of nations', or *ius gentium*, regulating the interaction among states (1970); the new word was to stay, though in 1999 John Rawls more traditionally, but with good reasons titled his work on international relations *The Law of Peoples*. We shall look here at the nation in the framework of the modern state's evolution, leaving aside questions such as the possible application of this term to biblical Israel or ancient Egypt.

In the context of modernity, the nation can be conceived of in two fairly different ways: either as an organic product of ethnicity that pre-existed, and also may survive the state, or as a *political construct* built up by political and intellectual 'elites', who select and put together elements already existing in the historical evolution and start a struggle for recognition in whose course the nation first becomes what those actors pretend it always was. The first view is called *primordialism* or essentialism and has been largely marginalised in the studies on nation and nationalism of the last forty years, while the second one, known as modernist, should be rather dubbed evolutionary. It sees the idea of the nation as having come up in the context of the European bourgeoisie's struggle aimed at enlarging the basis of existing territorial (France, Britain, Spain) or hoped-for (Germany, Italy, Poland, Hungary and others in Eastern Europe) states by transferring the source of sovereignty and legitimacy from the monarch's divine right to the people: popular sovereignty. The ignition of this processes came for all of Europe and later Latin America from the French Revolution, whose goal was – in the words of Emmanuel-Joseph Sieyès (1748–1836) – '*fonder la nation contre la noblesse*/to found the nation against the nobility'. At the turn of the eighteenth and nineteenth centuries, the idea of nation was very successful because it gave concrete shape to the more abstract political and juridical notion of the people as bearer of sovereign statehood – in the next chapter we shall see how consequential the merging of the *demos*/people with the *ethnos*/ethnic group was. That idea gave the new constitutional architecture roots in a community of living people that everybody could feel they belonged to. In this version, which is the antechamber of democracy, the *idea of nation* must be distinguished from *nationalism*, as it can be seen in the works and deeds of its most famous representative, Giuseppe Mazzini (1805–1872), who was a Europeanist in addition to being a leading figure of the Italian *Risorgimento*. Still in this light, the nation did not come up in politics without a measure of planned nation-building: by literary debates and exemplary action, sometimes in form of 'martyrdom', before it was established as nation state and recognised in the world, by education (elementary school in the first place) and military conscription afterwards.

Was the successive sliding of the idea of nation into nationalism, the most unfortunate event in modern history, inscribed in the nation's DNA, or was it the consequence of occasional factors or voluntary choices made by the ruling elites? I do incline towards the second answer, but again we cannot enter a philosophical inquiry in counterfactual history. That slipping move was energetically promoted by Europe's élites in a time of enhanced international competition and upcoming internal unrest due to the growing workers' movement, against which nationalism and military or colonial adventures were a welcome safety valve. Beyond the outspoken nationalistic ideologues and parties, the turn to nationalism included nearly all of the mainstream bourgeois (liberal) politicians and left the very workers' movement not unaffected. Unaware of the new destructiveness of industrial warfare, European 'nations' entered like sleepwalkers[26] into what later turned out to be the First World War, some of them even seeing in it 'the war to end all wars', which instead, left the continent and the world pregnant with the Second World War; in the course of this process, nationalism, the prime motivational force, was enriched with ideological conflict, xenophobia and state-operated racism in the *Shoah*.[27] At the end of this process in 1945, everywhere in Europe the nation states had lost their credibility and were supplanted by two empires, of which the Soviet Union was multinational and driven by a universalist ideology, while American exceptionalism cannot be seen as just another version of nationalism.

Among developing countries, nationalism has been and still is the unlucky road companion in the national liberation era and later in the often failed stabilisation of post-colonial regimes, sometimes accompanied by religious hatred; this has led, once again, to an arms race among developing countries that has gone so far as to not see the nuclear threshold as morally and politically insurmountable. India-Pakistan is the case in point, but nationalism has recently retaken the stage in post-communist states such as Russia, Poland, Hungary, even in states within the European Union, to date the most innovative and successful endeavour to get rid of its poison. Nationalist mobilisation also remains a tool of the art of government in the Russian Federation as well as the People's Republic of China. While globalisation has, in fact, further decreased the strength of nation states, its backlash on the subjective side of politics, the defensive appeal of nationalism, has been and will still be considerable. To strike a balance between global constraints, traded self-identification in local terms, weak universalist ideals and the temptation of resorting to the consensus-winning, if impotent appeal of nationalism remains difficult. Even more so in times in which liberal democracy, a valid vaccine against nationalist seclusion and hatred, is eroded by another problematic phenomenon: populism, which will be discussed in the next chapter.

5. The state and the law

It is a generally accepted doctrine that, while the state may or may not have goals to pursue beyond guaranteeing security and the minimal conditions for the citizens to thrive, it always has functions to fulfil, the first of which in the modern state is to *make, adjudicate and enforce laws*. This is the state on its performing side; in the section on identity, we have already encountered the basic standards of legality as one of the performances that allow for the legitimacy of an institution to become actual legitimation. On the side of the state's foundations, we have seen that the original, albeit fictitious, covenant is enshrined in a constitution that defines the matter of the covenant (what state and citizens are owing each other) and the limits to state's authority. In liberal democracies after 1945, the American model of a supreme court ruling over the conformity to the constitution of the norms passed by the legislative or executive power has spread as far as to the Russian Federation. The same holds with regards to the state's epistemic existence: constitutional law acknowledging the fundamental rights of citizens has occupied the place taken in the old German academia by the state-centric discipline called *Staatsrecht*/the law of the state. Seen in historical perspective, the *princeps legibus solutus est*/the prince is not bound by the laws norm, issued by the Roman Senate in AD 69 under Emperor Vespasian, and revived by modern era absolutism has disappeared; even the most heinous dictators of our time try to wrap their deeds in some kind of a legal form.

The law seems, therefore, to be a defining element in modern politics, even more than it was in Cicero's definition of the commonwealth. It gives it clothes (nearly all power comes in the form of laws), but it is also at the core of its operating and its legitimacy. The ancient dispute whether governance of the law (*rex sub lege*/the king is under the law) or governance by persons (*lex sub rege*/the law is under the king) is to be preferred seems to have been solved in favour of the first corner, in spite of all personalization of politics in the media. In most states, law graduates are still the preferred candidates for positions in the public administration, though economists, philosophers and political scientists would often be better at solving problems and fostering innovation.[28] New conflicts or impulses emerging from social dynamics are often not recognised as long as they do not find expression and regulation in a legal framework: this is an aspect of the phenomenon called *juridification*.

In the following, I shall not ask how far statute law (of Napoleonic-Roman or Germanic-Roman subtype) and common law differ as to the relationship between the state and its law. In law systems, as in continental Europe, deriving from the *Corpus iuris civilis* and issued by the state, that relationship is most evidently closer, and I will now refer mostly to this case. There are qualifications to the notion of law acceptable as expression of the legislative competence of the state within the social compact: it must have a *general and abstract nature*, as such refer to all citizens without exclusions or different treatments. Laws that under the clothes of generality are, in fact, tailored to a single situation (thus being an administrative measure[29] dressed as a law) are in principle not compatible with a constitutional system; even less so for laws, such as in racial legislation, that are conceived as exceptional measures aimed at excluding or disfavouring a single group of citizens. Totalitarian regimes excel in creating legislation of this kind, but the pure general character of the law is not completely preserved in all democracies either.

An analogue qualification must be specified with regard to the *rule of law* defined by the UN as

> a principle of governance in which all persons, institutions and entities, public and private, including the State itself, are accountable to laws that are publicly promulgated, equally enforced and independently adjudicated, and which are consistent with international human rights norms.[30]

This is the thick or substantive definition of the term, which also includes equality before the law, a principle already known to the Greeks as ἰσονομία/isonomy. In this version, rule of law means rule of the just law, including the protection of human rights. This makes it very different from its 'continental' pseudo-equivalents: *Rechtsstaat* in German, *état de droit* in French, *stato di diritto* in Italian, *estado de derecho* in Castilian. These terms used to indicate the conformity of the actions performed by the state to the existing legislation, whatever its origin or moral justification: a paramount example of legal positivism. Interpretations of both the rule of law and the *Rechtsstaat* have obviously varied over time: they have often constituted an anti-authoritarian barrier, and so they do in our time, but they have also been employed against new social legislation allegedly infringing upon civil liberties.[31]

There is a hidden truth in all of this: laws must be necessarily a general and abstract way of regulating social behaviour, otherwise they would lose their universal character. The law remains open to be twisted in one or the other direction, and can never be, by its own force, an insurmountable tool for preventing politically and morally infelicitous developments. Legal systems have a logic of their own, and are not mere side effects of social processes; but to believe that they can rule or change the world by themselves, without interaction with political decisions, cultural and ethical orientations and without reckoning with the economic structure, would be a case of what was once called '*Rechtskretinismus*/legal idiocy'. In a word, the rule of law as an indicator of legitimate statehood or effective democracy cannot be seen apart from these surrounding conditions.

A last complex of questions regarding the state and the law can only be briefly mentioned here. It must be held that the law governing the life of a state, that is the constitution and ordinary law, was not itself born legally, but rather out of political acts (war of unification, national liberation war, revolution) that subverted the existing order through violence.[32] Yet the *origin* is not the whole truth, unlike what philosophers in love with 'myths of origin' used to think: once established by a founding act, the legal order of the state perpetuates itself by its own force and the citizens' support, and remains in its legality unprejudiced by its violent origin (the shoot-outs at Lexington, Massachusetts, in 1775 and the Bastille in Paris in 1789, where the American and the French Revolutions started; the battles fought by national liberation movements before a successful post-colonial state-building). The same holds with respect to another major topic in state theory: even if the path-breaking revolution or liberation war was conducted by a narrow minority, the *constituent power*[33] in the state does not lie with it, but with the generality of citizens as gathered in the electorate or represented in a constituent assembly or parliament once they have invested themselves in that power by election or referendum. In the same line of thought, the excitement shown again in the new century by anti-democratic thinkers of the right and the left for Carl Schmitt's (1922) statement (in the first line) 'sovereign is he who decides on the state of exception' sounds necrophile, because its root – Schmitt's enthusiasm for Art. 48 of the Weimar Constitution, which in the event of an emergency conferred quasi-dictatorial powers to the president of the German Reich – vanished with the Third Reich in 1945.[34] Necrophile also because in our era and among democratic polities the problem has ceased to exist: all their constitutions provide for the state of emergency by non-dictatorial provisions, which do not deprive the liberal-democratic sovereign, the people, of its inalienable centrality – to pick up a notion astutely introduced by Schmitt, the problem has been 'neutralised'.[35] Also, at least in Western countries, political change has come about since 1945 by elections or mass movements reflected in elections, as in France 1958, and no longer by coups or revolutions – except in Greece's military coup of 1967. Positions holding that the (capitalist) state was not just born out of violence, but also lives on hidden or open violence, and must be therefore delegitimised and violently overthrown, fail to see that a democratic regime, though obviously still containing elements of socio-economic oppression and constraints, has realised the political order requiring the least amount of institutional violence seen thus far in the polity – an order that can be modified and has been often modified on a non-violent way. An intuitive worldwide comparison with other regimes of the present or the recent past (the 'real socialism' of Soviet brand) does not need to be detailed here.

6. State and values

Does the state have values to represent or to pursue?

We have seen that according to contract theory, it has one existential goal, to provide domestic and external security for its citizens; this may include making a minimum wellbeing possible, the lack of which would generate insecurity. Yet this goal is the state's *raison d'être*, not a particular goal, such as the uttermost realisation of individual freedom in classical liberalism, a classless society in Marxian socialism, or a racially pure society in German National Socialism. The upholding of these substantive, not merely procedural goals has, however, retreated in recent decades, and so have the 'comprehensive doctrines' (Rawls 1993) advancing them; where the latter still make resounding proclamations, the people are likely to pay, at best, lip service to them with the exception of those fascinated by fanaticism or resurrecting nationalism. In the present widespread, though non-universal conditions of recession, sluggish growth and high unemployment, the people rather pursue the goal to survive, if belonging to the poor or the lower middle class, or to get speedily much richer than they already are, if they are higher situated. Rapid gains in income and status are not an uncommon goal among the youth, and a self-centred strategy of personal success is often what the fall of lofty ideologies has left behind. This process is sometimes called 'loss of values' and happens in liberal capitalist countries as well as in China and India. It leads us to issues of normative political philosophy, in particular solidarity as one of the tenets that underpin the people's coexistence in the polity, and opens up the question: can polities live without a degree of shared values among citizens? What we have learned about identity suggests negative answers, but it depends on what type of values.

The great providers of (freely shared or imposed) values used to be and still are *religions* and *churches*. We are now looking at their relationship not to politics in general, which is too large a chapter, but to the state. This was built in Europe as an inclusive and (legally) egalitarian community by rescinding its ties to a church or more in general to religion, which happened in the aftermath of the embittered wars of religion of the sixteenth and seventeenth centuries and later under the mighty intellectual influence of the Enlightenment movement, a transnational Europe-wide phenomenon (less so in South-Eastern Europe, then still part of the Ottoman empire and/or dominated by the Orthodox Church). The peak of this process was reached in France with the law of 9 December 1905, concerning the separation of the churches and the state and affirming both the freedom of professing openly any religion and the individual freedom of conscience; the country remained bound to observe its 'republican values' only – *liberté, egalité, fraternité/* freedom, equality, brotherhood. In the French version, or in a less radical one, the *laïcité* or secular and neutral character of the state is regarded both as respecting the equality of all citizens and keeping the state away from the danger of ideological strife and oppression. The neutrality of the state and freedom of religion has been respected in liberal-democratic countries all over the world, not only towards various Christian denominations and Judaism, but also Islam and Buddhism, as immigrants can testify. This has not been reciprocated in some Islamic countries, such as Saudi Arabia, while religious communities are closely watched or hindered by the state in the People's Republic of China.

What the modern state cannot accept without giving up itself, that is its claim to include and protect all citizens, is to recognise an exclusive religious doctrine as state religion (confessional state) or to unify politics and religion by putting the state under the mastership of the clergy (theocracy). Vatican City and the Islamic Republic of Iran are the only existing theocracies, but the former, which has roots dating back to the year AD 752 and is extended over only 108 acres, is since 1870 no more than the material support to a spiritual power (the Holy See), while the latter, created in 1979, is a major regional player with a population of 80 million and a low human rights record.[36] This is to say that, given the present state of religions and religious organisations around the world, the constitutional and liberal state has fairly different levels of difficulty in coexisting with them. Nowhere can the state omit to fight with military and cultural tools against *fanaticism* such as Islamist jihadism, in which however the alleged religious justification for killing others and oneself in the name of God covers less spiritual motivations as well: homicidal instinct, neurotic quest for domination over enslaved women and children, revanchism. Even if we acknowledge that this extreme phenomenon is scarcely representative of mainstream Islam, the latter (both in the Sunni and Shia version) makes it difficult – at least in principle, since in single countries pragmatic solutions are being practised – to accommodate basic requirements of modern statehood: no or insufficient separation of religion and politics, uncertain acceptance of pluralism including conversion from one faith to another, no clear endorsement of modernity not only in technological and economic sense, but as a civic culture as well – of which effective gender equality is a tenet. An additional reason for Western scholars to be allowed to point at these elements is that the West is well experienced in the work of freeing itself from its own pathologies of fanaticism and bigotry: from Catholic and Protestant intolerance in early modern times, with 'heretics' and 'witches' burned all over the Old Continent and New England to murderous totalitarian ideologies in the previous century. On the other hand, there are enough Islamic or Buddhist communities in Western countries whose religious faith is practised in harmony with the Constitution and the laws.

To add a last consideration, state and values is not a topic limited to religion. With the secularisation of morality (divorce in Catholic countries, abortion, same-sex marriage, euthanasia) on the one hand, and the new moral scope of intrusive technologies (in vitro fertilisation, surrogate motherhood), the state is bound to legislate on *ultimate matters* on which neither consensus nor chance of mediation exists. It's worldviews against each other, a situation in which everybody could say, as Martin Luther is credited to have said before Emperor Charles V at the Diet held in Worms (1521) as he rejected the request to dismiss his theological opinions: 'Here I stand, I can do no other.' Now, individuals and parties act on an ethics of conviction, while states, if they are not theocracies or dictatorships, are expected to rule based on an ethics of responsibility – to use Weberian notions that will be clarified later in Chapter 10. This means that they have to find temporary arrangements that give full satisfaction to nobody, but also displease only extremists, well knowing that stable compromises (to be written into law) on deep-held beliefs are often impossible. It can be wise to procrastinate the legislative decision, provided this can favour a solution, or let for a while the courts rule in the single cases, whereas a vote by the parliament or the people (referendum), may disrupt the core political identity shared by the citizens. The deep beliefs of a people can change over time, and we have seen that abortion or same-sex marriage, though still divisive issues, are no longer perceived with the same degree of rejection as they were only a few decades ago.

This applies also to an ultimate issue that stands out as a permanent political question, at least since the European Enlightenment: does the state have the right to take the life of human beings, even if they have committed heinous crimes? Many states have *de iure* or *de facto* abolished the *death penalty*, first of all the Grand Duchy of Tuscany in 1776, and more recently all states belonging to the European Union, but also the Russian Federation, Cuba and South Africa (140 states in all, plus 19 states in the American Union). On abolishing capital punishment in Connecticut, the Supreme Court of the state ruled in 2015 that it 'no longer comports with contemporary standards of decency and no longer serves any legitimate penological purpose'. This is a utilitarian justification for the abolition; others prefer a principled one, in the sense that the state never has the right to take lives (self-defence being a different chapter).

Whatever the justification, *abolition* is now largely seen as a marker of civility and humanity, but this is not the place for examining the death penalty from the point of view of moral and legal philosophy. For political science it is interesting that the four countries that executed more people between 2007–2013 – China, Iran, Saudi Arabia, and the USA – belong to regimes and uphold values that could not be more different: a sign that the inclination to inflict death on presumably culpable humans has deeper – anthropological and ideological – roots than the political constitution of the state.

★ ★ ★

It is not possible to draw here conclusions about – I cannot avoid the pun – the present state of the state, because we have not yet acquired any knowledge about three other fundamental perspectives from which alone it makes sense today to look at the state:

- the present condition of democracy, now truly or allegedly the form of government of most states;
- the international perspective, or what happens to the state when we start looking at it in the plural – the states;
- globalisation and global/lethal challenges, which are essentially changing the stage on which politics and state politics play out their games.

The following chapters, particularly Chapter 5 and 7, will give some answer to the questions that must now remain open.

Notes

1 As a matter-of-fact, a curious and bloodletting hole in this essential monopoly exists in the most powerful democratic state, the USA, with its poorly regulated constitutional right for any citizen 'to bear arms' (the Second Amendment to the Constitution, which however originally tied this right to the training of a meanwhile vanished 'well-regulated militia'), now has come to mean in fact, the dissemination of violence in a measure hardly compatible with the protecting mission of the state.
2 *Res publica* has never lost its ambivalence of meaning both a commonwealth or a republic.
3 *Gosudarstvennoye*/state is the source of the G in KGB (*Komitet gosudarstvennoy bezopasnosti*/Committee for State Security), the post-Stalin name of the Soviet Intelligence Service from 1954 through 1991, whose possibly eternal fame is entrusted to the early James Bond movies.

4. Henry VIII broke with Rome and gave birth to the Church of England (1532–37) because (this was at least the *prima facie* causation) the pope rejected his request to regard his marriage to Catherine of Aragon as nil.
5. To give an example, England's public debt went up from £22mil in 1697 to £238mil in 1783, after the Seven Years War and the wars on the American continent.
6. The special jurisdictions for clergy and nobility were step by step dismantled; everybody became subject to the same law and the same judges.
7. *Ständestaat*, as the Germans, who invented this notion, say. It found a *post mortem* glorification in Hegel's *Grundlinien der Philosophie des Rechts/Basic Elements of the Philosophy of Law* (1821).
8. In England and later (after the Act of Union with Scotland of 1707) the UK, there were, and still are, two representative assemblies, one for the upper estates (the House of Lords) and one for the Commons.
9. These '-isms' will be more thoroughly examined elsewhere in this book.
10. By this word, I am hinting at the German *Staatsmaschine* or the Italian *Stato macchina*, which aptly convey the sense of the robot-like working of the huge impersonal apparatus of state bureaucracy.
11. So also in Italy's Fascist dictatorship from 1922 on, then in Germany's Third Reich (1933).
12. Also known in Europe as battle of Poitiers and in Arabic according to Wikipedia as Battle of the Palace of the Martyrs (Arabic: معركة بلاط الشهداء, transliterated as *ma'arakat Balâṭ ash-Shuhadâ*).
13. Dante's Ulysses travels on the high seas to his death driven by the invocation, addressed to his shipmates: 'Ye were not form'd to live the life of brutes, / But virtue to pursue and knowledge high' (*Inferno*, XXVI). Joyce's Ulysses's travel through Dublin is fairly less high-spirited and more inward-looking.
14. Post-colonial and subaltern studies, as they define themselves, can illuminate the reverse side of this story by revealing the costs paid throughout its course by the people of the colonies also with regards to the categories (gender, race, ethnicity, sexual orientation, beliefs, including their intersections) that help us describe their condition.
15. 'A commonwealth is a constitution of the entire people. The people, however, is not every association of men, however congregated, but the association of the entire number, bound together by the compact of justice, and the communication of utility.' (Cicero BCE 54, I, 25, 39). In Latin, the outset of this statement sounds much more plain and clear: 'Est igitur ... res publica res populi ...' (in my own translation: the public issue or commonwealth is therefore the people's affairs).
16. 'Give to Caesar what belongs to Caesar, and give to God what belongs to God', Matthew 22:21 at http://biblehub.com/matthew/22-21.htm.
17. In the Middle Ages, *societas civilis* was the Latin translation of Aristotle's πολιτική κοινωνία, which we now understand as political community.
18. Marx 1843. Things are made more elusive by the German language that used to merge two meanings, bourgeois and civil, in the same adjective *bürgerlich*.
19. Cf. Marx 1875.
20. In an interview released on 23 September 1987, she argued 'Who is society? There is no such thing! There are individual men and women and there are families' (cf. https://en.wikiquote.org/wiki/Margaret_Thatcher).
21. The emphatic use of 'the community' is more present in the USA than in Europe, where society is not as fragmented and the communitarians vs. liberals dispute hardly made any waves outside academic circles.
22. For the past half century, this concept has been often cited in its German original, *Öffentlichkeit*, made well-known in 1962 by Jürgen Habermas's first book (1962).
23. In the vocabulary – exit, voice, loyalty – of the great German American sociologist Albert O. Hirschman (1970), when members of an economic or political organisation or community are dissatisfied with the quality of its performances, they can either confirm their loyalty or voice their criticism or exit the group.

24 A scholarly instance of this use or misuse is the title of a classic work in the theory of international relations: *Politics Among Nations*, by Hans Morgenthau (1948).
25 Value-based in the sense of Weber's distinction between *wertrational* (value-rational) and *zweckrational* (ends-rational), which helps understand that the idea of nation can be upheld by rational discourse, as large strains of French, German and Italian literature bear witness, beyond being emotionally cherished – a view irrationalist thinkers are unable to accept.
26 Cf. Clark 2014.
27 I prefer to use this Hebrew word (the destruction) instead of the more current term Holocaust, a term made popular by the eponymous American TV series of the late 1970s.
28 It depends, admittedly, on the quality and the openness to other disciplines of the law school that a new civil servant comes from.
29 *Massnahmegesetz*/measure-law is the specific German name, and the trend towards this direction is common to many legislatures around the world.
30 See *The rule of law and transitional justice in conflict and post-conflict societies*. Report of the Secretary-General (2004), available at www.un.org/en/ga/search/view_doc.asp?symbol= S/2004/616, 4.
31 This was the case in the 1930s, as the US Supreme Court with a conservative majority tried to block many of Roosevelt's New Deal policies.
32 The only attempted exception, the founding in Europe of a new polity on a legal path (Treaties of the European Union), will be addressed at the end of Chapter 6.
33 Better known among scholars under its French name *pouvoir constituant*.
34 And so did by suicide the *Führer* of that Reich, Adolf Hitler, whom Schmitt had ten years before lauded ('the Führer protects the law') after in 1934 he let the leaders of an unruly faction of the Nazi party be murdered without any legal justification.
35 The notion of neutralisation is explained in Schmitt's article *Das Zeitalter der Neutralisierungen und Entpolitisierungen*/The age of neutralisations and depoliticizations, published as an Appendix to *Der Begriff des Politischen*, Berlin: Duncker & Humblot, 1963, 79–95 – no English edition seems to exist.
36 Cf. Chapter 2, note 1.

References

Alighieri, Dante (written between 1304–1321) *La divina commedia/The Divine Comedy of Dante Alighieri*, e-book available at http://oll.libertyfund.org/titles/alighieri-the-divine-comedy-vol-1-inferno-english-trans

Bentham, Jeremy (1789) *An Introduction to the Principles of Morals and Legislation*, Oxford: Oxford University Press, 1970.

Cicero (54 BCE) *De Re Publica*, available at http://oll.libertyfund.org/titles/546#toc_list.

Clark, Christopher (2014) *The Sleepwalkers: How Europe Went to War in 1914*, New York: HarperCollins.

The English Standard Version Bible, available at: http://biblehub.com

Habermas, Jürgen (1962) *Strukturwandel der Öffentlichkeit/The Structural Transformation of the Public Sphere*, Cambridge: The MIT Press, 1989.

Hirschman, Albert O. (1970) *Exit, Voice, and Loyalty*, Cambridge: Harvard University Press.

Machiavelli, Niccolò (1532) *Il Principe/The Prince*, New York: Cambridge University Press, 1988.

Marx, Karl (1843) *Zur Kritik der Hegelschen Rechtsphilosophie/Critique of Hegel's Philosophy of Right*, available at www.marxists.org/archive/marx/works/download/Marx_Critique_of_Hegels_Philosophy_of_Right.pdf

Marx, Karl (1875) *Kritik des Gothaer Programms/Critique of the Gotha Program*, available at www.marxists.org/archive/marx/works/1875/gotha/index.htm

Morgenthau, Hans (1948) *Politics among Nations: The Struggle for Power and Peace*, New York: McGraw-Hill, 1985.
Rawls, John (1993) *Political Liberalism*, New York: Columbia University Press.
Rawls, John (1999a) *A Theory of Justice*, revised edition, Cambridge: Harvard University Press.
Rawls, John (1999b) *The Law of Peoples*, Cambridge: Harvard University Press.
Schmitt, Carl (1922) *Politische Theologie/Political Theology*, Chicago: University of Chicago Press, 2005.
Tönnies, Ferdinand (1887) *Gemeinschaft und Gesellschaft/Community and Civil Society*, New York: Cambridge University Press, 2001.
Weber, Max (1922) *Economy and Society*, available at https://archive.org/stream/MaxWeberEconomyAndSociety/MaxWeberEconomyAndSociety_djvu.txt

Further readings

For the whole chapter, Bobbio's article *State, Power and Government* (44–132) from Bobbio 1989 (cf. *Preface*) is an invaluable reading. Also important are for the relationship to law the chapter *The Great Dichotomy: Public/Private* (1–21) and for the role of society the chapter on *Civil Society* (22–43).

For the transformation of the state in the perspective of historical sociology see:

Poggi, Gianfranco (1991) *The State*, Stanford: Stanford University Press.

5
GOVERNMENT AND DEMOCRACY

The state is an abstract entity, though a powerful one. Its only palpable existence is the person at its head, president or king/queen that it may be. Except in presidential regimes where s/he reigns or presides over the country, and does not govern it though. What the people come into contact daily with is the government: the member of the parliament voting for or against a law you like or dislike, the police officer you file a complaint with after your wallet was stolen, the judge who sentences you to prison because you evaded a remarkable amount of taxes. This is government in the broad sense of the institution (or set of institutions) managing our common affairs, not as the executive branch or the cabinet.

Given the relevance of government to the people's real experience of politics, it is no wonder that all across its history, political theory has been to a large extent an inquiry into the various forms of government and an argument on which of them is preferable. This debate *de optima republica*/about the best commonwealth, as it has been called since Cicero, is a point of contact between reconstructive and normative political philosophy; further elements of this debate resulting from the latter will come up in the corresponding last part of this book.

The conceptualization of government forms starts with Plato's and Aristotle's triad: monarchy or government by one, aristocracy or rule by the best, democracy or rule by the people. Aristotle also enumerates the degenerative forms of these regimes: monarchy can become tyranny, the aristocracy oligarchy or rule by the few, while he calls democracy the degeneration of the proper third regime, which he dubs πολιτέια/*politeia* or constitution of the *polis*, the city state.[1] Other degenerative forms are ochlocracy or rule by the mob and timocracy or rule by those loving honour and glory (Plato's version) or those possessing property (Aristotle's). With variations this triad remained the leading conceptualization of government in political studies until Machiavelli (1532) replaced it with the dichotomy of republics or principalities quoted in Chapter 4, §1. Whether it is one person or a body with internal rules that governs was, in his eyes, the relevant distinction. Though two centuries later Montesquieu reinstated a triad (monarchy, republic, despotism), in the centuries of modernity and particularly in the last and the current century the triad has lost its meaning in favour of a dichotomy, which is still different from Machiavelli's *democratic vs. authoritarian regime* – or democracy and autocracy, as others prefer to say.[2] Political scientists have outlined elaborated typologies of authoritarianism, from which it is not easy to draw a generally accepted definition; it seems that its main features are the non-acceptance of conflict and plurality as normal elements of politics, the will to preserve the *status quo* and prevent change by keeping all political dynamics under close control by a strong central power, and lastly, the erosion of the rule of law, the division of powers, and democratic voting procedures. Authoritarianism differs from *totalitarianism* in as much as this regime, based on one-party rule, goes a step further and tries to permeate the society with its own ideology and to reorganise it according to its doctrine – and to the vagaries of the leader. To do so, it must enact a violent and suffocating intervention in all societal interactions, which can go as far as to establish state terrorism.[3] Authoritarian regimes of various kinds abound in our present world, sometimes mixed with totalitarian, sometimes with democratic features such as limited or fictional party pluralism; while the only existing case of complete totalitarianism seems to exist in the Democratic People's Republic of North Korea.

For an authoritarian, and to a lesser extent, a totalitarian regime, further connotations such as *dictatorship, tyranny* and *despotism* are used. There is no universally accepted differentiation between these terms, and even the classical one, according to which illegitimate, limitless rule relies, in the case of tyranny, on unduly possession of the highest office (illegitimate *ex defectu tituli*/for lack of entitlement) and in the case of dictatorship, on the illegal handling of the instruments of power (*ex parte exercitii*/on the side of exerting power), is no longer observed by all writers. Neither is the etymological meaning of despotism as rule of the state as if it were a private possession of the ruler (in ancient Greek δεσπότης is the lord or master of house and business) still clear to everybody, and this word is rather used as pejorative or in the specialised sense envisaged by Montesquieu or in the notion of 'oriental despotism'. In the absence of a clear language convention using one term rather than another is left to the literary preference of the individual speaker.

We will now first differentiate in §1 between two understandings of democracy, then watch in §2 the link between representative democracy and its national format, while §3 will examine the pre-conditions under which democracy can work and preserve its meaning. The framework conditions that favour its development will keep us busy in §4, which will also discuss possible alternatives to it – at this time their existence is very unlikely, while on the other hand demythologizing democracy, as it is attempted in this chapter, seems to be a necessary passage in order to strengthen its credibility. A seminal question raised by this inquiry, the relationship between democracy and capitalism, will be discussed in the concluding §5.

1. Democracy one and two

A one-track explanation of democracy, say, as a procedure for governing a state, would give a clear-cut but impoverished picture of it, which could not cover the many instances in which a different version plays a role. In the following, two fundamental versions of this notion will be taken into consideration:

One: democracy as a set of values and principles, or as an ideal, and
Two: democracy as a method for governing mass societies – what the much quoted and praised Athens of the fifth century BCE was not.

Democracy One means power of the people (δημοκρατία) or, in a well-known formula used by Abraham Lincoln in his Gettysburg Address (1863), 'government of the people, by the people, for the people' – though Lincoln did not refer to it as a democracy, a word that became of general use only later. The standard interpretation of Lincoln's motto sees the people, rather than a king or the nobility, as the actor entitled to rule the state, that is the people itself (of the people); the people providing the governors, taking them from its very ranks according to norms established by itself (by the people); the people running government to the advantage of everybody, instead of granting privileges to a social class or group or geographical section of the state (for the people). We will see that in reality things are much more complex than in this standard view of democracy (and in Lincoln's clause), but this does not deprive the formula of its persistent fascination.

A first document about the fascination beaming from the democratic ideal is in the public eulogy Pericles pronounced for the Athenian soldiers who fell in the first year of the Peloponnesian War and retold by *Thucydides* (BCE 454–404 or –396) in Book 1, Chapter 2, §37 of his *History of the Peloponnesian War*:

> Our constitution does not copy the laws of neighbouring states; we are rather a pattern to others than imitators ourselves. Its administration favours the many instead of the few; this is why it is called a democracy. If we look to the laws, they afford equal justice to all in their private differences; if no social standing, advancement in public life falls to reputation for capacity, class considerations not being allowed to interfere with merit; nor again does poverty bar the way, if a man is able to serve the state, he is not hindered by the obscurity of his condition. The freedom which we enjoy in our government extends also to our ordinary life.[4]

In this account, the primacy given to the interest of the generality of the population, equality before the law, the superiority of personal merits over the social condition (meritocracy) along with freedom are the defining features of democracy. These are still now the basic reasons for *democracy's attractiveness*, or what still makes it a battle cry vs. personal or party dictatorship, oligarchs, corrupt and inefficient regimes. This came again to the surface in the Chinese protest movement of 1989, before the Tian An Men massacre, in the political upheaval in the countries of the former Soviet bloc (1989–1991), in the Arab Springs and the Iranian Green Movement of 2011, and in the democratic movement in Burma down to the election of 2015 – just to mention a few examples. In all these episodes, democracy is invoked less in its proper meaning as system of government and rather as an emblem for things such as the transparency of power or the rule of law that are not all strictly democratic in nature but originate from democracy's previous competitors, in particular liberalism and constitutionalism. In the time of its eighteenth century resurrection, 2,100 years after it eclipsed, the very idea of democracy, elevating the people's will to the rank of the only and unlimited sovereign, was indeed perceived as dangerous for the individual liberties that were being established against the absolute monarch. The conjoining of liberal values with democratic rule came later in the late nineteenth century and was again put to a stress test in the mass democracies between the two World Wars, a test failed in Italy and Germany. As we shall soon see, the conjunction of liberal and democratic principles is after the Second World War an accomplished fact in Western countries, and in our conventional wisdom we often call 'democratic' values or policies that rather stem from the liberal tradition.

In the modern version the core of the democratic idea is the *equal distribution of political power* as enshrined in the motto 'one man, one vote' – whose slightly sexist formulation (it should rather read 'one man or woman' or 'one citizen') aptly mirrors the time and the toil it took to extend universal suffrage to women, as it happened to an extent between the World Wars and definitely after 1945. This equality cannot be taken at face value because in order to do so several presuppositions should be met that not always are: first, formal equality on the ballot does not necessarily lead to equal power in government, because this operates not only along the lines indicated by the voters, but also very much under the pressure of other, non-democratic forces as well (high bureaucracy, big money, economic and party lobbies, the clergy or the military in weak democracies). This can hurt the promise of *autonomy* (to obey only commands and laws we have ourselves created by our vote) that is implied in the principle establishing equal power for all and everybody.

Second, tied *de facto* to formal voting equality is or used to be the mostly implicit expectation of higher social equality, due to redistributive or welfare policies pursued by the government. Empirical analysis disavows the expectation of this tie (Przeworski 2010), and the impressive rise of inequality in democratic countries since the 1980s puts, for the time being, a gravestone on it – though miracles (strategies reversing the rise of inequality while keeping the economy going; strong leaderships) can still happen. The much welcomed transformation of advanced societies into a 'knowledge society', has for the time being only added a new divide to the income gap between layers of the population. It remains true that in a democracy anti-poverty laws, fiscal benefits for low-income citizens and access to education for all are more likely to be passed than in an autocracy, thanks to parliamentary battles, an attentive public opinion and social movements. Yet the disappointment and resentment deriving from the gap between formal political equality and substantial, even rising social inequality can, over the long haul, push back the citizens' affection for the democratic regime, either by making them vote for strongly antidemocratic or at least populist parties or give up participation in public life. The peak reached by inequality in the middle of the Great Recession after 2008 seems to be putting an end to the prevalence of post-materialist values (autonomy, self-esteem, self-expression, sense of belonging) seen in the decades straddling the millennium divide and to shift attention again on jobs and salaries. Democracy as a method or procedure of government cannot be separated in the citizens' minds from the substantive policies and results it leads to.

Before we leave Democracy One I will briefly break up my abstinence from historical questions because I wish to clarify something that seems to me a popular misunderstanding concerning the theory of democracy, of which Jean-Jacques Rousseau is regarded as the modern founder. This is hard to reconcile with his condemnation of (direct) democracy as a system of government, in which the populace itself is supposed to manage the state affairs, blurring the distinction between legislative and executive power (Rousseau 1762, Book III, §4). Only a people of gods – Rousseau argues – could govern itself democratically. Equal participation is due only in the founding act of the polity, consisting of the total alienation of everybody's rights in its favour (Book I, §§6–7) – as it was already known to Hobbes and Locke. This gives the people the power to legislate, but how the *volonté générale*/general will expressed by the people creates laws remains undefined (Book II, §§6–12). This is enough to deprive Rousseau of the crown of 'father of democracy', which he would have himself certainly rejected. This gives him back his honour because otherwise, should his theory of the polity be mistaken for his theory of government, the accusation of having founded a totalitarian version of democracy would not be unjustified.

2. From representation to national democracy

The way it developed in Europe and the Americas in the eighteenth–twentieth century, democracy as a form of government would have not been possible without the framework provided by the representative state we have already met in the previous chapter. As John Stuart Mill put it,

> the meaning of representative government is that the whole people, or some numerous portion of them, exercise through deputies periodically elected by themselves the ultimate controlling power.... They must be masters, whenever they please, of all the operations of government.
>
> (Mill 1861, 68)

Mill's definition fits not-yet-fully democratic regimes, in which voting rights may be granted only to 'numerous' groups such as male citizens or those with higher income (census franchise) or belonging to the country's official religion, as in Britain until 1828–1829 or 1858 (when the exclusion of Jews was reversed), or with the accepted skin colour.[5] Also, the 'ultimate controlling power' fully resides with the people's representatives only in parliamentary, not presidential democracies, or those without a constitutional court. The main point remains that, unlike representation by estates, now all members of the polity are represented as *individuals*. More could be said about the philosophical implications of the notion of representation, but we shall limit ourselves to the once – in the time of Edmund Burke (1729–1797) – famous dispute as to whether the representative has to be a delegate of the constituency, only authorised to assert its wishes and requests, or rather a trustee, free from binding instructions and representing the whole of the people according to one's own best guess of what their interest is. This second image of the representative is now overwhelmingly prevalent, but proposals to go back to the imperative mandate pop up sometimes as a tool to bring back deputies to their job as allegedly true and loyal representatives of their own people, away from 'corrupting' political games. It is hard to see how the evils of representation in mature, ageing democracies can be cured by resorting to pre-modern forms that were characteristic of local communities or guilds.

Other proposals seem to make more sense than imperative mandate and regard the selection of representatives, with a view to make it less dependent on party bureaucracy, donors' money and personal lobbies. Draw – as in old Athens – and rotation in office are more debatable, provided they are combined with elections choosing who can enter the draw and even more necessarily those eligible for rotation. The combination, which we do not need to discuss in detail, is aimed at taking into account the will of the majority and the ideas emerging in the electoral debate, which cannot be ignored in favour of a redeeming mechanism. Generally speaking, mechanisms can help, but the poisons of politics such as love of power for power's sake, Godfather-like positions fed by cronyism, feudal management of party bureaucracy, still can neutralise them. A shift to a more rigorous civic culture among the actors, supported by less complacent laws concerning, say, the role of private money in the elections, can bring better and more stable results.

Beyond nature and selection of the representatives, the question of *accountability* is the other face of representation, its second pillar: the appointment by those represented is incomplete and only partly legitimate if it is not complemented by devices allowing them to test, to reward or to punish the representatives according to their performance. The basic device resides in the next election, in which the representative (person or party) can be confirmed or voted out of the job. In the history of both assemblies and political thought a more radical step, the *recall* of representatives, has been suggested or applied. This seems to bring the power back to the people, yet it evokes as well the danger of populism rather than the triumph of democracy: it would give a local constituency the power to recall a deputy who, once elected, voted in her/his assembly in a way aimed at protecting the interest of the nation rather than those of the local majority. It would be good neither for the nation nor, at the end of the day, for the local constituency, whose fate cannot on the medium-long haul be detached from that of the nation (or the Union, in the case of the European Parliament). Quite different is obviously the case in which a representative might be recalled because s/he reversed all of her/his original positions for motives of personal utility. In extreme cases a recall procedure should be possible, as it is at the state and city level in the United States.

Sticking to the idea that – at least in principle – constituencies elect representatives they deem capable of making good laws for the entire nation or union of nations makes sense self-evidently as long as the nation or the union exists. The fragmentation processes that go on in several Western and non-Western countries – not only in the direction of regionalism and secession, but also because the very tissue of society, for example the sense of confidence nourished by the youth, is weakened – affect the credibility of democratic representation as well. Decreasing participation in election, except in India, and political life altogether is one of the signs of this process. A degree of confidence in the future as well as of trust in fellow citizens and the institutions is crucial to the life of the polity. Where these two important categories defining the social and psychological background of politics are weakened, as they are for many reasons in the globalised world, consequences such as distrust vs. parliamentary turncoats and more generally politicians and parties do inevitably sneak into political life – organisational measures such as imperative mandate or obligatory step-down for MPs changing party are poor substitutes for structural reform of representation. It is in particular the crisis of the parties in many important democracies, their growing inability to design strategies and organise consensus beyond the short-term interest or whims of the electorate that contributes to the stagnation and lower quality of democratic life. In countries such as France, Italy, the UK in which workers' unions used to play a role in political life, their waning vitality is a further aggravating factor.

The path – a logical one rather than a historical sequence – leading from representative government to a full democratic regime goes through still another station, of which we already know some contours: the merging of *demos* and *ethnos*. The 'people', which was proclaimed to be the bearer of sovereignty in the American and French Revolutions, and later in other European and South-American countries, were an 'imagined community' of brothers and sisters (vs. kings and despots) in the political rhetoric and narrative as well as a legal or constitutional actor (the bearer of sovereignty, the generality of voters). It characterised and justified itself on lofty and abstract universalistic values. But at the same time this *demos* turned out to carry the very particular traits of an ethnic group or more often of a group consisting of several former peoples or tribes, not all too far from each other ethnically, largely merged into each other and now kept together by newly evoked cultural ties and a superior authority: the original ethnic core developed into a nation, as we have seen in the previous chapter. Democracy in France, just to mention a classical example among many, was and still largely is a French democracy, a democracy for French people.

This coincidence of *demos* and *ethnos*, universalism and particularism highlights one element and heeds its consequences. To begin with, a democratic regime always comes to be affected by a non-democratic element: he who is a citizen of a democracy is not the outcome of a democratic procedure, as this depends on historical and geopolitical factors – on the borders drawn by previous wars and the political evolution within them. With regards to immigrants, this nullified or greatly restricted the universalization of rights. As to the consequences, the merging of *demos* and *ethnos* in the nation facilitated the build-up of common, in particular cultural and legal institutions, in an atmosphere of national solidarity that helped overcome local egoism. It made possible that 'daily plebiscite' that Ernest Renan (1823–1892) thought to be the essence of a nation. This was true in the European nation states of the nineteenth century and again in some of the post-colonial countries. On the other hand, that merging fatally laid the groundwork for the later transformation or degeneration of the idea of the nation into *nationalism*, which claims the superiority of one's own nation, defined in opposition to all others, or even its right to dominate them, while asking from its own citizens to be ready to kill and to be killed for this purpose.[6] Under these circumstances, which dominated the first half of the nineteenth century, with the frequent addition of racism, 'patriotism is the last refuge of the scoundrel', as Samuel Johnson (1709–1784) is famously credited to have said – and is also known to be a mobilisation tool in the hand of authoritarian regimes in need of regaining consensus in the event of difficult times. In the new century, nationalism seems to have become a secondary component of populism, the most recent degeneration of democratic politics.

Lastly, the relationship between democracy and nation state contains the notion of *national citizenship* that reveals a necessarily non-democratic moment in democracy: determining who belongs to a democratic nation state is not itself subject to democratic decision. This is true, and most evident, in the spatial dimension, as immigrants painfully know, but also in the temporal one: Germans or Italians who lived between the wars and came too late (after the Fascists came to power and cancelled the previous liberal institutions) or too early (before the Fascist regimes were eliminated) in order to enjoy the advantages of democracy. It is not clear how far luck egalitarianism, a school of moral philosophy that regards as invalid and worth being corrected all inequalities deriving from pure luck and not from responsible choice, claims to apply to those being unluckily born in a poor or war-ravaged country. This would justify inviting immigrants from unlucky countries or at least not rejecting them, which is indeed an actual and controversial policy choice in affluent countries. We will leave this debate open until we come to Chapter 9, but take note again of the difference between an abstract moral and a political approach to the question.

3. Democratic government

We are now concluding our journey through some conceptual pre-stages of Democracy Two and come to the outline of democracy as a system of government: it is a *procedure that, based on the political (voting) equality of citizens and under certain preconditions establishes a government while settling conflicts by majority rule.* This definition is different from the most common ones.

Calling democracy a procedure means giving it a formal or procedural definition, at the first sight containing no substantive goals. This has been much criticized as impoverishing democracy, but here we are trying to catch the core element of it, which is common to its sub-types; to suggest what particular, time-related ends democracy should serve is not our business, as it belongs to political debate rather than political philosophy. Besides, we shall see that, once the definition has developed in all its implications, it turns out not to be as empty of values and goals as it may first appear.

The pre-conditions, which will be enumerated below, are *co-essential* to the procedure: without them the latter does not deserve the name of democracy.

Establishing a government (not just the executive branch) is the first performance of the democratic procedure, though it is often marginalised by theorists and ideologues: the much praised advantage of democracy, that is to deliver the most ample representation of the people's interests and ideals, is vain whenever the accent set exclusively on representation prevents democratic politics from providing a government that can really implement the projects based on those interests and ideals. That the country can have a government providing for its security and wellbeing is for the generality of citizens more important than giving every single group a share in ruling and legislating; access to media and the parliamentary tribune for its representatives meets the requirement of participation. All this is again, in another conceptual framework, the same complex we examined in Chapter 2 with regard to a legitimate regime's performances being necessary to its effective legitimation.

Turning now to the core question of democracy, its claim to assert the power of the people is ambiguous, even dangerous and should be reformulated. An actor called 'the people' does not exist; what exists are the citizens, each individual with their own rights, interests, passions and goals – which mostly differ from one another. In representative democracies, the citizens convene at the ballot box in order to establish whose will receives the highest approval, and it is on this ground that a government is formed that rules the country, based on the political obligation taken by both the majority's and minority's members. Politocracy, or the rule of the citizens (πολίτης/polites), would be a better name than democracy, as it would also dodge the *demos-etnos* equivocation, but I do not dream of introducing it straightaway.[7]

This is only possible under the following pre-conditions (A–C):

A1. Whatever the majority, the democratic procedure is neither terminated and replaced by dictatorship or theocracy nor disfigured by acts impeding the idea that everybody can – now and in the future – cast his or her ballot in freedom and equality and after due debate and information.
A2. Equal voting rights make sense only if the citizens have full access to free media and can at any and all times adhere to *parties* that assemble their demands and preferences in somehow coherent projects of how to govern the polity.

The sense of these pre-conditions is that the minority can accept the distribution of political power by majority rule only as long as it is reassured of the stable chance of becoming majority in the next election. Otherwise it may turn to other, more bellicose means of resolving differences or walk out of the community entirely.

This is the fundamental reason for the *superiority of democracy* over all other types of government: it makes government possible by assigning temporary asymmetric power by *peaceful* means, while at the same time preserving everybody's *freedom* as well as basic *equality* ('one citizen, one vote').

B. The fundamental civil rights of the citizens cannot be infringed upon by majority vote – which rights are intended by this definition will be examined in Chapter 8. This means that a number of issues are excluded from democratic decision making, which has to bow to limits required by liberalism and protected by non-elected bodies such as the courts of law and eminently the constitutional courts. The rationale for this is clear: citizens will participate in an open political game, unprotected by their own militias and fortresses, only as long as they can trust that they will not be hurt in body or have their property damaged because of what they have said or done. The uneasy marriage of liberalism/constitutionalism and democracy is also a wall against a totalitarian degeneration of democracy, enacted by a legislative branch that may want to assert the alleged will of the people by beheading the 'enemies of the revolution' (as it happened in France in the Years of Terror, 1792–1794) – or those sentenced for heresy in a theocracy. Still another institutional mechanism has been devised and also implemented in various forms in different countries to shield democracy against the poisons that it may itself generate: a system of *checks and balances* that adds to the democratic strife of parties and personalities a strong monarch-like figure such as the president in the US Constitution and/or a quasi-aristocratic body such as the US Senate or, previously, the House of Lords in the UK.[8] In historical perspective this can be seen as a modern resurrection of the doctrine of mixed government, put forward not only by Aristotle and Polybius (the Greek historian Πολύβιος, BCE 200–118, not the videogame), but also Machiavelli, Jean Calvin (1509–1564) and the *Federalist*.[9] Philosophically, democracy presupposes that everybody accepts the pluralism of conflicting views about God, the world and the polity, with the exception of doctrines preaching the destruction of tolerant coexistence among citizens such as Nazism or Islamist fundamentalism. *Politheism*, as we first encountered it in Chapter 1, is the foundation of democracy as well – what politicians seem to forget in the heat of the debate, when they dismiss the dissenting views of their adversaries simply as undemocratic or 'insulting the people'. Democratic governance is peaceful management of human conflict, and needs to be rooted in a culture of conflict fed by the acceptance of diversity. Democracy cannot be founded – except in a self-defeating mode – on the *truth* of a religion or philosophy. This has nothing to do with moral relativism, since government is a political, not a moral, issue and can justify its existence only by keeping peace among the citizens, not by submitting some of them to the 'truth' of another part – except in the case of fanaticism or bigotry. Nobody is hindered from believing whatever one wishes to believe, or from acting according to it, except if this means hurting others. On the other hand, in the case of verifiable and verified truths abstaining from cheating fellow citizens by falsifying statistics in economic policy or by denying research results in matters of technology and environment is a necessary premise of democratic procedures of understanding and bargaining.[10]

C. The will of the voters must effectively shape policy making and be superseded neither by the will of foreign powers nor by the influence or imposition due to non-elective factors[11] such as money or mono/oligopolistic media power. This opens the difficult question about 'democracy and capitalism', which will be addressed at the end of this chapter.

The examination that has worked out the pre-conditions under which democracy alone as procedure makes sense has confirmed that this model of government, despite its much contested formal character, involves a number of values and principles to be respected or implemented. When seen as a conflict-settling and government-providing scheme under conditions of freedom and equality, it may look less lofty and inspiring than democracy as 'power of the people', but is better focused on democracy's real achievements or failures and can better focus our sight on the dangers surrounding it. Before we begin examining them, let us however still dwell on its morphology, considering a number of dichotomies it is sometimes involved with.

The first dichotomy is between *ancient* and *modern democracy*.[12] The first type implied the direct participation of the citizens in the proceedings of the assembly as the only venue of sovereignty and government, leaving no room for any representative mechanism or free individual agency. Modern democracy is, as we now know, essentially representative and based on the exercise of individual freedoms.

The second dichotomy differentiates between *majoritarian* and *consensus democracy*, as defined by the Dutch-American political scientist Arend Lijphart. The first one comes close to the British or Westminster model of government (though this has been changing since Lijphart formulated his theory and may further change towards multipartitism) and entails a clear majority-minority divide; while in a consensus democracy all actors seek shared solutions that do not make the divisions of society sharper and rather try to include large political and social majorities in a 'consociational' way of governing.

The third dichotomy is the most significant, and comes up here only because it furnishes a bridge to another thematic complex, which we could put under the heading of the downsides of democracy. It's the dichotomy between *representative* and *direct democracy*, and contains an argument both normative and historical in favour of the former, while explaining most of the present evils from the confusion between the two models. The argument maintains that direct democracy, in which all citizens participate in frequent or daily decision making, is far from being the ideal democracy; that it is wrong to believe that we must replace it with the representative one only because of the size of our polities, or that representative democracy has to come as near as possible to the direct one. There is a weak and a strong reason for this argument.

The weak reason says that in modernity, in our late modernity in particular, governing an extremely complex mass society surrounded by an even more complex and precarious international environment can be managed only by a political leadership and an administrative apparatus that have learned the vision, the skills and the sense of balance adequate to the challenge. This remains true even if the fundamental choices are made every fourth or fifth year by the entire population – or rather by those who believe that voting is still better than abstention. By voting (but also by non-voting, which favours candidates and parties more adept at mobilising voters) citizens not only choose representatives, but also the strategies and policies they or their parties stand for. There remains, however, a difference for the electorate between expressing its prevailing will by electing a candidate (or a party) and conferring her or him an imperative mandate. This does ordinarily not happen, while her or his conformity to the mandate could also hardly be checked, for legal and technical reasons.

The strong reason is that, confronted with policy making, the electorate, especially the swinging wings that do and undo majorities, more often than not chooses to support its immediate *self-interest*, disregarding the likely needs of people too far in space (the poor of the world, say) and time (future generations) who cannot make their voice heard. The presently much lamented short-termism of democratic politics has one of its roots here. Giving immediate, daily policy-making power to the broad electorate would block innovation and reform, which are often advanced by small avantgardes without the stable support of the majority.

On account of these two reasons combined, the idea of representative bodies being replaced by this version of e-democracy with daily or weekly voting looks very much like a nightmare, a *Nineteen Eighty-Four* with a collective and impersonal Virtual Big Brother.[13] In addition to the previous considerations, the learning process taking place among active citizens, politicians and bureaucrats in the debate occurring in public opinion and parliament is worth being preserved and not discarded in favour of the fictional competence of every isolated individual to shape policy. Even in mature democracies the web seems to have become primarily the venue used by parts of the population to vent their dominating approach to politics, that is anger and resentment against rulers and fellow citizens as well, all spiced with falsehoods, unfounded claims and inflammatory language. Traditional voting has been also influenced by these attitudes, as in the 2016 Brexit referendum in the UK.

In other words, the cook whom Lenin in 1917 wanted to make eligible for running the country – we met her already in Chapter 1 – would have led it into disaster much swifter than the Communist regime did, and extreme egalitarianism is, in general, not to be taken seriously in its claims, because of its counter-intentional effects (the Russian Revolution rather produced a self-perpetuating bureaucratic elite) and because it denies the specificity and complexity of political activity. In the practise of democratic countries, cooks or actors or grocers or professors of both sexes have become eligible for public office only once they have learned the art of politics on the field – as politicians, not as defined by their former profession or social status.

These arguments in favour of representative democracy resonate in part with those against the tyranny of the majority made by classical liberalism, eminently by

Alexis de Tocqueville (1805–1859) in his masterwork *De la démocratie en Amérique/ Of Democracy in America* (1835). Focusing on the downsides of democracy, we should rather direct our attention to recent experiences such as the deterioration of democratic processes due to the overwhelming pressure stemming from the massive spectacularization of politics or to what the Columbia scholar of democracy Giovanni Sartori has dubbed 'videocracy'. This all comes down to political will-formation and communication being subjugated under the logic of televised entertainment, far beyond the inevitable percentage of theatrical self-presentation that already played a role in the Greek *agoras*. Another distorting factor lies in the polarisation of political conflict that occurs in some countries, most notably in the USA, with electoral campaigns whose core has been summarised as 'who hates who'. This seems to weaken or to erode the political identity of the citizens, which is in a democracy more vital than elsewhere since more than others this regime must be able – as we have seen – to rely on a universally shared belief in certain values and principles.

★ ★ ★

We have thus examined the presently more influential downsides of democracy that emerge on the subjective side of politics. They converge in creating the terrain for one of the two greatest dangers surrounding democracy itself: *populism*, the other danger being its low efficacy in policy making, as we shall see. By populism I mean the belief in the 'people' being the sole owner not just of sovereignty, but of any actual power, the touting of this entity against any limitation set by liberal-democratic institutions and the proclamation of its morally superior rights against any elite.[14] Since the beginning of the twentieth century onwards, universal suffrage made the masses of voters co-protagonists of political life, both a rightist and a leftist populism[15] have popped up time and again in most countries, with the exception of countries with previous and engrained autocratic traditions such as China and, to a lesser extent, Russia; we cannot possibly explore here the historical phenomenology of this attitude, nor can we discuss the epistemological problems arising from a notion that, while indispensable, is sometimes overstretched.

Populist movements and initiatives can be revealing signals of social pathologies, such as the sky-rocketing income inequality within most countries, and political failures in managing the ordinary citizen's problems. Populism as a political project can be dangerous for the domestic democratic stability, leading not only to the de-legitimation of the institutions protecting fundamental rights by the rule of law, but also to the undoing of democratic peace as well as international peace, since right-leaning populism in particular mostly comes paired with eruptions of nationalism. Not to forget is the tendency to authoritarian leadership or caesarism residing in the 'people' of populism, which can by its very nature be led only by bosses and demagogues adept at creating political myths and distortions and using the media for the mobilisation of masses.

Populism would not represent such a relevant threat to democracy if it did not happen to re-emerge[16] in a time marked by what we may call the *objective downsides* of democracy, which are obviously interconnected with the subjective ones, their distinction only being analytical. In Western countries, but not only here, the difficulties in reacting to the effects of globalisation, in particular (youth) unemployment, job precariousness and bad jobs with low pay go hand-in-hand with the demise of welfare entitlements and the weakening of social safety nets – along with the loss of social capital highlighted by Robert Putnam (Putnam 1993, 2000) for the USA, but not limited to America. Islamist terrorism and its grasp on second generation immigrants, along with the never-ending wave of new migrants have grown into an additional problem, along with the constitutional questions arising from the inevitably enhanced security regimes. Also, whatever the real grasp of these phenomena, renewed talks of secular stagnation and of an emerging and job-cutting Fourth Industrial Revolution add to the subjective disorientation of citizens. This, along with the justified 'indignation'[17] caused by rising inequality, is the breeding ground for one or the other shape of populism, whose dangerousness lies in its ability to pick up existing and justified elements of protest against governments while proposing to tear down the institutional safety nets protecting any politics based on rational debate and shared rules of the game.

On the whole, populism seems to make the worst out of the ambivalent notion of 'the people' that lies at the core of democracy: one more reason to abandon this hypostasised notion along with all the surrounding rhetoric and put instead in place 'the citizens'. But it is also true that the present state of affairs in democracies – not to mention some of the other troubles we will address later on – seems to provide fuel for the populist fires that erupt time and again in several countries. As long as this fuel is not neutralised by redesigning democracy, there is little chance that the fires cease to erupt. One could even ask if the type of mentality (made of manichaeistic simplifications, disregard for complex arguments, rancour and self-righteousness) prevailing in populist electorates is not going to occupy more and more minds, voiding democracy of its meaning and values. On this front the only proposal so far is to complement or (in radical formulations) replace the voting procedures of representative democracy with deliberations involving all stakeholders, in which reasonable arguments capable of finding solutions adequate to the common good are exchanged rather than relying on bargaining or mediating between positions based on self-interest. Participants in *deliberative democracy* – as its theorists intend by drawing on Habermas's thought – present their arguments relying on the 'claims of validity' that are common to any linguistic exchange among competent citizens. Those theorists have meanwhile set out a large literature containing models of deliberative democracy that seem to satisfy their normative perfectionism rather than to tackle the troubles of democratic regimes around the world. More helpful for the future of democracy among citizens who are a mix of income maximizers (be the actor a millionaire or a low-income pensioner) and partisan political philosophers are the experiments of deliberative processes in local communities, which can be in this way more broadly involved in consultations that prepare for the formal decision making of representative bodies such as city councils. In these cases the *quality* of democracy is enhanced, with regard to both the procedure and the substantive outcomes – policies that are often better than those resulting from mere voting. Also, the range of deliberative democracy remains obviously limited, as it cannot apply to, say, the national budget or foreign policy decisions. Overblown confidence in it is not a good service to what it could do for the troubled democracy of the present time.

★ ★ ★

Do these very cautious and demythologizing views about democracy mean that this book identifies with the famous definition formulated by Joseph Schumpeter?

> the democratic method is that institutional arrangement for arriving at political decisions in which individuals acquire the power to decide by means of a competitive struggle for the people's vote.
>
> (Schumpeter 1942, 269)

This definition is not only elitist, in the sense that it views politics mainly as a business among smart and powerful individuals, but also peers into it with economic notions such as competition for a sought-after scarce good – the majority of votes. The definition is a pinnacle of political realism and has, ever since its first formulation in 1942, caused rejection as well as attraction. It comes closer to how democracy really functions than its definition as 'government of/by/for the people', which taken literally materialises nearly nowhere – also because of the ambiguity of the 'people' notion explained above. On the other hand, also in Schumpeter's formula the people or the generality of citizens remains the bearer of sovereignty or ultimate power, which confers the (derived, secondary) power to make policy decisions on the individuals (or parties) that have gained more votes. In an ironical sense the formula has regained validity: while in the decades after the last World War, power was rather conferred upon parties, it is now again in many countries the individual leader, along with her or his staff, to play – in the so-called personalization of politics – the main role in the electoral game and the formulation of policies. The demise of the party format as the pivot of the political process in democracies has degenerative effects on the latter, as it deprives political decision making of an orderly connection to problems and disfunctions in the society as well as protest or new ideas among citizens.

A concluding remark: the image of democracy resulting from this chapter focuses on it as a procedure, though the substantive implications of liberal democracy have been also highlighted. In a procedural view on democracy we are in the good and large company of the likes of thinkers as different from each other as Joseph Schumpeter, Hans Kelsen (1881–1973), Norberto Bobbio and Jürgen Habermas – to mention just a few. In the political history of the nineteenth and twentieth century, however, to be 'democratic' has mostly implied not just loyalty to a method, but also a position left from the centre, implying wealth redistribution, job creation and protection, more rights for women and minorities – in a word, a preference for equality over liberty. The word still keeps much of its symbolical or label-like function, in America as well as in Europe and elsewhere. It has survived the misuse done to it in the former Communist bloc, as 'democratic' was the official standard definition of the countries that were not allowed to claim to have attained 'socialism' as the leading power, the Union of Soviet Socialist Republics, did. The name of the Democratic People's Republic of Korea is a remnant of those times, in which a further, now largely vanished dichotomy – *substantive vs. formal democracy* – was used to argue the superiority of the socialist system. The countries allegedly ruled by the working class through its Communist (or, as in the German Democratic Republic, Socialist) party were deemed to be truly in the service of the people instead of only granting citizens civil and political rights that must remain empty in the absence of social policies and power allocation capable of making them real. This was hardly anything more than an ideological cover for a privileged party bureaucracy's often incompetent management of a society under authoritarian rule and with bogus elections. The problem of what social condition can make democracy work existed and will continue to exist,[18] but the only acceptable, if problematic, solution has turned out to be historically the welfare state established within pluralist and liberal democracies: social policies such as the creation of a national health service can only complement the full respect of procedural democracy, not replace it (see Figure 5.1). What has proven wrong is the belief that

FIGURE 5.1 The creation of the National Health Service in the UK (1948) – here as it was remembered in the opening ceremony of the London Olympics 2012 – was a major step in the transformation of the liberal-democratic state.

cutting down on the free procedures of 'formal democracy', or undervaluing them, is conducive to more 'substantial' results.

'Substantial democracy' as superior substitute for 'formal democracy' was a formula quite similar to the 'brotherly help' by other Communist parties, which in the ears of the Austrian writer Ernst Fischer (1899–1972), a former Communist, sounded – he said – very much like the caterpillars of the tanks sent under that alleged rationale by other Soviet bloc states into such unruly places as Budapest in 1956 and Prague in 1968. In hindsight, the systems of government based on 'substantial democracy' (or 'real existing socialism', as the USSR and its allies loved to be called) have been a nearly total failure, since they have either collapsed, giving leeway to a democratic rule that is not free from authoritarian temptations, or led to a satrapy with dynastic government, or – the more puzzling and mixed outcome indeed – established a technocratic party dictatorship while substituting a communist economy with a mixed one, in which aspects of ultra-capitalism seem now to prevail (more on China in the next section).

4. How is democracy possible? Does it have alternatives?

Apologists of democracy tend to believe that it is the best possible choice everywhere and at any time; some go as far as to mark it as an export good. Most people would indeed rejoice if democracy, the best or rather the least defective system of government to date, were available under all possible conditions and regardless of the stage in evolution; lamentably, this is not the case, since democracy is itself the product of earthy, variable circumstances, and its assertion is futile if these are not considered – provided we understand democracy in the complex sense described so far rather than as majority rule in polls. We are now going to examine four of the framework conditions (as different from the pre-conditions mentioned above) that are either indispensable or highly favourable to the establishment and thriving of liberal democracy.

First. A degree of (moral) *individualism* in the cultural background of the society: important as groups and communities may be, the individual remains the ultimate bearer of rights and values, which are not at the disposal of the state or church or tribe or electoral majority. This is not to say that democracy is reserved to populations with a background in the Judeo-Christian and Enlightenment tradition, in which the individual and the person, two major philosophical notions, were first developed; but the philosophical and religious environment cannot be ignored as the factor that is hospitable or not to a decent version of democracy.

Individualism is conducive to democracy only if it is paired with belief in the basic equality of all individuals, irrespective of their income or status. Equality of men and women, or gender equality as it is now standard language to say, is fundamental in this sense, and remembering how long it took to implement it, or the equality among citizens of different skin colour as regards suffrage, shows how tortuous the road to a full-fledged democracy was, and in the many countries that treat women as B-citizens still is. It is also known that equality between sexes or ethnicities at the ballot box does not mean equal treatment in the family or the working place, let alone salary levels.

Second. Tolerance of other reasonable faiths or doctrines or interests, in other words *pluralism* or Weber's politheism is indispensable. If you think that a person believing in another religion or an atheist or a member of a minority or the supporter of market economy vs. state intervention (or vice versa) is intellectually or morally less worth of being understood in her/his reasons and respected, you are not going to share a stable democracy with them. This requires, besides tolerance, an attitude towards compromise instead of fighting holy wars; the *compromise* may come from either the recognition of the partner's understandable reasons or the consideration that stepping back today can preserve the conditions for tomorrow's cooperation.

By 'reasonable' we understand doctrines not aimed at hatred and destruction, racial superiority, fanaticism – nor at the cancellation of democracy and fundamental rights once fanatics or anti-democratic populists have achieved a majority. This limit must be set for theoretical considerations and out of historical experience: the inability or unwillingness of Italian and German democratic politicians to put above all the fight against the rise of totalitarian movements in the 1920–30s remains an unforgettable lesson of history – though in general, history does not have lessons to teach, unlike what European scholars believed from the Renaissance to the Enlightenment.[19]

In the democratic theory of the last century the relevance of pluralism has been most forcefully highlighted by the leading American political scientist Robert Dahl (1915–2014), who introduced *polyarchy* (πολυαρχία/rule by many) to denote what a democratic society is like, in which diverse social forces and interests interact with each other in the framework of representative institutions.

As a meta-condition to these two framework conditions a certain degree of *education* must be present among the public destined to go to the ballot box. Both the awareness of one's own individual rights and the respect of plurality in the human and cultural environment require a literate general population and a political leadership capable of arguing reasonably and not fanatically with each other. By a vote a citizen does not only express her or his will by making use of the equal share of political (electoral) power distributed in democracy, s/he assumes at the same time responsibility for the lot of all co-citizens and is required to do so in knowledge of the premises and consequences.

Third, both the scarcity of goods and the inequality in their distribution have to be moderate if people are to choose debate and struggle in a democracy as the dimension in which to assert their will to improve their condition. Poverty, both absolute and relative, but more forcefully the former, keeps people away from political participation or drives them to fruitless rebellion. Further up in the social ladder, the flourishing of the middle class stabilises democratic regimes more than, say, the dominance of the divide between haves (business people, high bureaucrats) and have-nots (unskilled working class, low-level clerks, small farmers). Rising inequality, as in the last decades and years at least in Western societies, is a blow to democracy's credibility.

These points lead us back to the problem of economy and democracy. But before we deal with it in the last section of this chapter, the question must be raised: what if the framework conditions for democracy are not met?

It is difficult, if not impossible, to answer this question with a general rule, which would then be superseded by the specificity of any singular case; besides, this is not an operational treatise in the art of government. Nonetheless, we can perhaps say that the introduction of democratic institutions should not be hurried where most of the conditions mentioned are absent, while a traditional non-representative regime should not – as a transitional solution – be easily dismantled where the introduction of democratic mass mobilisation for parliamentary conflicts is likely to break up internal peace and to reinforce civil strife. For cases like these, John Rawls (1999) used in his work on international society the expression 'decent hierarchical societies' and saw them as possible members of international society along with 'free and democratic peoples'. Still another reason for not treating democracy as a salvific remedy to be spread around everywhere is that bestowing the label 'democratic' on a regime in which essential conditions are missing, just because it holds some kind of election, confers upon it an undeserved legitimacy. There is hardly something as false and distorting as the equation 'election = democracy'.

We can push our questioning a little further and ask in a first step: is the picture of democracy painted here the only one available on the market of political ideas? Is there a non-Western form of democracy? We are not discussing here the merits of existing democracies, but the emergence or absence of an alternative model to Western democracies – which in their real contours lag often behind their own claims, in domestic as well as foreign policy.

The answer is negative for the time being. There are, around the world, different national versions of democracy, none however that raises the ambition to represent an alternative model. Such is not the democracy-cum-theocracy ruling Iran.

What seems to be up and coming is an alternative not within, but to democracy. Leaving aside Fascism and Soviet communism, this was in the 1990s the vindication of 'Asian values' as set in the Bangkok Declaration of 1993: primacy of the community over individual human rights, respect for traditions and elders, preference for authoritarian government as well as for harmony over pluralism. Not even in East Asia, however, did these principles find widespread acceptance, thus remaining limited to countries applying them such as Singapore and Malaysia. In this century theorists from the People's Republic of China have stressed the superiority of an anti-individualistic model of government, based on meritocracy, technocratic problem-solving and conflict-avoidance, over the Western model relying on the will of the citizens and the appreciation of diversity and mediated conflict. This latter element, they argue, is dysfunctional to efficiency in economy and administration; it would have made the huge and rapid growth impossible that lifted 400–500 million people from poverty in the post-Deng Hsiao Ping[20] era – certainly a historical achievement. On the other hand it must be said that democratically regulated conflict would have helped China identify early enough roots of malaise such as pollution, corruption and unregulated urbanisation. To be an early warning system for social troubles is an additional virtue of democracy.

How far the Chinese self-appreciation is linked to China's newly revived Confucian tradition cannot be discussed here. This model is clearly opposed not only to democracy, but also to the idea of politics that is being developed in this book out of the belief that good and stable government has to provide not just the satisfaction of the material needs of the population, but also its request of a balanced and freedom-enhancing governance. In any case, in order to gauge the robustness and attractiveness of the Chinese model, it is advisable to wait until its contradictions, to use a Hegelian-Marxian term loved by Chairman Mao, will have worked themselves out: I mean the contrast between the still authoritarian rule of the Communist Party and the emerging middle class as well as the sub-optimal, not to say perverse side effects of (high-carbon) growth. The student and youth movement of 1989 and the ensuing massacre on Tian An Men in Beijing at Deng's order, along with the more recent sprawling of initiatives in the field of environmental, labour and human rights policies, bear witness to the resilience of democratic aspirations within the alleged Chinese alternative to democracy.

This notwithstanding, the cultural differences between different civilisations must be kept in mind when discussing the pretended universality of government models, even if it is wrong to ossify them into a 'clash of civilisations', as Harvard political scientist Samuel Huntington (1927–2008)[21] and, even more, his followers did. It remains here an open question whether or not cultural roots make China and other South-East Asian countries impermeable to liberal democracy; but the belief in its universalizability that spread across the USA and to a lesser degree Europe in the second half of the twentieth century was not only naive, but arrogant, as it projected in an uncritical way a Western experience into the rest of the world. This attitude generated disasters, last but not least for the very credibility of democracy.

Furthermore, what possibly lies behind this simplistic approach to the universalization of democracy is the confusion with human rights as defined in the Universal Declaration of Human Rights of 1948. These are best protected in a democracy, but this does not mean that they can live only in a full-fledged democracy, as they can be asserted and to a degree protected also in regimes that do not choose their leaders by democratic procedure. For both individual wellbeing and international peace, the protection of human rights is more crucial than how power is distributed and government structured. In a normative sense, being intransigent on human rights is universally justified, while the call for democracy everywhere and at any time is not.

5. Democracy and capitalism

If we want to address this thorny topic in a rational way, it is wise first to clarify our language, steering away from the understanding of capitalism the reader may have drawn from political struggle and propaganda, in which words are bent to the particular interest of any actor in order to influence the debate in her/his/its direction.

By capitalism let us understand an economic system producing commodities, which is driven by *profit* expectations and based on private ownership of the means of production as well as wage labour being itself a commodity exchanged on the job market.

This is the core definition of capitalism, of which many versions have existed in modern history and the contemporary world. Some of them bring, in extreme cases, to development the pathological elements that are – given its core structure – possible, but not necessarily always active. The sometimes recurrent cry 'abolish capitalism' seems to be aimed at these pathologies rather than at capitalism as such.

Against historical determinism, and in the sense of a multi-factor conception of history, we can hold that, while the rise of the modern state was almost contemporary to the rise of capitalism, the former was not caused by the latter, and even their interrelationship cannot be enshrined into a formula. As to democracy, its relationship with capitalism has been ambivalent.

On the one hand, so far capitalism has been the economic system that has best accommodated democracy; the same can be said neither of pre-capitalist economies nor of the state socialism of Soviet or Chinese brand nor of the economies almost exclusively based on the selling of their natural resources and incapable of normal capitalist development (countries affected by the 'oil-curse'). As the revolutionary force that was recognised as such by Marx himself, capitalism has set traditional societies upside down and created the terrain for modern political dynamics. The private powers created by early capitalism were able to counterbalance those of the absolutist state and to loosen its grip on a country's wealth, especially in France; the creation of economic growth also generated the urban middle class and the civil society based on it, which were the fitting environment in which liberal, democratic and later socialist ideas and movements were able to thrive. After the Second World War, the capitalist reconstruction of Western and Southern Europe under democratic governments created the premises for the implementation of the workers' social rights – obviously not without conflicts with entrepreneurs.

On the other hand capitalism, if left unbridled, can become a threat to democracy for at least three major reasons:

1. It creates global and national non-political powers that can overwhelm the policy-making ability of democratic governments and severely limit their range of options, especially after the primacy achieved by insufficiently regulated financial capitalism.
2. Those extra-democratic powers can heavily influence policy by poorly regulated money donations to parties and politicians as well as by corruption of representatives and civil servants, which sometimes occurs across borders. The funding of anti-democratic parties and rebel groups is another example; one of the many examples was the funding by wealthy donors of rightist militias in the process that led to the upsetting of Latin-American democracies in the 1970s–1980s.
3. Capitalist powerhouses or oligopolies, seeking to expand their profits without economic wisdom and due consideration to the human and environmental

externalities[22] of their activity, can constrain legislation in the direction of voiding or limiting social security, thus eroding one pillar of the democratic state and creating social unrest, or even letting conflicts degenerate into a threat to domestic peace. The market, to put it in the words of Robert Dahl, needs to be civilised by democracy.

This view is based on a balanced appreciation of the market along with the rejection of the attitude called market fundamentalism. Looking back at the debate 'market economy vs. planned (or command) economy' of the early 1920s in Germany and Austria (cf. Cubeddu 1993), there is little doubt that the liberal or free trade party was right in seeing the market as better equipped to provide an efficient (thanks to the price mechanism) provision of goods for the society, even if they were wrong in rejecting any state intervention in the economy – as the New Deal in America and the social market economy of the European reconstruction proved. By the way, planned economy also was relatively successful, but only in the initial phase of industrialization and modernisation of underdeveloped countries such as the Soviet Union in the 1920s and China in the 1950s and 1960s; it proved later an incorrigible obstacle to development, so that Deng's China shifted later to capitalism in order to kick off poverty-staving growth and reinforce the Communist regime.

To be clear, one thing is the superiority of market over plan, another one altogether the alleged autonomy of the market from all politics, which has resurfaced as neoliberal myth since the 1970s and contributed – along with the new global dimension – to taking away economic processes from regulations passed by democratic decision making. The Asian crisis of 1997 and more decisively the first financial, then economic crisis that started in New York in 2008 and led to the nearly worldwide, year-long Great Recession, has proven the fundamentalist faith in the market wrong not only in theory, but in economic practise as well, as remedying it required a lot of intervention by governments and international institutions. Nonetheless neoliberal ideologues are rarely ready to give up their exaltation of the market and their treatment of the state as their *bête-noire*.[23]

We will come back to the 'democracy and capitalism' topic in the chapter on the two moments of globalisation, which will have something to say also on how democracy comes to terms (or fails to) with scientific and technological advancements, be it nuclear physics or the unveiling of climate change. But we need to first enter the two fields of international and global politics and make ourselves familiar with the state of affairs and its language. Then we will be able to complete our image of democracy with the issues challenging it today and tomorrow.

Notes

1 The same word is the title of Plato's main work on politics and is in his case translated as *Republic*. As to democracy, till the 18th century this word meant either government by the populace led by demagogues, as in ancient Greece, or direct democracy.

2 This is clearly not even a recapitulation of the long and variegated evolution of the typologies of government, for which the reader is invited to turn to both a history of political thought and a history of political institutions.
3 Philosophical reflections on totalitarianism – a word introduced by Italian fascism, which unlike Nazism did however not fully succeed in realising a corresponding regime – were first formulated by Max Horkheimer (1942, 15), though under the label of the authoritarian state, and later Hannah Arendt (1951).
4 Thucydides BCE 404. That the author ended his writing in the year BCE 404 (the year of his death? or 396?) is only a conjecture. We also ignore the original title given by him to his work that was traded down to us as ἱστορίαι/histories or. Περὶ τοῦ Πελοποννησίου πολέμου/The Pelopponesian War.
5 Voting rights for African-Americans, established by the Fifteenth Amendment passed in 1870, only became effective nation-wide with the Civil Rights Act of 1964 and the Voting Rights Act of 1965, a combined if conflictual achievement of President Lyndon B. Johnson and Dr. Martin Luther King Jr.
6 This was the prevailing direction in which the doctrine of the nation state expanded, though not the only one, as the cases of Mazzini and later Otto Bauer (1881–1938), the leader of the so-called *Austromarxismus*, prove.
7 Here I am reminded of Norberto Bobbio's suggestion, in a talk given as early as in the 1980s, to replace 'the people' by 'the citizens' in constitutional texts.
8 In the case of the USA, the quasi-aristocratic role is now said to have passed from the Senate, which until 1917 was not elected by popular vote, to the Supreme Court. *Bundesverfassungsgericht* in Germany and *Corte costituzionale* in Italy were given from their very beginning an analogue function.
9 In Cicero's formulation the three forms of government were interconnected by ἀνακύκλωσις/anacyclosis, the dynamics that let the three forms of government cyclically change into each other by degeneration.
10 I shall briefly come back to the issue of lying in politics in Chapter 10, §1.
11 With the obvious exception of constitutional authorities such as supreme courts that are not elected by popular vote.
12 The classic document for the differential description of ancient (Athenian) and modern politics is the essay by the French liberal thinker Benjamin Constant (1767–1830) *De la liberté des Anciens comparée à celle des Modernes* (Constant 1819).
13 Addressed here are hyper-democratic illusions and self-delusions about the use of IT in political affairs, not at all the use of e-government procedures for the sake of public information and education, transparency of administrative processes as well as in local policy deliberation. On the other hand the rising role of 'big data' and algorithm-driven strategies in social life and electoral campaigns is problematic.
14 In EU member states, populism is nowadays accompanied by euroscepticism or europhobia aimed at 'those in Brussels' or 'eurocrats'.
15 One should perhaps add a third, more centrist type: regionalist populism, centred on the claim for autonomy or secession of the region's 'people' from the nation state. My use of the term populism connects to its meaning in the European history of political vocabulary.
16 Italian Fascism originally had populist traits, as did Peron's movements in the Argentina of the Forties; much less so National Socialism. In Europe after 1945 episodes of populism were the 'Uomo Qualunque' movement in Italy in the Forties and in the French *poujadisme* of the 1950s (led by Pierre Poujade 1920–2003). Fascinating is a comparison between present-day populism and its comparable predecessors in the Athenian democracy, the demagogues. An eloquent document of populism is Donald Trump's inaugural address (20 January 2017) as President of the USA, available at www.whitehouse.gov/inaugural-address. As to the element of 'post-truth' present in populist rhetoric cf. Chapter 10, endnote 6.
17 This is a hint at the Spanish *indignados* movement of 2011. All the factors mentioned were at work in the Brexit referendum of June 2016, a striking example of how entrusting a

historic policy decision to the 'people' runs against all the reasonable criteria of deliberation in a representative democracy.
18 It was first addressed polemically by the young Marx in *Zur Judenfrage/On the Jewish Question* (1844), a critique of bourgeois revolutions.
19 On the *topos*, going back to Cicero, of *historia magistra vitae*/history is life's teacher cf. Koselleck 1979.
20 He lived from 1904–97 and was the country's supreme leader from 1978–1992.
21 See Huntington 1996.
22 'An externality is the cost or benefit that affects a party who did not choose to incur that cost or benefit' (Wikipedia); diseases among the workforce that with the enforcement of more preventive measures by the factory owner could have avoided or the pollution of a river due to toxic industrial side-products are typical externalities.
23 This attitude did not prevent them from using a strong state in order to implement neoliberal reforms, cf. Schmidt and Woll 2013.

References

Constant, Benjamin (1819) *De la Liberté des Anciens comparée à celle des Modernes/The Liberty of the Ancients Compared with that of the Moderns*, available at https://mises.org/library/liberty-ancients-compared-moderns

Cubeddu, Raimondo (1993) *The Philosophy of the Austrian School*, London: Routledge.

Hannah Arendt (1951) *The Origins of Totalitarianism*, New York: Schocken Books.

Horkheimer, Max (1942) *The Authoritarian State*, New York: Telos Press, 1973.

Huntington, Samuel (1996) *The Clash of Civilizations and the Remaking of World Order*, New York: Simon & Schuster.

Koselleck, Reinhart (1979) *Vergangene Zukunft: Zur Semantik geschichtlicher Zeiten/Futures Past: On the Semantics of Historical Time*, New York: Columbia University Press, 2005.

Machiavelli, Niccolò (1532) *Il Principe/The Prince*, New York: Cambridge University Press, 1988.

Marx, Karl (1844) *Zur Judenfrage/On the Jewish Question*, available at www.marxists.org/archive/marx/works/1844/jewish-question/

Mill, John Stuart (1861) *Considerations on Representative Government*, Indianapolis: Bobbs-Merrill, 1958.

Przeworski, Adam (2010) *Democracy and the limits of self-government*, New York: Cambridge University Press.

Putnam, Robert D. (1993) *Making Democracy Work*, Princeton: Princeton University Press.

Putnam, Robert D. (2000) *Bowling Alone*, New York: Simon & Schuster.

Rawls, John (1999) *The Law of Peoples*, Cambridge: Harvard University Press.

Rousseau, Jean Jacques (1762) *Du contrat social/The Social Contract*, ebook available at www.constitution.org/jjr/socon.htm

Schmidt, Vivien and Cornelia Woll (2013) *The State: The Bête Noire of Neo-Liberalism or Its Greatest Conquest?* in V. Schmidt and Mark Thatcher, eds., *Resilient Liberalism in Europe's Political Economy*, Cambridge: Cambridge University Press, 112–142.

Schumpeter, Joseph (1942) *Capitalism, Socialism and Democracy*, London: Routledge, 2003.

Θουκυδίδης/Thucydides (404 BCE) Περὶ τοῦ Πελοποννησίου πολέμου/*The Peloponnesian War*, available at http://classics.mit.edu/Thucydides/pelopwar.1.first.html (404 BCE is Thucydides's presumptive year of death; title attributed in the Hellenistic era).

Tocqueville, Alexis de (1835) *De la démocratie en Amérique/Of Democracy in America*, available at http://classiques.uqac.ca/classiques/De_tocqueville_alexis/democracy_in_america_historical_critical_ed/democracy_in_america_vol_2.pdf

Further readings

Three fundamental works on democracy, between political philosophy and political science:

Dahl, Robert (1989) *On Democracy*, New Haven: Yale University Press.
Held, David (2006) *Models of Democracy*, third edition, Cambridge: Polity.
Sartori, Giovanni (1987) *The Theory of Democracy Revisited*, Chatham: Chatham House Publishers.

On populism, no new encompassing research work has been published after:

Meny, Yves and Yves Surel (2002) *Democracies and the Populist Challenge*, London: Palgrave Macmillan.

An interesting survey is:

Baracani, Elena and Roberto Di Quirico, eds. (2013) *Alternatives to Democracy: Non-Democratic Regimes and the Limits to Democracy Diffusion*, Florence: European Press Academic Publishing.

PART III
World politics and the future of politics

We are now coming a step closer to the full reality of politics by shifting from the singular, the state, to the plural, the states. Since the beginning of politics as a specific human activity, members of the political community had to put their mind to the needs and troubles inside the group as well as to the threats or opportunities coming from the inevitable contact with other groups. Policy has always been essentially foreign no less than domestic policy, as great even if diverging thinkers such as Hobbes, Kant and Hegel – but not their epigones – knew. Globalisation has eventually put an end to the shortsightedness of less recent textbooks, in which politics pretended to be all explained once the origin and the working of the state (singular) had been dealt with.

What follows in this Part is therefore not an application of or a marginal addition to the categories we have seen so far, but rather their re-examination within a new context along with new categories that will all lead us not only into the worldwide dimension of politics, but also to a revision, pressed by substantial novelties, of the very notion of politics we made the acquaintance of at the outset of our journey.

In this Part we consider two further dimensions of politics: international and global. They are still merged by most authors into one big chapter called 'international relations', but I deem the sphere called 'global affairs' to have its own specificity, as it will be shown in the following chapters. The first, Chapter 6, deals with the classical themes of international politics: the nature of international relations, war and peace, and the restraints to war. Chapter 7 comprises the two, largely unrelated areas in which the word 'global' occurs: economic, but also social, cultural and political globalisation; global, or rather global and lethal challenges in the particular sense I am giving to this expression.

6
THE STATES
Power, peace and war in anarchical society

The journey we are going to undertake has two intentions. It is going to check the validity of the fundamental categories examined in the first three chapters of this book outside of the domestic realm and facing the present state of the world. But it also wants to build up a batch of conceptual knowledge related to the evolution of peace and war, poverty and cooperation in order to know what we are talking about when we deal today with the normative problems that come up with these issues and require more than a generic ethical answer.

The journey unfolds in this chapter in four stages. In §1 it draws a general picture of international relations in the modern era under the label of an 'anarchical society', while §2 focuses on war, a crucial feature of those relations. How to restrain war or how to establish and protect peace is discussed in §3, but also in §4, in which a paramount example of pacification by political means of previously bellicose populations is presented, also in its theoretical aspects: the process of European integration.

States face each other in the international arena as *sovereign* states, though in our time not all actors that confront each other in the international arena are states: think of liberation movements, terrorist groups, worldwide advocacy groups, powerful multinational corporations (MNCs), and, of course, international institutions, whether political or economic or scientific – the so-called 'epistemic communities' such as the IPCC (International Panel on Climate Change).

In this dimension, states exert the external dimension of their sovereignty: external with respect to other states or actors, in the sense of a state's recognised claim to autonomy that is to govern itself by its own statutes, held valid in the same territory and over the same population, as we saw in Chapter 4. We also remember that sovereignty, in particular external sovereignty, depends very much on the *recognition* granted by other states (since 1945 it is a vote in the General Assembly of the UN that makes the difference). In other words, sovereignty means independence from other countries or superior bodies and allows for autonomy or self-rule. External sovereignty is a pre-condition to the domestic one: a community can succeed in giving itself a state-like power structure, but without recognition even its domestic sovereignty remains uncertain and subject to anybody else's claim or intervention. Sovereignty as recognised international actorhood lastly entails *equality* among the states, a formal or legal equality that matters regardless of different levels of individual wealth or might.

This first description makes the two opposing sides of external sovereignty neatly visible. On the one hand, it signals the state's ability to act as it pleases on the international stage: it can wage war, break up peace or negotiate a truce, invade and occupy, withdraw from treaties and deny cooperation or burden-sharing. On the other hand, as far as it seeks and achieves the recognition of other states, it is expected to bow to elementary diplomatic rules and to reshape its behaviour according to international law. Yet, if it falls short of those expectations, there is, or rather used to be (before institutions such as humanitarian intervention, the responsibility to protect and international criminal justice were created), neither an enforceable law that can restrain and punish it (except in certain cases) and no superior and common power that can impose the law. It is now clear that sovereignty is not a matter-of-fact feature, but rather a legal category: relations between sovereign states are clothed in international law, which is different from domestic law, being nevertheless a law that gives shape to and even constrains those relations.

1. The anarchical international society

In this picture of international relations, a number of independent states share under themselves the world in an adversarial way, as it is defined at any given moment. This element differs a lot over time: in early modernity the world was still the European-Mediterranean area of the Roman empire plus its 'Holy' medieval extension to Northern and Central Europe, though confronted on its southern rim with a new civilisation and polity (first the Caliphate, then the Islamic follow-up states) and opening up in the direction of the Americas; in this century it's the planet, plus the outer space and perhaps in the future one or two other planets where humans may try to settle. Every state looked after its chief's and its citizens' interest in survival and welfare, in a competitive environment in which nearly everything is permitted. Cases of cooperation and alliance existed, but the absolute primacy of self-interest made them shaky. Self-reliance remained the safest resource and *anarchy* (ἀναρχία/ lack of government), meaning the absence of a common superior power – a *tertius super partes*/a Third over the parties – the fundamental connotation of this world. Historically, this became more visible as the old universal forces, the Holy Roman Empire and the Roman Church, which in the Middle Ages were theoretically entitled to settle disputes and wars, lost all their power; they however acted mostly as particularistic rather than universalistic instances, though it took centuries before the other powers or countries felt free to behave regardless of what the emperor or the pope had to say.

In this scenario disagreements between international actors found settlement in diplomatic action or could not lead but to *war*. This has always happened – let us look back for example at the city states of ancient Greece. But the structure we are now outlining came about with all its features only in modern Europe, as a true if restless polyarchy of fully independent and equal states, fairly different in its constitution not just from the Greek *poleis*,[1] but also from the warring kingdoms of ancient China or the likewise warring tribes or nations of Native Americans. A war is still an event in which human beings kill other human beings, but being or not the killing embedded in a grid of legal norms and diplomatic customs (formal and informal institutions) may change the frequency, the duration, the intensity of the war and the procedures for peace.

The concept of war will keep us busy in the next section, but let us now note that going to war in order to solve a dispute is tantamount to admitting that both diplomacy and the system of international law and tribunals has failed: in the absence of a judge and of an enforcement authority it is military (supported by economic) *force* that decides whose right will prevail. Every body's asserted right is admitted to the race, and force will design the winner. International anarchy is the sheer *state of nature* among nations. Once war has broken out, as a bottomline, *silent inter arma leges*/the laws are speechless among arms, as the Romans said.[2] The Thirty Years' War, which ravaged large swaths of Europe and along with the ensuing pestilences caused enormous suffering to the population, came near to the regression of social relationships into a state of nature.[3]

We have so far outlined the structure of international relations as it can be reconstructed by their history in various epochs and regions, and with the help of formulations drawn from modern classics of political philosophy, primarily Thomas Hobbes. This anarchical core structure is and remains a substantial help for the understanding of international politics. But to grasp its configuration in our time we have to pay attention to three major revolutions that occurred between early modernity and now:

- the rise of the anarchical society after the Peace of Westphalia, which set an end to the Thirty Years' War (1648)
- the two World Wars of the twentieth century and the birth of collective security and international organisation
- the globalisation of politics, both in the aftermath of economic globalisation and as emergence of global/lethal challenges that require rethinking politics altogether.

We are going to now examine only the two changes high on the list, but this will be enough to modify the all-anarchical image of international relations we have just described. The core structure does not disappear, it was full at work in the Second World War and could under (for the time being unlikely) certain circumstances regain the central stage, but its modifications seem to be here to stay.

What is *anarchical society*?[4] It's first of all an oxymoron, in which the adjective 'anarchical' contradicts the noun 'society', whose meaning indicates peaceful coexistence or even cooperation aimed at everyone's advantage. We could likewise say 'societal anarchy'. In it the absence of a higher power adjudicating controversies remains, but is tempered by a common interest in stability (lest one's own position is damaged) and by shared norms, followed as long as they serve one's own advantage and the costs for breaking them imposed by the partners exceed the gains one could receive from freeriding. In anarchical society, we meet again the notion of political order we have learned about in Chapter 3, along with the goals *political order* pursues, though not in a planned way: reduction of violence and inflicted death, observance of covenants. One of the norms, or rather habits, underlying it is to try as far as it goes to solve controversies by diplomatic means and to go to war only as a last resort. This is all possible only because the actors have recognised each other as sovereign states, and sovereignty remains the first conceptual pillar of the anarchical society. They, and they alone, not whatever group can legitimately go to war, since the *compétence de guerre* – as the entitlement to do so was called in French, until the Second World War the language of diplomacy – is reserved to them.

A further consequence of this 'societal' element is that war is conceived as a clash of legal personalities, the states, not of peoples, being therefore clothed in legal forms – though combat remains the opposite of a legal relationship. Fighting happens only after the formal declaration of war, and is restrained on a voluntary basis by the rule to not attack civilians and to not loot their properties, to not kill wounded enemies or prisoners and to not impose the occupier's religion over the vanquished. These provisions belong to *ius in bello*/law within war, that is the law – we will soon come back to it – that still has a voice among armed clashes, unlike in the Roman sentence quoted above.

Let us now recapitulate what we have learned so far and situate it in the context of history: just as with the notion of the state, international anarchy as a structure already existed in antiquity and the Middle Ages, but came first to full life in modernity with the wars for hegemony between the Holy Roman Empire (comprising Austria, Germany, Bohemia, Slovakia, parts of the Baltic states, Northern Italy and was for a while in the sixteenth century in the person of Charles V connected to Spain and the Netherlands) and other European states in the late Middle Ages and the sixteenth–seventeenth centuries, then was reshaped as anarchical society in the process that started with the Westphalian Treaties. In the eighteenth century, officially with the Treaty of Utrecht of 1713, which contains the clause *iustum potentiae equilibrium*/just balance of power or might, a new element came to define the modern political order. Balance of power as opposed to hegemony was intended to describe a situation in which a limited number of great powers could coexist with military force and diplomatic influence approximately in the balance; attempts at acquiring a hegemonic position by one or two powers were legitimately rejected by the other powers joining in the common effort, including if necessary by war, to counterbalance the hegemonic move. This scheme of order is almost a constant in history and remains still now one component of international politics along with others, though severely limited by nuclear armament; its most linear manifestation was the European system of the eighteenth century.

The war of revolutionary, and later Napoleonic France, brought a first moment of perturbation to that order: ideology. This had been largely absent from European conflicts after the end of the religious wars, and came up again, on the one hand, as the revolutionary ideology of bourgeois France, on the other, as the traditionalistic doctrine of the Holy Alliance (since 1815). Later the preservation of the balance of power as well as of the anti-revolutionary order (the Restoration) was entrusted to a new tool, a first glimpse of what became in the twentieth century the international organisation: this was the (informal) Concert of Nations, which made its first appearance at the Congress of Vienna (1815) and then again at the Congresses of Paris (1856, after the Crimean War) and Berlin (1878, on the Balkan question). In the new scenario created by the Great War, as the First World War was nicknamed, the creation of the League of Nations at Paris in 1920 marked the beginning of a new international order based on the notion of collective security.

What is *collective security*? It's a system of relations in which political and military security is no longer the business of the single actor, but rather everybody's concern. A potential enemy must know that, if it attacks one of the system members, it will have to do with the reaction of the entire alliance, an expectation that deters it from waging an aggression and stabilises the environment. The first worldwide collective security system, the League, then renamed the Society of Nations, failed miserably, as it made no serious attempt at stopping Fascist Italy's invasion of the Kingdom of Ethiopia (1935–1936); the second one, the United Nations Organization, has done much better, either authorising military action by a 'coalition of the willing' against invaders (two examples: Communist North Korea invading South Korea in 1950, Saddam Hussein's Iraq invading Kuwait in 1990) or keeping peace by interposition forces and aiding civilians in crisis areas (one of the many examples is UNIFIL operating in Southern Lebanon since 2006). However, the worldwide security system is a weak Third, hardly a Third above the parties, as it depends on the will of the majority in the UN Security Council and can be paralysed by the veto of one of the five veto-holding powers. Much better results are on the record of regional security systems such as NATO (the North Atlantic Treaty Organization, in force since 1949) that can reckon on a deeper homogeneity among members and/or the presence of a leading partner.[5] Lastly, collective security can be reinforced by *common security*, in which two potential enemies reassure each other and prevent overreactions and misperceptions, a factor known for igniting wars, by communicating steadily with each other and taking confidence-building measures.

This is all we have for keeping peace among the states, which was one of the major problems with which the modern classics of political philosophy from Hobbes to Kant were concerned. It is not much, it remains below what seemed to be the optimal solution of a law-abiding and peace-imposing Third, but it has transformed sheer anarchy into an anarchical society or even an international community in which at least in principle almost every state is interested in peace and cooperation.

Even this modest but real progress is however almost powerless when confronted with both nuclear war and the wars that are not interstate clashes. To better grasp this present reality we shall now linger for a while on the concept of war.

2. War

War has been the central problem for modern political philosophy, whose leading authors often lived among foreign and civil wars. Hobbes reinvented the good biblical monster Leviathan as remedy to *bellum omnium contra omnes*/war of all against all dominating the state of nature as well as opponent to Behemoth, the nasty monster of civil war,[6] but in his realism saw no alternative to international anarchy but war preparedness. On the opposite, idealistic side of the spectrum the ageing Kant wrote his last famous work immediately after the peace treaties signed in Basel by revolutionary France, Prussia and Spain, arguing the reforms he deemed necessary to make peace finally perpetual (Kant 1795). John Rawls, himself an infantryman in the US Army on the Pacific Front from 1943 on, wrote, at the end of his scholarly activity, his view on the international order that may best secure peace (1999).

But what is *war*? Empirically speaking, an armed conflict between states or other organised political groups with at least 1,000 battlefield casualties – as statisticians used to have it. For a philosophical definition we must turn to the celebrated 'philosopher of war', the Prussian general Carl von Clausewitz (1780–1831), whose *Vom Kriege*/Of War was published in 1832 by his widow Marie von Brühl: 'war is ... an act of violence to compel our opponent to fulfil our will' (Clausewitz 1832, 1).[7] On this account, war as violence is a means for a goal that is not itself military but political in nature: to have the opponent do what we want her/him/it to do. This comes very close to our initial relational and substantive definitions of political power; but in the case of war, violence does not remain in the background as a last resort guarantee and rather intervenes as actual violence.

Clausewitz's famous formulation of these relationships 'war is simply the continuation of political intercourse with the addition of other means' illuminates his entire analysis of the several aspects and stages of war, which he sees as shaped by a 'trinity': hatred and enmity, rooted in the population (Clausewitz was deeply influenced by the anti-Napoleonic Prussian liberation war, in which he fought); probability and chance, which is the business of the commanders; the war's nature as a political instrument, therefore governed by intellect. In this philosophical account the emotional side of war is considered, but also relativized, far from seeing war – as conventional wisdom sometimes still wants to have it – as the inevitable outcome of 'natural' aggressiveness.

Clausewitz's philosophy of war was, up until the Great War, an excellent intellectual tool for the understanding of interstatal war in anarchical society. Then, things started changing with war and politics, and that conceptual grid lost some of its analytical strength. In the years from 1914 through 1918, two aspects popped up that came to full development only in the Second World War: one was the total engagement of a country in the war effort, requiring a restructuring of the economy in the sense of planned mass production and changes to social life, particularly regarding women. Second, with the fledgling use of the great novelty, aviation, for military purposes, began the weakening, then the disappearance of the distinction between armed forces and civilian population, now explicit target or 'collateral damage' of aerial bombardment. It was the beginning of the process that in the wars fought after the First World War has seen the ratio of civilians' casualties vs. the fighters' more and more reversed in comparison to previous wars, thus *de facto* voiding the distinction of combatant and non-combatant, the pillar of *ius in bello*.

The step further was the massive re-entering of *ideology* into politics and war, in a dimension and depth unattained in the religious wars of early modernity. The Spanish Civil War of 1936–1939 was the prologue to the following world war clashes between Fascism, Nazism, Communism and democratic doctrine, which made the war bloody and cruel well beyond any former example. The *Shoah* (destruction) of the Jews, or Holocaust, went far beyond any military logic, and is a watershed moment in the history of civilisation rather than an event in war history – along with the extermination of Slavs, Roma and Sinti, gays and Jehovah's Witnesses in Hitler's death camps. The *Shoah* cannot just as easily be regarded as political conflict, because it includes dynamics of paranoid identification or invention of the 'enemy' and industrial destruction of human beings deprived of all human dignity that escapes the usual categories of politics. On the other hand the prevention of similar events by all possible cultural and administrative tools has become after 1945 an elementary task of all politics.

The Second World War ended in August 1945 with the atomic bombings on Hiroshima and Nagasaki, a step that opened a new era in human history and to which politics has not yet provided an adequate response. The Third World War indeed did not come about and was replaced by the Cold War, but in any case we know that at stake is now not victory, but the survival of humankind. In a nuclear war, which is always an implied potentiality in the deterrence regime, the instrument of war turns against its owner, since starting a nuclear war or participating in it is suicidal beyond being omnicidal; the weapon is no longer a means for a political goal and becomes the element dominating the outcome of the game well beyond the intentions of the players. Although never fully experienced,[8] already the perspective of nuclear war put an end to Clausewitzian war as the war in which deadly violence remains under the control of political actors and their finality. We will come back to nuclear war and deterrence in Chapter 7.

The transformation of war has gone further after the invention of nuclear weapons. Beyond interstate war fought with conventional weapons, which after the Falklands War of 1982 has become a rarity, and nuclear war, which has never been fought (otherwise we would not be here writing or reading about it), the actually fought wars fall into the category 'wars of the third kind',[9] which comprise ethnic, tribal, religious, secession, civil, and drug wars presently fought by actors that can be states, parties, movements, sects, terrorist groups and criminal gangs. A war of this kind can hardly be neatly attributed to just one of these types and is rather likely to result from a mix of them and to be 'asymmetric' in the tactics chosen (laser-guided bombs from supersonic fighter-bombers on the one hand, suicide terrorists with explosive belts on the other). In either case, asymmetric conventional warfare of the third kind has made big advances in destructiveness even if remaining under the nuclear threshold.

This is all tantamount to the collapse of the picture of international order as found in international relations classics from Hobbes to Waltz. It is not easy, for example, to readapt the latter's authoritative framing, some sixty years ago, of the phenomenon of war in three 'images' to the later evolution – authoritative because it shaped the language of international theory for decades and is still worth being learned (Waltz 1959). In the first image the roots of war are seen in human behaviour, as it results from 'selfishness, from misdirected aggressive impulses, from stupidity' (Waltz 1959, 16), or in other words, from human nature as seen through optimistic or pessimistic lenses. In the second image or level of analysis it is the internal regime of states to determine their bellicose or peaceful attitude. The third image places the *cause of war* in international anarchy, in the terms seen above. This is regarded as a permissive cause of war: the international system makes it possible. Image One and Two, in whatever version or combination, provide the efficient causes, which make the possibility of war an actuality based on a given occasion. Neither image taken by itself can explain any war.

Having enriched our view on international affairs and war, let us now briefly recapitulate by linking this chapter to the general categories of politics as defined in the previous chapters. Politics here too can be seen as the re-allocation of material and relational resources by means of power, as we saw in its first definition in Chapter 1; and *power in the international arena* does not appear to coincide with sheer economic or military force, because a mighty actor still needs political skills (alliances, inclusive management of one's own points of strength, soft power) in order to not misuse and disperse its elements of superiority. Even in the conduct of a war – history teaches – diplomatic ability remains a fundamental asset along armies, fleets and healthy budgets.

What lacks – at least *prima facie* – in the anarchical society is another basic element of our definition of politics and power: *legitimacy*. Power among nations is primarily *de facto* power, building on the pillars mentioned above; it does not need to correspond to models of good governance that peoples and their elites may have in mind. Neither does – except in the EU – a region-wide or worldwide covenant exist, similar to a domestic constitution, under whose rules the legitimacy of old or new powers can be discussed and evaluated. The only universally accepted category, national sovereignty, goes in the opposite direction of justifying only (formal, legal) equality among nations. This is however no longer the whole truth: to begin with, a formal mechanism of legitimation of international behaviour has been introduced in 1945 with the UN Charter, which we will come back to in the following section. Second, a weak form of legitimacy pops up when peoples (or their majorities) which are not high on the ladder of international politics approve – perhaps willy-nilly rather than enthusiastically – of a regime of relative peace, prosperity and stability guaranteed by an overwhelming leader or imperial country or bloc. In their best days, Rome with the *Pax Romana*, the USA with the *Pax Americana* of the decades following the Second World War and the European Community or (since 1993) Union with the peace and prosperity it contributed to on the continent until 2008, are examples of what the (weak or second-grade and half-hidden) legitimacy of power in international politics means. It must be noted that we are now speaking of the effective legitimacy of international power in history and presently. A fairly different question regards the criteria of legitimacy for a hoped-for transformation or regeneration of government/governance in the international realm; we will briefly touch upon this area of questions in Chapter 9 under the heading of 'global justice'.

3. Restraints to war, or peace?

Can war be limited in frequency and cruelty? Or can war be erased from the future and peace established? How, and to what extent?

The containment of war has been seen by theorists and statesmen as a goal that should be strived for by (a) restructuring international relations, or (b) imposing normative (legal) constraints on the behaviour of states.

Under (a) the tools known so far are:

- hegemonic peace. A hegemonic or imperial power keeps peace under the countries within its sphere of influence and, thanks to this control mechanism, with competing powers as well. The Cold War was a last example of this bipolar hegemonic system, complemented by the balance of terror.
- the balance of power as explained above.
- the nuclear balance of terror relying on deterrence as mutually assured destruction; but also the high degree of technological destructiveness another conventional world war would set out works as a deterrent.
- collective security, including common security, as previously explained.
- *democratic peace:* democratic countries do not go to war against each other. This is a theoretical claim, first raised by Kant (1795) in *Perpetual Peace*. If you want peace, he suggested, you must change the international system, making it federative in the sense of a league of states; but also eradicate the cause of war in the domestic regime, switching it to republican, which for Kant means based on the freedom and equality of all citizens under the law; we, living in democratic countries, say now democratic instead of republican by looking at the origin of the law from the citizens' will. A republican or democratic regime lacks the eagerness for war that characterises absolute or authoritarian or totalitarian regimes. Beyond an arguable theoretical claim democratic peace has to date been also an empirical fact, since there is not a single case of liberal-democratic countries waging war against each other, while they can be – and have been – fierce fighters against non-democratic regimes. Needless to say, neither Kant's argument nor its updated version justifies any war to 'export democracy'. Also, an evolution towards populism can spoil democracy and democratic peace also in the sense of making a country xenophobic and aggressive.

Under (b), that is from a normative perspective, we re-encounter in full size the *just war* tradition. Just war means justified, admissible war, and this theory is aimed at checking the reasons for going to war, strictly defining and limiting them; it has nothing to do with holy war, being instead its contrary, that is containment of war rather than enthusiasm for it. Every civilisation has its own standards for admitting or rejecting war; we can only briefly illustrate the Western tradition, which goes back to St. Augustine, but was in modern times secularised and in this version influenced the norms regarding war in international law. The tradition includes *ius ad bellum* and *ius in bello*.

Ius ad (or *in*) *bellum* regulates the right to go to war and has been the least effective part of the doctrine, since states have often waged war only pretending with captious arguments to respect it. In modern times, as we have seen, that right is co-extensive with sovereignty, but is now strictly defined by the UN Charter in Chapter 7. War is only permissible in self-defence or to support the self-defence of a country being attacked, which is what has sometimes occurred since 1945 and represents a legal support to collective security systems.[10] Otherwise, military action can only be taken by the Security Council 'to maintain or restore international peace and security' (Art. 51) with forces provided by the member states and with the help of UN Military Staff Committee – which is the provision never enacted in over 70 years because of the opposition or lack of interest of the great powers. Even the armed forces intervening in Korea 1950 and Kuwait 1990–1991 were just a coalition of national forces authorised to intervene by the Security Council.

Ius in bello (the laws of war) is now defined by the Geneva Conventions of 1949 as far as the distinction of combatants and non-combatants with all its corollaries is concerned, and by other conventions with regard to non-permissible weapons such as chemical and biological ones. This part of the just war doctrine has been more successful than *ius ad bellum* and was to an extent respected even in the battles of the Second World War in Africa and on the Western European front – except in partisan warfare. It was more successful, however, only in the wars between 'civilised' nations, while on the fringes of European civilisation, in the campaigns against native populations in the colonies or on the American frontier, the laws of war were disregarded on purpose.

Yet, war has, since the end of the Cold War, changed so deeply that in its new reality the just war norms sound surreal. The numerous wars or rather armed clashes around the world reflect a degree of cultural fragmentation that makes a shared, or at least convergent view, of situations and norms very difficult if not impossible to attain. Ethnic or religious hatred or nationalist revenge have taken the place of more usual motivations (territory, energy resources) and are hardly conducive to a rational conduct of war; they are rather fit to being poles of attraction for fanatics and bloodthirsty criminals, who would have otherwise spent their life on the margins of society and seek a meaning to their own life in hatred and destruction. As to the conduct of war, not only mass rape and forced marriage, but the enslavement of women and the spectacular execution of prisoners and civilians have become frequent practises, as well as, on the other hand, the indiscriminate use of artillery and aerial bombardment in densely populated areas.

In this situation it is senseless – except in the sense specified in Excursus 2 – to deprecate war altogether: as against Nazi Germany the war against Islamist fanaticism cannot but be fought and won, because beyond all geopolitical aspects it contains the core instance of 'civilisation against barbarianism'. It is by no means Christian vs. Islamic civilisation, as followers of the clash of civilisations doctrine, or the Islamists' 'cleansing' the Middle East of Christian populations would like to have it. In Christianity, fanaticism also existed, but retreated at the dawn of modernity and with the Enlightenment; Fascist and Nazi fanaticism was a secularised one.[11] To eradicate armed fundamentalism and to contain the unarmed one also means preserving the great Islamic culture of previous centuries from any involvement with this farcical degeneration. In wars of the third kind like this, the very nature of warfare makes it extremely difficult to apply the laws of war or *ius in bello*; which is not a good reason for ignoring them altogether.

Against this backdrop *peace* is the absence of war. Peace research, a school of thought initiated in the 1950–60s by the Norwegian sociologist Johan Galtung, characterises the absence of fighting as negative peace, whereas positive peace includes collaboration among nations as well as the struggle against structural violence, such as sexism and racism that generates open clashes. But in a philosophical perspective Hobbes's definition maintains the advantages of clarity and simplicity:

> so the nature of war consisteth not in actual fighting; but in the known disposition thereto, during all the time there is no assurance to the contrary. All other time is peace.[12]

In other words peace is regarded here as the absence of killing because this is an existential cleavage, as anybody who was alive in 1945 knows. Also, this cleavage speaks for itself, while the attributes of positive peace must remain controversial.

We encounter peace and pacifism on two levels: as a moment in politics that has to be actively pursued (political pacifism or peace-building politics) or as a meta-political goal that must at any time be unconditionally affirmed (absolute pacifism). A third, although unauthentic type exists, which makes instrumental, lop-sided use of radical, universalistic pacifism in order to give partisan support to one of the conflicting parties or to assail another, mostly the USA or NATO or the EU, or Western values when used against armed humanitarian intervention in defence of human rights (instrumentalist or pseudo-pacifism).[13]

On the first level we have seen peace or pacification and containment of flaring conflicts to be an intrinsic, if unplanned aim of international society or community; but what is meant here is *political pacifism* as a determined and proactive peace-building policy on the side of the actors that want to accelerate or stabilise situations of peace. This remains, however, a peace for the time being, with little guarantee of lasting or being transformed, as Kant wished, into perpetual peace. Is this perspective still open, given that two hundred years after Kant war continues to ravage the planet, even if not on the same scale as in the first half of the twentieth century – while the threat of nuclear war to destroy civilisation still exists? There is ground enough to be sceptic. More will be said about nuclear war as a lethal challenge to politics in Chapter 7, but we can note here that this kind of scepticism means neither that the efforts to strengthen international institutions working for pacification (institutional pacifism, a specification of political pacifism) nor that those aimed at neutralising the hubris of war such as cultural, ethnic, religious enmity (cultural pacifism) should be abandoned or downsized. The UNO remains in many regards an unkept promise, but without it the world would be much worse.

Still in the realm of peace-building politics or political pacifism one of its basic conditions is *multilateralism*, that is the (normative) recognition of the equal importance of the participants in international governance, including the principle that solutions are to be sought as far as possible through everybody's participation. This goes far beyond multipolarism (the analytical acknowledgement that world power is distributed among a number of key players) and is a rejection of unilateralism, in particular if ideologically laden like the neoconservative version that inspired the George W. Bush administration (2001–2009) on an American mission in allegedly spreading democracy. This blindness due to an excess in ideology led in 2003 to the most stupid war – much more stupid than the Vietnam war – ever waged by the USA in its history, with disastrous consequences for the whole of the Middle East and later Europe (terrorism and mass migration being among its long-term effects). Multilateralism is a logical premise for lasting collective security systems (they falter under unilateralist efforts of a member) as well as for federative processes at the regional/continental level, which bind the member states together in a degree of economic and political integration that is the best background condition for stable peace – but also for regaining the full-fledged sovereignty lost by the weakened individual nation states. The European Union is the unprecedented example of this *regionalism*, somehow a vindication, beyond democratic peace, of the second reform – federative relations among the states – Kant suggested as a step towards perpetual peace.

Another version of the federative principle, *cosmopolitanism*, takes it very radically and makes the case for the 'world republic' Kant praised as the worldwide realisation of the democratic or republican regime, though acknowledging at the same time its impossibility and resorting to a more realistic league of states. Cosmopolitanism is found in various shades, from a world state or world government or world parliament to less doctrinarian proposals aimed at building up levels of decision making more adequate to the increasingly global dimension of the issues. Scepticism about it has two reasons: even in the global era politics does not work the way that the expanded dimensions of the problems gives by its own force birth to a corresponding level of decision-making institutions. This will not happen before the previous institutions have proved their exhaustion in everybody's eyes, which is not yet the case (the Paris climate agreement of December 2015 has been reached through negotiations among states, modest that its policy effect may be). Besides, the intellectual and political forces have still to be identified that under the given historical circumstances may find enough determination and power to build a new edifice. In international politics the need to find consensus (and its premise, leadership) is no less important than domestically, but consensus can from time to time be found on very few relevant issues and after many failures, as the history of climate policy or the Millennium Development Goals (2000–2015) have shown – hardly establishing a binding world government for which no consensus is in sight. Where consensus is unattainable, cosmopolitan institutions could be only imposed by war, thus reaching the most counter-intentional effect of cosmopolitanism. Without keeping all of this in mind, designing blueprints for new institutions just out of concern for the world and good will must remain an idle exercise. Besides, cosmopolitans appear to underrate the danger Immanuel Kant already indicated as he spoke (in the second definitive article of *Perpetual Peace*) of the 'soulless despotism' of a universal monarchy: the homogeneity that world government would bring in its wake collides with the huge diversity of civilisations and traditions, which is a premise of conflict and ingovernability as well as freedom and creativity. More and better governance, which the globalised world certainly needs, does not necessarily mean more government; this can be counterproductive, not only unattainable – proven by the fact that not even a modest UN reform has been agreed upon after decade-long debates.

Let us now turn to the pacifism of the extra-political type or *absolute pacifism*. This posture is not ready to acknowledge politics as a sphere including force as an element that can be restrained but not excluded from it, and wants to reshape the world from a religious or philosophical perspective as found in Buddhism, St. Francis and the Mahatma Gandhi or several other creeds. Leaving Gandhi and his struggle for India's independence aside, this type of pacifism does not make political choices and participates in wars only to take care of the victims. It finds its place in religion or philosophy, as a testament to one's own rejection of any violence and any responsibility for a social order based on force. It accepts responsibility for not joining active or armed resistance to murderous regimes. It also values the purity of radical distance from violence over the efficacy of coordinated action aimed at spreading peaceful regulations and checking aggression and genocide – a task that only political peace-building, including the use of force to stop aggressors and torturers, can implement.[14] In 1932, still under the impression of the Great War's massacres, Sigmund Freud, on answering the question 'Why war' raised by Albert Einstein, recognised the superior value of building new ties of affection among humanity as a preventive medicine against war, but concluded that these methods 'conjure up an ugly picture of mills that grind so slowly that, before the flour is ready, people are dead of hunger.'

We add that it is not even safe to assume that those mills effectively grind a relevant amount of flour, because – to stick to a Freudian language – Eros (the force building ties of affection) and Thanatos (Greek for death; the force of destructiveness) are very much entangled with each other; though the idea that the aggressive component of human psychology must at all times lead to war is a piece of conventional wisdom lacking any scientific foundation.[15]

Absolute pacifism may not qualify as an effective force in order to bring about peace as a political outcome, but preserves its dignity as long as it sticks to its refusal of violence and war under whatever circumstances and from whatever actor they may come; as long as it observes a *super* (or rather *extra*) *partes* universalism. It loses its dignity as soon as it pretends to brandish the lofty reasons of universalism to condemn wars fought by just one party and forgets about the others. This kind of pseudo-universalistic pacifism is but one partisan position among others in the political game.

4. The pacification of Europe

A discussion of peace and war cannot ignore the European Union (EU), so far the only successful case of institutional pacifism applied among nation states in modern history. It has come into being by the word (intellectual debate, diplomatic talk, wording of the treaties), not the sword (Napoleon's artillery, or Hitler's *Panzerdivisionen*) – though this origin may be one reason for its weakness.

Now known as an economic giant with low political capacity, Europe was, on the contrary, born as a political project in the minds of its founding fathers: the French Jean Monnet and Maurice Schuman, who as Foreign Minister started the process with his declaration of 9 May 1950, the German Konrad Adenauer, the Italian Alcide De Gasperi and the Belgian Paul-Henri Spaak. The paramount goal of the project was to bring stable peace to Europe, shaken by two world wars started and fought on this continent, by bringing the countries closer together in a federative process. The strategy, however, did not start with political moves, whose acceptance was unlikely among recent enemies, but rather with economic integration, pooling basic resources (European Coal and Steel Community, Treaty of Paris 1951, later complemented by the European Atomic Energy Commission) and opening the way to a customs union (European Economic Community, EC, Treaty of Rome 1957), which generated a common, and later, in the 1980–1990s, a single market. The leading idea was that integrating the economy of the member states would have generated a prosperity that European peoples and governments would have found more attractive than enmity and war: it was somehow a resurrection of the belief heeded in the eighteenth and nineteenth century by thinkers of the Enlightenment and Manchesterian liberals in the *douce commerce*/sweet commerce as an evolutionary alternative to war. This time it worked because it was embedded in a political project.

The governance of this integrated, but not unified Europe was and is as complex as the architecture of the process itself. It is also little known, even to European citizens; it seems therefore advisable to start with some information. The European Union is a federative but not federal institution: there is no overwhelming central power, sovereignty is not transferred to Brussels, but is rather 'pooled and shared', and the EU is not, nor can it be expected to become the United States of Europe, even if this remains the dream of old-fashioned federalists. European nation states are still too important hubs of political will formation to be restricted into a classical federal frame. We should rather regard the EU as a post-national or post-modern version of the mixed government model well-known to the ancients, as we saw in Chapter 5, §3: it comprises

- an intergovernmental (European Council, made of the heads of state or executive, plus the area-specific Councils of ministers) and

- a supranational or 'communitarian' (EU newspeak) level, which is made of
  - the Commission (which can be likened to the executive, but has some more power than this)
  - the Parliament (which has more power than before the Lisbon Treaty of 2007, but not yet as much as a national parliament does)
- the European Court of Justice, whose jurisprudence in European legal matters supersedes that of the national courts and has constitutional rank (the ECJ has nothing to do with the European Court of Human Rights, which refers to the Council of Europe, an intergovernmental convention of 44 states, not linked to the EU)
- the European Court of Auditors
- only for the countries that have adopted the euro (€): the European Central Bank, at the time of writing the most powerful supranational instance in the EU.

This so-called *multilevel governance* includes the permanent interplay of twenty-eight (in 2016) national governments and parliaments and innumerable regional instances, represented in the Council of Regions. It is, in principle, necessary in order to regulate a single market, which requires a certain amount of uniform rules protecting everybody's legitimate interest, though the Eurobureaucracy in Brussels sometimes indulges in pathological over-regulation. On the other hand, it determines a very slow process of legislation and regulation, with too much veto power given to single actors, in particular national governments, in matters requiring unanimity and not legally entrusted to the EU by the Treaties such as foreign, defence, internal security and economic policy.[16] A shift from multilevel governance largely operated by diplomatic and bureaucratic actors to a more determinate political leadership is unlikely to be chosen by unanimous consent of the twenty-eight member states, and could be obtained only by a coalition of the willing (for example, the six original founders: Belgium, France, Germany, Italy, Luxembourg and the Netherlands), capable of enduring – even more after the English decided to walk out – an eventual paralysis or break-up of the Union.

Having given priority to the economy, the 'peace through prosperity' path chosen for the pacification of Europe has left as structural legacy the tension between the market regulating function of the EC/EU (privileged by countries such as the UK and Denmark) and its inevitable development towards a post-national polity, supported by Germany, Italy, the Iberian countries and only half-heartedly France.[17] This odd beast with two natures struggles to assume the full political actorness that the world, and in particular, neighbours would expect from an economic and cultural giant, often leaving a vacuum that is not favourable to keeping or restoring peace to the world. A peace-setting function was still exerted by the EU in the 1990s, as after the collapse of the Soviet Empire the former satellite countries were prevented from entering into nationalistic clashes by the will to enter the EU having satisfied the Copenhagen accession criteria of 1993. The accession of ten

Eastern countries in 2004, which on the one hand watered down the cohesion of the Union, was, on the other hand, a successful case of 'structural foreign policy', the instrument mainly used by the EU, which lacks autonomous military power, for conflict prevention through integration of neighbouring and economic incentives to developing countries.

As early as 1946, Winston Churchill encouraged European leaders to 're-create the European family in a regional structure called, it may be, the United States of Europe', however, not including the UK that had to remain the leader of the British Commonwealth.[18] This process has granted the continent seventy years of peace at the time of writing, with the appalling exception of the Yugoslav wars of 1992–1995, as the EC/EU and its member states – along with the UN – proved unable to stand firm against murderous warlords, and the attempted genocide of Bosnian Muslims was stopped only by the military initiative taken by US President Bill Clinton in August 1995.

The 'success story EU', which is undeniable, has blind spots and – what is more – its future remains unpredictable in the midst of the revival of nationalism and populism in several countries, first of all the now departing UK; this is aggravated by the lack of leadership and vision in Brussels as well as in the national capitals under post-recession problems, the pressure of mass migration from the failed or semi-failed states on the southern Mediterranean rim and Africa, lastly by the new role played by Russia and possibly the USA under the Trump presidency. Nonetheless, the European process remains to date the most advanced case of regionalism as continental pacification via economic and political integration, which makes it an unprecedented quasi-polity, far away from both world government and traditional local confederation. Even if the centre of world politics and economy has moved towards the east, the lot of the European Union in the coming years and decades, now endangered by a number of external and internal factors, will impact heavily – positively or negatively – on world peace and the shaping of political structures around the planet.

★ ★ ★

The European experiment is important also from a theoretical point of view. Along with other cases of institutionalised interstate cooperation, it disproves the neo-realist fixation on the nation state as the sole substantial actor of international politics, to which alone human groups in search of protection and interest representation can turn to; this actor, driven only by its momentary strategy of utility maximization and relying only on its own strength, makes anarchy the permanent axis of international relations. Others oppose that international anarchy is reduced, though not eliminated, by the frames of formal and informal cooperation rules (also called by some international regimes) on which states agree for the advantages deriving from it and to which they mostly stick to instead of constantly freeriding, because their expectations and action patterns are more and more shaped by those rules and institutions. This *neo-institutionalism* in international relations (some add 'liberal', to mark its difference from realist foreign policy as exemplified by Henry

Kissinger or, on a lower level, the neocons around George W. Bush) has been able to explain phenomena such as the European process or the spread of political and economic international institutions much better than classical realism or neo-realism did.[19] It is not a vindication of idealism, *scil.* of norm-driven behaviour for the sake of justice, in international politics, but it fosters understanding and stimulates the forces that may shape state behaviour along lines of peace and cooperation to everyone's advantage. While states are not on their way to becoming angels, they have made some progress in understanding that wars such as the Second World War, let alone nuclear war, are too costly, while regulated coexistence and cooperation bring more advantages than an unattainable military victory. Essential to this posture is the notion that world politics is not necessarily a zero-sum game, in which the gains of the winner are all made of the losses of the losers, because cooperative interaction can make all parties win something. States are not dropping *self-interest* as guidelines, they are reinterpreting it in a way adequate to the new circumstances of world politics, which will be further examined in the next chapter.

Notes

1 Plural of *polis*.
2 There is a nuance of complacency in the similar English saying 'all is fair in love and war'. The panhellenic Olympic games however took place in any case, interrupting the state of war.
3 Two later masterpieces of European literature contain vivid pictures of episodes from that Great War: Friedrich Schiller's (1759–1805) *Wallenstein* trilogy (the political, religious and personal intrigues behind the battles) and Alessandro Manzoni's (1785–1873) *I promessi sposi / The Betrothed* (the plague in Milan, brought by German mercenaries).
4 This notion emerged in the so-called English School of International Relations and spread around especially after the publication of Hedley Bull's *The Anarchical Society* in 1977.
5 In today's international relations lexicon NATO is more exactly dubbed a defence community.
6 *Behemoth*, written in 1668, is Hobbes's account of the English Civil War, covering the years from 1640–60.
7 Much on war, but not its definition is contained in the Chinese treatise *The Art of War*, written in the sixth century BCE and credited to an author called Sun Tzu or Sunzi; its first accurate English edition came out in 1910 (Sun Tzu 1910).
8 In Japan 1945 no nuclear war as a bilateral exchange was fought, and only in the mid 1950s did the two main nuclear powers attain massive retaliation and second strike capability.
9 This term, a container rather than a category, was introduced by the American political scientist Kalevi J. Holsti (1996).
10 More precisely, Art. 39, Chapter VII of the UN Charter regards 'the existence of any threat to the peace, breach of the peace, or act of aggression' as matter of concern for the Security Council, which may justify military action (Art. 41).
11 It is true that colonial genocides or massacres were perpetrated by Germany against the Herero and Namaqua in Namibia (then Südwest Deutschland, 1904–1907), the British Empire at Amritsar, India (1919) and Italy in Libya and Ethiopia in the 1930s; this happened however without much religious fanaticism in the background, but rather as an outcome of racist arrogance and contempt for the laws of war.
12 This famous quote is from Part I, Chapter XIII of *Leviathan* (Hobbes 1651).
13 'Humanitarian intervention' belongs to the same family of legal terms as 'responsibility to protect' and in French 'droit d'ingérence'.

14 A radical pacifist alternative, if this wording is adequate, was sketched in 1946 by Gandhi, who famously wrote: 'Hitler killed five million Jews. It is the greatest crime of our time. But the Jews should have offered themselves to the butcher's knife. They should have thrown themselves into the sea from cliffs. . . . It would have aroused the world and the people of Germany. . . . As it is they succumbed anyway in their millions.' (https://en.wikipedia.org/wiki/Mahatma_Gandhi)
15 This book is only concerned with war as a political phenomenon and must regrettably leave aside what ethology, psychoanalysis and cultural anthropology have contributed to its knowledge.
16 The Schengen countries have open borders, but no central intelligence authority; the Euroland countries have no common finance minister.
17 What consequences the withdrawal of the United Kingdom, which can in the process become less united, will have on the balance between the two natures of the EU is impossible to forecast.
18 This he said in a speech given at Zurich and available at http://www.churchill-society-london.org.uk/astonish.html.
19 The main representatives of neo-institutionalism are Stanley Hoffmann (1928–2015), Robert Keohane, Joseph Nye, John Ruggie. Classical realism in the twentieth century had Edward Carr (1892–1982), Hans Morgenthau and Reinhold Niebuhr (1892–1971) among its principal authors, mostly on reformist positions. Waltz's *Man, the State and War* quoted above still belongs to classical realism, while his later work *Theory of International Politics* (1979) inaugurates neo-realism, which includes its author's conservative stance. To remember is still the research attitude called constructivism (or reflectivism), which tends to dissolve the classical unit in IR, the state, into the processes leading to its build-up and actorness. Alexander Wendt is one of its relevant representatives.

References

Bull, Hedley (1977) *The Anarchical Society*, New York: Columbia University Press.
Clausewitz, Carl von (1832) *Vom Kriege/Of War*, e-book available at http://www.gutenberg.org/ebooks/1946
Freud, Sigmund (1932) *Why War? The Einstein-Freud Correspondence (1931–32)*, available at at www.fd.unl.pt/docentes_docs/ma/FPG_MA_27510.pdf
Hobbes, Thomas (1651) *Leviathan*, e-book available at www.gutenberg.org/ebooks/3207
Hobbes, Thomas (1668) *Behemoth*, New York: Burt Franklin, 1963.
Holsti, Kalevi J. (1996) *The State, War, and the State of War*, ebook available at http://ebooks.cambridge.org/ebook.jsf?bid=CBO9780511628306
Kant, Immanuel (1795) *Perpetual Peace*, ebook available at https://archive.org/details/perpetualpeacea00kantgoog
Rawls, John (1999) *The Law of Peoples*, Cambridge: Harvard University Press.
Tzu, Sun (1910) *The Art of War*, available at www.gutenberg.org/cache/epub/132/pg132-images.html
Waltz, Kenneth (1959) *Man, the State, and War*, New York: Columbia University Press.
Waltz, Kenneth (1979) *Theory of International Politics*, New York: McGraw-Hill.

Further readings

A pluralist variety of views on world politics:

Held, David (2010) *Cosmopolitanism*, Cambridge: Polity.
Kissinger, Henry (2014) *World Order*, New York: Penguin.
Lebow, Richard Ned (2010) *Why Nations Fight*, New York: Cambridge University Press.

Russett, Bruce (1993) *Grasping the Democratic Peace*, Princeton: Princeton University Press.
Schmitt, Carl (1951) *Der Nomos der Erde im Völkerrecht des Jus publicum Europaeum/ The Nomos of the Earth in the International Law of the Jus Publicum Europaeum*, New York: Telos, 2003.
Telò, Mario, ed. (2014) *European Union and New Regionalism: Competing Regionalism and Global Governance in a Post-Hegemonic Era*, Farnham, Surrey: Ashgate.

7

THE GLOBALISED WORLD

A challenge to politics

Though states play an important role in the field we are now entering, this cannot be adequately defined as resulting from their international relations. The dimension, the causation and the effects of what happens here supersede the agency of states. We speak therefore of global affairs, whose space is the globe, along with forces such as the warming of the atmosphere that ignore borders, rather than acting within the grid created by states interacting with each other.

It is not too early to see all of this as a shift in world history and to make our eyes wide open to the deep changes politics is undergoing and will have even more to manage in order to repair its already indented ability to govern human societies. A philosophical scepticism as to whether this ability will actually not only materialise, but do so in time, is more than appropriate.

The amount of novelty we are now watching and tentatively conceptualizing is boosted by the ambivalence of all discourse containing the notion of 'global'. By 'globalisation' we currently mean by default economic (and technological, social, cultural) globalisation. But this is only one facet of the truth, the part that will be discussed in Part 1 of this chapter. My point here is that the globalised world has a second component, which has little to do with economic globalisation and consists of man-made lethal threats to civilisation; it is up to politics to transform them from threats into challenges. Of these global and lethal challenges I shall examine, in Part 2, the political consequences of the only two which we have a sufficient scientific knowledge of: the nuclear weapon, whose globalising effect that started in 1945 pre-dates economic globalisation, and anthropogenic climate change.

Part I looks first at the essentials of economic globalisation in §1, then in §2 at its connection with politics, finally in §3 at global governance.

PART I

Globalisation and global governance

Globalisation is of interest to us in as much as it influences politics, not as an economic, social, cultural event; nonetheless it is useful to establish a couple of basic points that clarify what we are talking about.

1. What is globalisation?

The globe has become the easily accessible dimension of many economic activities thanks to technical and policy factors. The first include the invention and rapid spread of both IT (information technology) and containers and container ships, which have hugely increased the size of communication and trade among societies, enterprises and individuals; by the second, the policy factor, I mean the tearing-down of protectionist trade barriers and the opening of more and more free markets, not just for commodities and financial capital, but wage-labourers as well (the latter with limitations to migrations, and a low level of social protection for migrants). What defines globalisation is, however, not just the planetary dimension, but likewise the growing level of *interdependence* among its participants.

The main areas of globalisation are:

- the economy, as already seen; this area relies on highly innovative and easily available technology.
- culture, in the broad sense, with the creation of a 'global village' and the local integration and modification of cultural patterns coming from far away – the 'glocal'.
- the sphere of social and interpersonal relations, in which formal and informal transnational networks – from photography clubs to mafia-like associations – facilitate previously unthinkable exchanges.
- politics, to be examined in detail.

A comprehensive, well-documented and unbiased history of globalisation is still to be written. In the sense of the widening dimension of knowledge and exchange among humans, it has always existed, with leaps forward in the Mediterranean area in Roman times and in all of Europe and beyond at the time of early capitalism, as a world market was created.[1] But we are here only interested in its last chapter, which began in the 1970–80s and for the first time in history made the planetary dimension easily available to everybody every day (I can read every morning the newspapers published everywhere, buy stocks on any stock exchange on the planet in real time and fly anywhere, whenever I wish – granted I have enough money and own the appropriate passport). The specificity of the present globalisation wave is undeniable, whereas all insistence on globalisation being a constant in human history and therefore hardly a novelty is of little help – more interesting is the study of retreating or waning globalisation in periods such as the early Middle Ages.

On the one hand, the modern push to globalise was and is inscribed in the logic of capitalism since the creation of a world market, and now particularly in the presence of technological leaps forward and a favourable environment as it was created by the General Agreement on Trade and Tariffs (GATT 1947, which became in 1995 the World Trade Organization, WTO). In this sense, a new wave of globalisation at the conclusion of what the French call *Les Trente Glorieuses* (the thirty glorious years of reconstruction, growth, full employment and rising welfare between 1945–1975) was to be expected and inevitable. On the other hand, the new wave was also the result of policies devised by the Bretton Woods institutions, such as the World Bank and the International Monetary Fund, and entangled in cultural if not policy coordination with the US Department of the Treasury in the framework of the so-called *Washington consensus*.[2] This was a mix of common sense directives and neoliberal dogmas (trade liberalisation, privatisation of state properties, deregulation), whose massive and uncritical application in developing countries created much economic and social havoc and made globalisation the target of protest movements around the world; they were later reunited in the World Social Forum, originally held in Porto Alegre, Brazil, in 2001 as a counter-event to the mainstream World Economic Forum, organised every year in Davos/Switzerland. But even critics do not reject globalisation altogether and rather propose an 'alter-globalisation', which would change its rules and goals.

2. Globalisation and politics

Having sketched the essentials of globalisation, we shall now examine

a. the impact of globalisation on politics, and
b. what political globalisation may mean.

a. Globalisation's effects on politics are double-edged. On the positive side, it has substantially contributed to economic growth in developing countries, thus lifting hundreds of millions from *poverty* and *illiteracy*, as in India and China, and promoting the build-up of a middle class: all conditions that are favourable to political participation and democracy, where this exists and is not spoiled by populism. Another huge advantage of globalisation is that growing interdependence tends to foster peaceful relationships among states, as it replaces hegemony or imperial dominance. It is true that the degree of interdependence existing during the *belle époque* did not prevent the First World War from erupting, but this time interdependence seems to work hand-in-hand with the deterrence created not only by the nuclear balance of terror, but by the fear of highly destructive conventional warfare as well.

On the problematic side, we meet first the *losers* of globalisation: all those who have lost their jobs or seen their income dwindle as a side effect of it. Peasants from the traditional agriculture of poor countries or older skilled and unskilled workers from wealthy countries' factories that have been shut down because of the competition from energetically developing countries are only the best known representatives. For these losers, the trouble is the new political powerlessness of the nation state that would have previously addressed social crises by industrial protectionism or generous social policies; these are now ruled out either by the sharper international competition and/or regulations barring state intervention in the economic life. Besides, what used to be the first tool of redistribution inside a country, fiscal policy, is now severely limited by the free transborder flow of capital, which is pumped out of countries as soon as they try to fund social policies compensating globalisation by imposing more taxes on businesses and the wealthy. Keynesian deficit spending for social purposes is made difficult if not impossible; the attitude towards budget deficit and public debt depends in part on the economic doctrine or ideology followed by the nation's government. Lastly, inside countries' income inequality as measured by the Gini coefficient, in other words the gap between the very rich and the very poor, has gone up with globalisation, which has in the core capitalist countries unleashed protest movements eager to delegitimise a social and political system privileging – as they say – the uppermost 1% against the 99% of the people. While social conflicts are healthy for democracy, the feeling – particularly in the youth – of being marginalised and politically powerless against the dragons of globalised financial games is not.

Not to forget are the future, indeed imminent effects of the globalisation of health care, due to both the penetration of pharmaceutical corporations into developing countries and the work of international institutions such as the World Health Organization. This has hugely and rapidly extended life expectancy almost everywhere, which along with other factors will further expand world population, thus creating possible food and water shortages and increasing global warming: one more global problem that politics-as-usual is poorly equipped to address.

In terms of the human condition, the balance is, on the whole, likely to tip in favour of globalisation because of the enormous and swift job it did in lifting hundreds of millions out of poverty, something that could have not been otherwise achieved. The price paid by the losers we have mentioned was high and could have been softened if less ideological radicalism had been deployed by the neoliberal supporters of globalisation and the governments had put in place timely compensatory policies such as retraining measures for the workforce. But these considerations or speculations do not address the true problem: can globalisation be politically governed?

b. *Political globalisation* means two different things: which political structures have been globalised, and if and how the globalised world can be politically governed.

Globalisation has so far regarded democracy, human rights and terrorism. After the fall of the Soviet regime and the dismemberment of the Communist empire, *liberal democracy* has remained the only model of polity with universal appeal around the world. Alternative claims are raised, as in China, but – as we have seen in Chapter 5 – none with the same degree of acceptance and legitimacy as the democracy of Western origin. It is true that this circumstance says nothing on the real democratic quality of the present regimes that label themselves democratic, nor on democracy's ability to govern the globalised world. What is stunning, is that after the demise of the European regimes that in the Middle Ages all claimed to be Christian, neither Europe nor the world had ever known such a degree of alleged homogeneity. The consequences of this circumstance on political allegiance and participation are still to be seen.

Human rights, or rather the debates and the struggles aimed at codifying them and making them respected all over the planet, have also been boosted by globalisation, which has brought labourers and union activists in the developing countries closer together with the liberal public opinion of Western consumers. In the remaining Communist regimes (China, Vietnam, North Korea, Cuba) and in some African dictatorships or plebiscitary democracies, little has changed, but there is no longer an alternative empire, like the former Soviet Union, to deny the primacy of liberal democracy in the name of 'substantial democracy'. The right of women to not be marginalised or kept as men's servants, to not be sold as child brides, to not be excluded from education and deprived of bodily integrity by genital mutilation is more widely and loudly asserted, though not much seems to have changed in traditional societies. In a backlash against cultural modernity, Islamist fanaticism has even revived the enslavement of women – questionable or outright faked that their attempted resort to Islamic religion may be. In light of these events, a differentiated analysis of the relationship of human rights with the various religions and cultures on earth appears to be more fruitful than philosophical speculations; while the question of their universality or relativity will be discussed in Chapter 8.

With the unrelenting change it has promoted in all societies and its modernist, rationalistic culture, globalisation has created an environment opposite to the religious fundamentalism that since the beginning of the new century has become the main inspiration of international *terrorism* as a global phenomenon.[3] Where does then their connection lie? It is, on the one hand, characterised by international terrorism being, to an extent, a reaction to devastating (for traditional cultures) advances of globalisation. On the other hand, globalisation of trade and communication has greatly facilitated the spreading of terrorism, having created an open, complex and fragile world society, which is easy to attack or even to paralyse by applying the asymmetric warfare of suicide bombers, with its de-globalising effects (on air traffic and tourism, for example). It is not even safe to assume that another piece of asymmetric warfare, a possible nuclear device built by terrorists maybe in the form of a 'dirty bomb', can be prevented from ever being created. In general, militarization and war are verifiably anti-globalisation forces (cf. Acemoglu-Yared 2010).

3. Global governance?

Can globalisation be governed?

We now begin discussing this question, but will be able to complete the discussion only after considering global/lethal challenges in Part 2 of the chapter.

Globalisation means a *cleavage in politics*, in as much as the problems it raises belong to a dimension for which no government exists. This gap between the size of the issues and the size of the existing governing activity occurs for the first time in history, and makes any political theory obsolete that does not rethink politics and government taking the new conditions into account. On the other hand, the gap also leads many to the illusion that, given the size of the issues to address, a corresponding new size of government and authority will also soon materialise in the shape of world government or global governance. This is the residual outcome of a comfortable, but shortsighted philosophy of history that states that humanity only sets itself tasks it can also manage. Peoples and politicians are reluctant to change their habits and systems of government as long as they still see enough advantages in sticking to the old, and are not driven by compelling forces to change their routes. Are the global challenges of Part 2 compelling enough?

This remains to be seen, while on world government we have said what is necessary in the previous chapter. It is now time to discuss in detail the notion of *global governance*, which has already popped up somewhere in this book. At first glance, governance looks like a stopgap notion where no government is possible; but it is indeed more than this. Globalisation makes us ask if government as a formal institution is possible and desirable under all circumstances, and think that in the global dimension the absence of government may not necessarily be a deficit. In essence, what we need is that the globalised world is somehow governed rather than having this done by a government – in the sense of a national government writ large.

Now, to make sense of the notion of global governance, it is wise to keep its two prevailing meanings from each other. In the first *analytical meaning* it is understood as a performance of the international system, provided by the accidental combination of various forces and actions in an impersonal and, as it were, actor-less way; this combination of myriads of actions driven by the most different motives and goals brings about a degree of governance that takes place behind the actors' back.[4] Not unlike what goes on in the concept of anarchical society, it is 'as if' actors had agreed to work for certain shared goals (in this case the governing of global processes), whereas we know that they certainly did not. On this count, global governance is a problem that finds unstable and varying solutions in a world in which the space for goal-oriented political management of affairs has become minimal.

Who is unsatisfied with global governance as extra-political performance of the social system handles it as a *normative project* that has chances to change things and needs to be defined. Here, governance results from the planned actions of the actors; the open question is how the best (best under a general principle such as justice or efficiency) global governance can be brought about. In some versions, global governance is more explicitly presented as an anti-neoliberal project, as it means providing governance for the otherwise anarchical and therefore unjust globalised world, instead of relying on what worldwide market forces and national governments driven by the idea of national interest may bring about; it means to organise solutions for what would otherwise remain an anarchical reality, much to the disadvantage of the weakest. In this direction one – not necessarily the most productive – development is found in the literature related to the topic of global justice, which will be dealt with in Chapter 9.

Global governance, however, is not limited to the two theoretical views we illustrated, but was and remains also a fledgling activity of international, mostly inter-governmental institutions such as the Commission on Global Governance, which worked between 1992 and 1995, and the UN Global Compact Governance Board/Office; not to speak of the bodies that, though not working under that headline, provide some amount of global governance such as G7/8, G20, the Financial Stability Board, as well as two UN-based projects: the Millennium Development Goals (2000–2015) and the Sustainable Development Goals (2016–2030). It is not our task to find out which conception of global governance these bodies heed. Needless to say that, through all of this, it is obvious that no form of global governance of political affairs is on its way to becoming world government, but rather a piecemeal attempt at providing governance of some essential single issue such as health or web addresses or missile technology.[5] Instances of global governance are neither universal (not all of the countries participate) nor compelling nor always felt as legitimate.

★ ★ ★

At midway through our review of global affairs we stop for a while and draw some provisional conclusions regarding capitalism, the state and democracy.

Capitalism has once again proven its vitality by globalising itself and changing the framework conditions of the economy and politics in the many ways we have tried to sketch. But it has failed to rethink its own governance rules under the new circumstances, in particular after the Great Recession, started in 2008 in America and Europe. This event has disproven the myth of the self-regeneration of the market as far as it was left free to follow its logic of profit disjointed from production and consumption of real goods. Financial capitalism, the motor that cracked in 2008, has been largely successful afterwards in impeding a re-regulation capable of preventing a rerun of the crisis. The capitalism of the twenty-first century has not been so far up to its own Schumpeterian definition as 'creative destruction'.

The *nation state* has, on the one hand, acquired unprecedented tools of control on the life of society, for example in fiscal, health and security issues; government techniques, or what Foucauldians would call governamentality, have become more refined due to both technological and organisational advances. On the other hand, the weakening and perforation of borders, in a physical (migrants) and what is more in a virtual (financial transactions) sense, have deprived states of control mechanisms that were an important instance of sovereignty. As we have just seen in the case of financial capital, mechanisms nearly as robust as those once put in place by national governments have not been established at an interstate level. The only still effective national actors in financial and economic policy are the central banks via monetary policy, but only in an indirect and limited measure. In a global perspective, the erosion and partial impotence of sovereign statehood has created a void that is not being refilled by global institutions, but rather left to extra-political forces such as financial markets or multinational corporations. This *retreat of politics*, which resonates with the 'retreat of the state' analysed by Susan Strange (1996), is one of the most significant side effects of globalisation.

Democracy's fate in globalisation is highly ambivalent: on the one hand, the prevailing state of affairs seems to be democracy's victory parade across most of the planet, though the non-availability of alternative models does not guarantee the quality of democratisation.[6] On the other hand, *democracy* has been losing effectivity and credibility, in the first case because not only of the dimensional gap between national democracy and issues requiring global governance, but also of the mentioned retreat of politics as human agency in shaping communal life. These factual changes have percolated into the voters' minds, particularly among the youth in developed countries, and generated waves of disaffection from democratic procedures and proneness to populism or extremism. For situations in which the democratic institutional framework remains in place, yet the citizens no longer feel they can determine the course of public affairs, the keyword 'post-democracy' is being put into circulation (cf. Crouch 2004).

What democracy can take advantage of is, however, not any effort of an impossible return to its social-democratic or liberal stage in the nation state, but rather the invention of a new architecture, both domestic and federative, that fits the complex globalised world. This will yet not happen if politics, and democratic politics in particular, does not stand up to the lethal threats that undermine them even more than economic globalisation. Rather than complaints over 'de-democratisation', a profound and innovative shift in the theory and culture of democracy is required.

PART II
Global/lethal challenges: politics after modernity

New realities require new concepts, while these are supposed to generate clarity in our otherwise confused look into the new realities confronting us. This is why I have introduced (Cerutti 2007) the concept of global challenge, a philosophical concept that intends to break with the common parlance use of these words. I have seen later that the adjective was not telling enough to define the concept, and have modified the language highlighting the severity of the challenges, which are global and lethal at the same time. Global challenges are therefore not an array of things, but only those that meet the following conceptual standards: *lethal, physical, and man-made threats that can hit everybody on earth and can be addressed with some chance of success only by the joint effort of all peoples or countries.*

Lethal for whom? They endanger the survival of civilisation rather than the biological existence of the human race, although this danger cannot be excluded in the case of a large nuclear war followed from a worldwide nuclear winter. *Civilisation* in what sense? Not as a lofty treasure of values and ideals, but as the set of social and technical institutions (agriculture, trade, communication, plus the legal and political conditions that uphold their regulation and protection) that enable the human race, which lack any specialised organ, to survive on the planet.

But why the stress on 'physical' and 'man-made' or anthropogenic? Because the physical nature of the threats makes them not dependent on any questionable theory of society, obligation, salvation or justice, and subject only to state-of-the-art methods of scientific discovery and verification. Why this may become important will emerge later. Also, the anthropogenic nature of global challenges is fundamental because it does not only open the chance (nothing more than a chance) of working on them, but also underlines how relevant they are for reinterpreting, now on a global scale – humankind's contribution to good and evil, in other words for reassessing the relationship of politics and morality. As noted above on more than one occasion, what worldview we have in mind is far from indifferent to the way we act politically.

Global challenges seem to contain a compelling push toward solidarity and cooperation in the global dimension, this being the main reason why defining and highlighting them has become relevant to politics and political philosophy – though political philosophers have hardly taken note of them as philosophical issues. Examining that reason, we will also get out of any ambivalent interchangeability between threat and challenge and speak more exactly of challenges only as far as a scientifically verified threat is taken into consideration by politics and treated as a challenge politics has to stand up to. How large the range of that push may become cannot be discussed before we have applied our definitions to the items that seem to fall under them.

After analysing in §4 the characteristics of global and lethal challenges, we shall address their impact on future generations (§5), politics (§6) and democracy (§7).

4. The two present challenges

Which threats qualify as potential global challenges is an empirical, not a philosophical question; the answer is therefore subject to the changing scientific evidence. Human biotechnology or nanotechnology or artificial intelligence or other items may have chances to become global challenges; but not even a thin body of evidence that one or more of these developments are on their way to becoming so is available at the time of writing, and I may surmise that this is going to remain so for some further years. With other items that are often presented by the media with the label of global challenge, such as AIDS, an unstable worldwide financial system, cyber terrorism, water scarcity and the like, at a closer view they are neither global (a part of humanity can shield itself) nor lethal for civilisation; or actors are not in sight that are likely to become able and want to make a catastrophic usage of that possibility in order to establish their worldwide domination. It is true that advances made by science and technology in the last decades offer – well beyond nuclear physics – various chances for humans to modify or subvert the structures of matter, life and the mind; but political philosophy does not speculate like futurology or literary musing on the future and sticks to what normal science offers as evidence at the time of writing.

Mention must be made of non-anthropogenic lethal and global threats such as the collision with a large asteroid or comet or a volcano explosion of a size never seen, the latter with consequences similar to a nuclear winter. Not being manmade, they are politically not relevant, but they become so as soon as a technical chance is identified to prevent or minimise them, as is the case with attempts at deflecting the asteroid's trajectory. To put it on the agenda and mobilise the global governance resources necessary to take action would truly be an ultimate challenge.

A last remark before we address the only existing man-made lethal challenges. As the reader may have noted, I do not use the notion of risk with respect to them, as otherwise typical, and also advise against using it. To fully explain why would require too long an epistemological discussion.[7] Instead, let us plunge into the specifics of α. nuclear weapons and β. climate change. They are not examples of a wide array of global challenges, but the only two cases that are presently recognisable as such.

α. Hardly any reasonable person would doubt that the presence of *nuclear weapons* on the planet (perhaps even on satellites) satisfies the criteria for being regarded as a global threat. It is not only the immediate effect of a nuclear exchange, but even more the ensuing nuclear winter that would let civilisation unravel, primarily by destroying agriculture and food trade, not to speak of the long-range radiative side effects on all living beings. The few safe havens for wealthy people and dignitaries would either not hold or later be submerged by masses of desperate survivors. But, as more optimistic observers believe, this would never happen, because nuclear weapons (or nukes, as they were flippantly called in the 1950s) are there not to fight a war, which everybody concurs should never be fought and could never be won, but on the contrary to make war impossible, because everybody knows that a nuclear war would be lethal for both sides. Those weapons' existence in the hands of rational state actors is thus seen as a guarantee for peace.

This is the theory of *nuclear deterrence*, which by some theorists of extreme realist orientation[8] has been further developed up to the proposal of putting all relevant states, such as Germany and Iran, in the possession of nuclear weapons ('More may be better', was Waltz's motto in Sagan and Waltz [2003, 45]) in order to let all participate in the nuclear balance and responsibility. This theory claims to find confirmation in the sixty or so years in which the balance of terror, which dates from the mid 1950s, has had the appearance to work.

Sixty years is however too short a time for testing the robustness of nuclear deterrence, which is supposed to work for centuries. As a variation on one joking analogy by Thomas Schelling, the most astute nuclear theorist since 1945,[9] to feel perfectly safe after the Cold War and episodes such as the Cuban missile crisis of 1962 is to think like the guy who, after just one round of Russian roulette, tells his friends 'It's not that dangerous after all!' It is rather true that the longer nukes are around, the higher the chance of a war by misperception or technical failure may become. More importantly, nuclear deterrence still entails nuclear war as the answer to its own failure; the alternative, that is doing nothing if attacked, would mean that deterrence is bluff, in which case deterrence would be definitively toothless. Also, deterrence may work between rational actors like states and empires, as it did during the Cold War despite the sharp ideological war that divided West and East; but is less credited to do so if the number of nuclear armed actors (not just states, but also less accountable groups) grows, which will probably happen despite all attempts to stop proliferation. In this regard, we must remember that the problem for humanity is not *nuclear proliferation*, which is a side-phenomenon, but the sheer existence of nuclear weapons. Checking nuclear proliferation and the chances of nuclear terrorism eliminates a minus to nuclear deterrence, *pace* Waltz, but entails no plus to the solution of the problem of nuclear weapons. This problem, while less sharp for the contemporaries of this book, written in a relatively stable nuclear situation, is likely to become more worrying as time goes by, and to represent the most poisoned legacy the twentieth century has left to future generations.

What would the solution be like? The elimination of nuclear weapons altogether seems to be the optimum solution, but still has dangers: first comes the cheating by one or more states, which would then become the Masters of the world, and could be contained only by the strictest monitoring and control regime, regardless of the complaints of the states, which would see the rest of their sovereignty vanish. Then comes the non-eliminable nature of technical knowledge, which could be re-used in later times by pact-breakers – though the journey from a re-activated know-how to the effective production of weapons is verifiably long and tortuous and could be interrupted by a determined control authority. We can say that the solution has technical aspects, but is primarily – how could it be otherwise? – a political and institutional problem: how to establish a *supranational authority* capable of keeping existing weapons, technological knowledge, would be-cheaters under control? It needs to be supranational, because an intergovernmental body, which can act only on unanimity, would be too weak and disruptive as to assert itself in such a deadly and supreme matter. Even if supranational (with qualified majority and weighted vote), the authority would still fall short of a world state, which nobody would accept, and would refrain from invading any other field than nuclear security. This is, on the other hand, the supreme dimension of power and order, and its actions would, by default, spin off to all issues of world politics. On the whole, it is a puzzling job of designing a new worldwide authority (the UN throughout their history does not qualify as a supranational institution), while making it acceptable to all major players, keeping possible not-yet-nuclear free riders at bay and containing its tendency to expand its power beyond the nuclear issue and into an unauthorised world government. Unlike cosmopolitanist thinkers, I am not going to outline a blueprint of such an institution; I only want to underline that, unlike climate change, it is the very nature of the nuclear weapons issue that makes a mere convergence of national (disarmament) policies coordinated in an international treaty insufficient and requires a central authority capable to act swiftly on its own and without much bargaining with the states, for example in point sanctions to freeriders.

The record of both politics and philosophy in front of nuclear weapons and war is disappointing, not to say appalling. The endeavour to put nuclear arms under binding international control flared up briefly between 1945–1946 and soon collapsed in the environment of the dawning Cold War; it was never seriously resurrected, and even the intention to do so expressed by Barack Obama in his speech at Prague in May 2009 could not be implemented. World leaders have long since adapted to deterrence as the best available regime in which to frame nuclear weapons, whose 'overkill' capacity has been reduced while they remain numerous enough to ignite a planetary catastrophe. Nuclear arms come on the agenda of international politics only in the shape of initiatives against cases of proliferation, but the existing nuclear powers have never moved towards that 'treaty on general and complete disarmament' they pledged to work for in Art. VI of the Non-Proliferation Treaty of 1968 – thus making the Treaty less palatable for nuclear have-nots.

Only in the first two decades of the nuclear era have a few philosophers (Günther Anders, Norberto Bobbio, Karl Jaspers, Bertrand Russell and later the British historian Edward P. Thompson musing on 'exterminism, the last stage of civilisation') made the possible suicide of humankind in a nuclear war a crucial theme of their reflections. In later years, all possible novelties and evils (alienation, commodification, gender oppression, intolerance, imperialism of the social system, distributive injustice, pervasiveness of bio-power and others) were made the matter of philosophical consideration and complaint, while a veil of ignorance or denial came to cover the existential questions: how could humankind bring about its possible self-destruction? What does it reveal about the human being and its civilisation? Is a change of course still possible? What are the cultural, motivational and political forces – if any – to count upon for a change?

β. Anthropogenic climate change due to global warming, discovered in the mid 1970s, became a political issue shortly thereafter: in 1992 the first summit of the United Nations Framework Convention on Climate Change was held in Rio de Janeiro, in 1997 the first agreement aiming to reduce greenhouse gases (GHG) emissions in developed countries was signed in Kyoto. Yet it took eighteen more years for a follow-up agreement including nearly all of the countries on Earth to come to fruition (Paris Agreement, December 2015). In the time between 1992 and 2015, worldwide emissions have only gone up and the side effects of climate change (mass migration, climate wars, desertification, drought, spreading of diseases) have worsened; the Kyoto Protocol was politically a step forward, signalling the possibility of international climate cooperation, but was physically not particularly relevant. The 2015 Paris Agreement – of modest relevance because based on voluntary pledges to bring down emissions by single countries and lacking robust mechanisms of monitoring and compliance – is again a political step forward, all countries having recognised the necessity to act in concert, while its physical effects are expected to fall widely short of the announced goal of keeping the increase of Earth atmosphere temperature in 2100 by 2°C. Hence, more, further reaching and more binding agreements will have to be negotiated and implemented in order to slow down global warming. If this does not happen by the deadlines set by climatology, that is by nature, the already serious consequences of the warming threaten to go beyond certain thresholds and generate in the next century catastrophic effects that would bring down food production worldwide, drive hundreds of millions out of their regions and continents, worsen global health and generate wars around resources, borders and welfare levels.

Unlike nuclear war, which can happen or fail to happen and unleash a global catastrophe if it happens, global warming already happens – as a wealth of scientific evidence regarding, among other things, greenhouse gases proves – and will continue at least for a long time as it still grows incrementally, thus making the prediction of its effects on humans and nature more and more reliable, the more climate models are refined. Please see Figure 7.1.

More explicitly than the nuclear threat, climate change affects our responsible or irresponsible attitude towards *future generations*. The threat of nuclear war and the threat of major climate-related catastrophes, though different in many regards, can be subject to joint consideration because of their global dimension and their involvement of the generations of the far future.

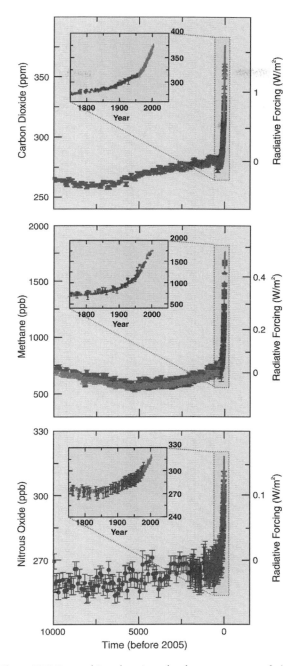

FIGURE 7.1 These IPCC graphics showing the huge upsurge of three greenhouse gases in the atmosphere in the last century in comparison to the preceding 10,000 years are a vivid picture of one of the global and lethal challenges politics is recently confronted with.

5. What to do with future generations?

The novelties in world politics we are analysing raise problems modern politics was and is not equipped to address, while we are reminded of the changing civilisational roots of politics. Do we have reasons to speak of post-modern politics?

By *modern politics* let us understand politics as it has been managed for the past five centuries by territorial states (later nation states) on an increasingly representative and democratic basis and having the wellbeing of their peoples as separate entities as official and legitimate purpose. The totalitarian monsters of the twentieth century were the distillate of the failures of this process and hopefully the last devastating reaction to it.

Other features of modern politics are:

- politics had to come to terms with moderate challenges, which endangered nothing more than the individual life or freedom, though in the colonies entire populations were exterminated.
- technology was a morally neutral tool or regarded as an instrument of progress.
- politics (remember its definition in Chapter 1) was the activity settling distribution conflicts around divisible goods, which it allocated authoritatively.
- distribution or identity conflicts unfolded in a narrow timeframe and a relatively stable civilisational environment; even after the ruinous Second World War it was possible in fifteen-twenty years to rebuild Berlin, Dresden, Warsaw, Stalingrad and Hiroshima.
- the external security of the states was entirely entrusted to the sovereign state and was by nature disjunctive (my security weakens whenever you feel fully secure and vice versa) until the rise of common security, which is however still a fragile and infrequent component of international politics.
- the Roman principle *salus reipublicae suprema lex esto* (the safety of the commonwealth has to be the supreme law) presides over all domestic and foreign policy.

What is different in post-modern politics? Please remember that my hyphenated wording signals that my use of this expression differs almost completely from the (mainly French) postmodernism of the 1980–1990s, which was, in my view, a reproduction of modernity with a negative mark rather than an effort to radically rethink the human condition after modernity.

We are in a transitional time, in which features of modernity coexist but also collide with new elements, among which we note the following:

- global and lethal challenges, at least the two we are examining.
- technology – not just nuclear, but, say, reproductive technology – becomes morally significant.
- we have some solid knowledge about the future of our actions and omissions, not in the sense of the all-inclusive scenarios designed by futurology, but with

regard to well-defined physical processes and their immediate social consequences (for example desertification→mass migration).
- in particular we know that we are putting global commons in danger, which are to be saved or lost as a whole, that is not subject to adversarial distribution.
- the *salus reipublicae* (safety of the commonwealth) is now possible only within the *salus humani generis* (safety of humankind), which to be preserved requires everybody's participation.
- the modern state has turned out to be an insufficient provider of security and has rather created supreme insecurity by disproportionately widening the destructiveness of its weapons, and failing to keep the perverse effects (global warming) of 'progress' under control. The first of these shifts can be regarded as the nuclear culmination of the 'security dilemma' that has always accompanied international politics: to enhance its own security state A has grown so powerful that its adversaries B, C, and D see A as a potential aggressor and enter an arms race with it or wage war in order to undercut its might before this has overgrown theirs.[10]

It is sufficiently clear that the tools of modern politics cannot match the severity and novelty of the new threats; we have displayed above the theoretical reasons and the empirical evidence for that. Politics-as-usual does not even seem capable to come to terms with the problems created by economic globalisation. But it is not enough to proclaim the necessity and rightness of a turn to a new understanding of politics: the political philosopher as I conceive of this figure is neither a preacher nor a persuasive politician seeking consensus, though both these professions are respectable and useful. It is the philosopher's task to investigate the *motivations for a change* and the counterforces and counterarguments that may oppose it. Every change, even the exit from a no-longer manageable situation, entails material costs and mental efforts that not everybody is ready to pay, in particular not the social groups entrenched in the pre-existing power structure. There must be good arguments for convincing the people affected by change to accept and proactively pursue and govern it. One could otherwise determine what would be just or ethical to do with regards to certain values and relying on a view of human beings as subject to Reason, call it 'ideal theory', while leaving to practitioners ('non-ideal theory') to come to terms with non-compliance. This is not the method followed in this book, as Chapter 10 will make more clear.

★ ★ ★

The usual motivation for political action is the self-interest of a nation, a social class, a generation; in the best case the self-interest is 'enlightened', detached from the immediate preferences of the living generation and taking into account its future and the future of its children and its children's children. Both shortsighted and enlightened self-interests are indeed among the main motivators of political behaviour, either in opposition or in a mix. But not even the most enlightened self-interest would suffice to drive today's decision-makers to give up the present arrangements with global threats (the nuclear deterrence regime, the regime of voluntary emissions cuts) for a truly new governance of those threats. Cost-benefit analysis is, for many reasons, a poor oversimplification of these complex existential questions, but is still prevailing in the mentality of politicians: applied by people led by (enlightened) self-interest it would never lead – and it has in fact not led – to costly decisions in favour of a different nuclear and climate governance. Let us see why.

Change is costly in more than one regard. Leaving the deterrence regime to an authority capable to oversee disarmament and to keep residual nukes locked up may be regarded as a sacrifice of one's own security for an uncertain new regime. Agreeing on mandatory and enforced emissions reduction, as it may become necessary in the likely case that voluntary reductions fail to slow down the warming of the atmosphere, means not only losing one point of GDP per year, but restructuring technology and economy in a low-carbon key. Taking upon ourselves these and other costs is justifiable not out of any version of self-interest, but only if we put the interest of the *generations of the far future* in the lead, since they would be severely or tragically damaged if we do not perform a radical change. But why should we do so? Not out of supererogatory generosity extended to dwellers of future centuries, but because we the contemporaries (as well as our forefathers since 1850 in the case of global warming) have, by our very own actions and omissions, prejudiced the life conditions of those generations in a measure we would by no means accept for us or our grandchildren, and because we are informed about this causal link. Between us (or any generation behaving like ours has done so far) and posterity a relationship like that between plaintiff and defendant in tort law can be assumed to exist, with the obvious difference that the plaintiff does not yet exist and his or her interest has to be protected by ourselves as stewards of global commons. Whether or not we are going to take the step from business-as-usual to the representation of future generations damaged by our behaviour is a moral and philosophical question we have to decide ourselves; there is no superior judge sentencing us to bear responsibility for the damages we have possibly inflicted upon the global commons that will be inhabited by future generations.

Leaving all similarity with legal procedures aside, the reasons for taking that step require reconnecting politics (an eventual new course addressing global challenges) with philosophy and morality (which motivations for including future generations among those whose interests politics is bound to protect?). Politics has, at its best, come to regard the interests and rights of all present dwellers of the planet as worth being protected (*space universalism*). The step to be taken would recognise the equal dignity of future dwellers: *time universalism*. To do so, two difficulties are to be hurdled: on the *cognitive* level, it is difficult to consider persons of the future as similar and close to us, therefore as possible addressees of either our obligation or empathy. This is a cultural and psychological question that no persuasion strategy can target; only good novels such as Cormac McCarthy's *The Road* (2006) and good movies such as Stanley Kramer's *On the Beach* (1959) can stimulate our moral imagination in that direction.

On the *normative* level we can choose among various options, which lamentably I cannot discuss here to a full extent because they involve a complex reasoning in moral philosophy. Given that the motivation for taking action should be accessible to informed citizens all around the globe, a first requirement is to avoid 'thick' theories that involve notions and mental procedures open only to professional elites within a single cultural realm. A second requirement favours options as transcultural as possible. This makes philosophical heavyweights from the West, such as the theory of justice, hardly eligible, even regardless of this theory's own difficulties with the problem of future generations.[11] In the choosing of a foundation of our care for future generations, the options must remain open according to one's own cultural and philosophical orientation, and all claims to possess a trump card in this competition are not productive. It is in this spirit that I am now giving a brief account of my own choice, which moves from the fact of the transgenerational chain of parents who at every turn of the age have generated and raised children, always trying to protect and improve the conditions for their children to grow up in. Except in cases of genocide and enslavement, each generation has acknowledged to the following ones the right to protect and improve those conditions, while the assumption that the chain can be continued over time is a hidden presupposition of all cultures – a very few nihilistic thinkers excluded. Now, doing nothing in order to prevent global commons from being spoiled either by nuclear explosions or catastrophic climate change means accepting that the chain can be broken up and future generations left on their own in a life-unfriendly environment causally dependent on our acts and omissions. But why should we not accept this outcome? For two reasons.

If we accept it, we would infringe the most elementary and universal obligation: 'what you hate, do not do to anyone' (Tobit 4:15). I have quoted this formulation of the Golden Rule from the Old Testament, but it can be found also in the Gospels as well as in Confucianism and in ancient India; apart from religions, Kant's categorical imperative can in rough terms be seen as a secularised reformulation of it. Further elaborations on the reasons for preserving the transgenerational chain, which cannot be unfolded here, would include the notions of responsibility, vulnerability, trust.

The second reason is that not standing up to our responsibility to the generations of the (far) future risks making our own life poor of meaning, which is an impalpable but essential resource, since if men, women and civilisations were not able to give their life a meaning, this would much more frequently end up in self-destruction or aggressiveness and despair. Now, not only raising children, but counting on the continuation of human reproduction as cultural, not merely biological perspective is a condition that helps most persons make sense of their lives.

6. Politics after modernity: another definition

All things considered, politics as defined in Chapter 1 – the allocation of shares of divisible goods among conflicting parties, performed by a legitimate power or authority – reveals itself as inadequate to a situation in which the resources in critical condition are not divisible and physically unfit to be allocated in an adversarial way – you cannot divide the atmosphere and give more to one than to another. On a second track, the classical definition was unaware of the responsibility we are now asked to face towards future generations since we are endangering their life conditions.

All this seems to require a second definition of politics or Democracy Two, as *the activity aimed at saving and managing our global commons also on behalf of future generations*.

Let us recapitulate and explain. Under the heading 'global and lethal challenges' we analysed two actual threats (others may come) to the survival of humankind as a species in need of civilisation in order to survive. At first glance, one could dub them Hobbesian in the sense that they endanger the life and limbs of human beings and drive them to seek an exit from this situation and to establish a superior protective power like Hobbes's Leviathan – in this case a worldwide Super-Leviathan. Global challenges in a word may seem to provide a *compelling motivation* to make room for Democracy Two in the still classical way of creating a state. This is not exactly the case, because – as we shall see at the end of this section – the theoretically compelling motivation finds obstacles hindering its ability to change the real behaviour of individuals and states. Unlike life in Hobbes's state of nature, which is 'solitary, poore, nasty, brutish, and short' (Hobbes 1651, I, 13), life under nuclear or climate threat can be agreeable (less in the second case), as long as no catastrophe occurs. Also, what is at stake is not so much the survival of self-centred individuals, but rather the survival of humankind in civilised conditions, and worrying about particular goods is easier than about global ones.

Nonetheless, at least in principle, global/lethal challenges are incomparably more compelling than needs of global governance deriving from economic globalisation and, since the 1960s, have produced more global governance than the latter: nuclear non-proliferation and deterrence regimes, unsatisfactory though they may be, are just one example as is the sheer fact that, after the Cuban missile crisis of 1962, nuclear states have carefully avoided coming into dead-end situations in which resorting to nuclear weapons could have been a real choice. The same holds for climate deals such as the Montreal Protocol of 1987 on the protection of the ozone layer, the Kyoto Protocol of 1997 and the Paris Agreement of 2015.

These tentative piecemeal answers to the requirements raised by global commons and future generations being now issues of politics make clear that Democracy Two or politics for post-modern times is not just a project, even less a utopia or a matter of hope, but something that is tentatively getting under way. How can we otherwise explain the tortuous process of climate negotiations, insufficient that their outcome may be? Democracy Two has not just *normative*, but *explanatory* value as well.

The same holds for another element of change. The notion of humanity has so far been evoked and put to work in philosophy, religion and literature; as such it had no status in politics and attempts at introducing it were fiercely rejected as a 'zoological notion' (cf. Spengler 1922). With global/lethal challenges things are changing: if all presently living and future men and women are subject to the same condition of potential victims of man-made lethal events, a link of necessity or necessary cooperation arises among them if a shield has to be built. In philosophical terms, we recognise only a non-voluntary association with compulsory membership as political; associations which everyone can get in to and out of at one's own pleasure are not, because their decision making is not binding. With regards to the destiny of the global commons in which it lives, and only under this regard, *humankind* is now potentially such a non-voluntary, political association or community: living on the planet makes us all subject to the same lethal threats. Whether this potential unfolds and makes humankind actually capable of acting politically to the extent necessary to address global challenges remains to be seen. If this happens, it will create a pattern of robust and successful cooperation among states in the form of treaties and new institutions, but it will not introduce a world state by stealth. In this process regional associations may come to play a major role.

One corollary of the second definition of politics as it emerges in post-modern times still needs to be made explicit. It will not replace the classical definition, but coexist and collide with it. It is not a new step in the 'foundation of a new politics' or the rejuvenation of it occasionally announced by would-be prophets. As long as scarce and unequally distributed divisible goods will exist, there will be conflicts between parties over their distribution. In the process leading to more or less successful climate agreements (Montreal, Kyoto, Paris), we have already seen the interplay of the logic of global commons' protection with the particularistic logic of parties in the struggle for the allocation of burdens; the latter has for long strides blocked or hampered the former, thus causing dangerous delays or a lower effectiveness of the agreements. Understanding and managing this interplay, orienting it towards goals benefiting everyone, is now the puzzling new skill people interested in global politics will have to develop. It is perhaps less shining, but intellectually more interesting and politically more beneficial than waging great designs of 'global justice'.

7. Global troubles for democracy

The ability of today's politics to stand up to global threats and transform them into challenges leading to a rethinking of government or governance under the new conditions is severely limited by a number of factors. Finding answers to the challenges may fail, and traditional politics remain powerless before them, as long as actors are incapable of shedding their particularism and short-termism in favour of a time universalism that is careful of global commons. All these dangers, while related to politics in general, have a heavy impact on democracy, because they compound with specific downsides that this regime shows under the pressure of global threats. Let us first examine these factors one by one, starting with a premise.

Threats, challenges, problems, policy indications are not yet politically relevant at the time in which they exit the mind of their formulators, like Pallas Athena being born full grown and armed from Zeus's forehead. They become it in the moment in which they are received, endorsed and transformed by real political actors, common citizens and/or elites. This is what I have dubbed the subjective moment of politics; in it the way how issues are communicated is crucial. *Communication* is a constitutive element of politics, especially in modern polyarchies, and without keeping this knowledge in mind, all discourse about politics must fail to grasp its reality. Reasons of space make lamentably not possible to reconnect diverse themes present in this book (political identity, symbolic language, public sphere/opinion, and – with due scientific caution, given the slippery terrain – imagination) into a discourse regarding political communication, in which analytical and empirical contributions overwhelm anyway what philosophy has to say.

The first reason why objective, (highlighted by science) lethal threats have so far been neutralised in their possible impact on subjective perception and on policy is their abstract nature. The atomic bombing of 1945 lies more than seventy years behind us, and the new generations have fortunately a paling image of what nuclear war would mean; tales of MIRVs (missiles with multiple warheads), megatons, nuclear winter and crop shortages require a degree of concentration on the issue that few can be expected to show. Climate change is a statistical entity made of measurements of phenomena happening now and even more figures resulting from a mathematical projection of present processes into the future. Mass migration comes onto TV monitors, but only in the Mediterranean and (some) European countries is perceived as a problem affecting everybody, while its causal link with the changing climate is indistinguishable from the causation of migration due to pending civil wars. For the rest, climate change has so far been poor in sizeable, impressive phenomena that hit large populations in the highest GHGs-emitting countries. This abstract appearance of the two global threats, so different from the event-based communication style of TV journalism, has sidelined them from public attention for decades. Since the Internet has so far failed to dispossess TV as the preferred source of political information, things have not changed much. Only the interventions of powerful communicators such as President Barack Obama and Pope Francis with his Encyclical (2015) *Laudato si'* have had some effect on public opinion.

A second factor neutralising the political effects of global threats are the *denial mechanisms* actively or unconsciously set in motion. The campaigns launched by the oil industry or the military-industrial complex in previous decades belong to the first type, actively playing short-term interests (industrial jobs, nuclear security by supremacy) against those of future generations. Groucho Marx's famous quip 'What has posterity ever done for me?' represents a counter-argument based on *ad absurdum* reasoning rather than mere denial; if obligations require reciprocity, it is manifest that we can enter none toward a partner who does not yet exist and will therefore never be able to exhibit his or her reciprocating performance. More powerful seem however to be the unconscious denial mechanisms, such as the refusal to stand up to threats perceived as too big to manage or terrifying.[12] Thoughtless confidence in nuclear deterrence or shortsighted belief in 'national security' to the tune of old, state-centric realism belongs here too.

Connected with the denial mechanisms, but not identical to them, is the growing inability to come to terms with *fear*, an important cog in political mechanisms as seen in Chapter 3. Far from rejecting any fear as irrational and dangerous, the appropriate attitude to lethal challenges is a reasonable fear that takes stock of the real size of the threat and designs viable measures to meet it, while falling into neither catastrophism nor the phobic fear that targets heretics, strangers and marginal groups as culpable by imagined causation of the fearful phenomena. Due to psycho-social mechanisms we cannot examine here, such as narcissism, reasonable fear has retreated in the globalised world giving leeway to indifference and fatalism or moving the attention to other, real or fantasised targets: joblessness, migrants, but also vaccinations causing autism, chemtrails controlling minds. In short, even rational constructs such as policies for the global world do not work politically if they cannot mobilise beneficent emotions aimed at protecting ourselves and those we care for. Real actors do not act on rational choice patterns alone, rarely do so primarily, and sometimes not at all (cf. Epilogue).

This is not say that political communication as it is cannot but block the transformation of global threats ascertained by science into challenges that politics can work upon. I rather want to point out specific difficulties that must be taken into account and possibly modified if the philosophical or religious motivation against the threats burdening the present and future life of humankind is to generate political identity and action.

Let us now come to *democracy* and consider its troubles caused by both economic globalisation and global/lethal challenges. Under the first, due to the merger of *demos* and *ethnos* and the exclusive national dimension of this regime, democracy has lost much of its power, since important matters for its decision making are now pre-formed by decisions made at the global level by markets, large global corporations and international institutions, whose legal legitimacy is only indirect and partial (only some of their officials are appointed by democratic governments). National sovereignty, whose management is periodically subject to electoral verification in democratic countries, has lost chunks of its realm by giving them away either to impersonal market dynamics or to international bodies.

Lethal challenges can undo one of the hidden presuppositions for democracy as the most fair and advantageous method of conflict resolution to work: a high relative *stability* of the social and natural environment in which democratic societies live and reproduce themselves. This has been guaranteed so far and never put into question; change has unfolded, for example from the agrarian-industrial stage of early capitalism to the present service economy, but at a low pace over generations, and societies were able to adapt, though not without pains. Whatever majority may have come out of the elections, that environment could be expected not to be significantly or irreversibly damaged or upset; the successive majority or coalition may have had something (at worst, the damages of an unsuccessful war) to redress, but not to restart in a waste land. This stability is no longer a safe and implicit assumption (and that presupposition, which was in fact obvious, needs to be investigated and found to be absent). Change affecting global commons can happen at high speed; ten years from the Manhattan Project to the establishment of a balance of terror, a few decades between the discovery of global warming and the increase of

GHGs in the atmosphere up to 444 parts-per-million CO_2 equivalent (+60% compared with pre-industrial levels). Politics in general and democracy in particular, have so far proven incapable to match these challenges in an energetic and timely way. Wrong decisions, significantly postponed decisions as well as omissions (such as the refusal – upheld for decades – to put global environmental challenges on the agenda) can spoil the natural environment more than it is already, and contribute to the cause of irreversible damages. Some critics of democracy go as far as to suggest that, due to its procedures and pace, this regime is structurally unable to meet the speed of technological progress and its consequences for the shape of societies and individual destiny. For all these reasons, *the converging assault of economic globalisation and lethal challenges* seems to erode the truth of democracy's claim to be the regime in which human beings can best and effectively take their lot into their own hands. Paralysis is not a good foundation for credibility.

This credibility is also under stress from another corner. A further claim made by democracy used to be the identity between voters and those affected by their decisions, a guarantee for everybody not to see burdens resulting from decision taken by others fall on his or her shoulder. This pillar of *democracy's legitimacy* is now shaken by the circumstance that democratic decision-makers of today have been making decisions, or endorsed omissions, that constitute a grave prejudice to the life conditions of future generations. The inability shown by democracies in the past decades to forcefully address the nuclear, as well as the climate threat, can disavow their claim to ensure equal consideration for everybody's rights, since this finds application only among contemporaries; and this could be seen as the worst case of the short-termism affecting them anyway, as we saw in Chapter 5. Needless to say that future generations are not here and will never be present to make their protest heard, but living generations, first and foremost the youth, have already begun to perceive democratic short-termism as going against the promises of democracy and its legitimacy. Whether steps taken in the second decade of the new century, such as the Paris climate deal, can be taken as signs of a new effort by democratic and other regimes to combine time universalism and space universalism, also involving non-democratic countries in the cooperation, is, at the time of writing, too early to say. Should this effort be successfully pursued, it will have to find sooner or later an institutional anchorage, an example – just an example – of which could be an *ombudsman* checking new legislation and major administrative acts with respect to their consequences on future generations and alerting parliament and public opinion whenever dangers are to be expected.[13] But whatever institutional innovation will only work if embedded in a changed political and ethical culture as sketched in this chapter; and this still fledgling force of change cannot be said to receive much support and inspiration from today's political philosophy in most of its many versions.[14]

Putting together what we saw in Chapter 5 with the troubles of democracy under global and lethal strains, it seems fair to say that democracy as a concept, as well as many of its local applications, are in need of a profound *revision*, while democratic triumphalism is misplaced. This revision, including its timing, is important if democracy is to remain the alternative to dictatorship and populism, as we saw at the end of Chapter 5. The people's choice for democracy, as the time between the World Wars has shown, cannot be taken for granted; reversal is possible wherever democracy proves unable to come to terms with unprecedented challenges.

This book does not offer any recipe as to how to perform that revision. Unlike other political philosophers, I do not regard this discipline as tasked with constitutional engineering, which is rather up to political actors to engage in, while facing needs for reform or revolution in any given situation. A critical attitude that limits itself to find conceptual names for thus far untold problems, threats and alternatives, and highlights false or obsolete solutions – similar to the highlighting of the 'negative side' in Hegel's dialectics – is more conducive to productive inventions and agreements than the issuing of blueprints for a better or perfect world.

Notes

1 Two names are to remember in this field of research: the French historian Fernand Braudel (1902–1985) and the American sociologist and historian Immanuel Wallerstein.
2 So defined later in 1989 by the economist John Williamson.
3 Defining exactly what we mean by terrorism and describing its evolution is not an easy business and cannot be pursued here.
4 See Cerutti 2012.
5 A typical case of international regime, the Missile Technology Control Regime (MTCR) is a voluntary association among 35 countries aimed at preventing the proliferation of military missile technology.
6 According to the Democracy Index compiled by *The Economist* (2016, 41–42), out of 167 countries only 12% consist of full democracies (the Anglo-Saxon and Scandinavian countries plus Germany), while 35.9% are flawed democracies, 22.2% hybrid regimes and 30.5% authoritarian regimes. Freedom rather than democracy is measured in the Freedom House 2015 report, which rated 46% free, 28% partly free and 26% not free. These figures are to be taken purely as an indication, while the parochial Anglocentric assessment criteria remain questionable.
7 This is available in Chapter 1 of Cerutti 2007.
8 See Sagan and Waltz 2003.
9 His *The Strategy of Conflict* (Schelling 1962) has been for the rationalization of nuclear deterrence, a contribution to humankind's survival as long as abolition is not possible, what Machiavelli's *Il Principe* was for the conceptualization of politics in Renaissance Europe.
10 This was according to Thucydides (Book I, 23) the mechanism – sustained by fear – that ignited the Peloponnesian war; on fear cf. Chapter 3, §2.
11 For all of the questions addressed in this and the following section the full argument is developed in Cerutti 2007, Chapter 5, §§2–3. See also Pogge 1994.
12 In refined philosophical terms this inability has been analysed by Günther Anders in the first decade of the atomic age as the 'Prometheic gap' consisting of lack of imagination and emotional involvement in front of a potential nuclear holocaust, see Anders 1956.
13 This question is detailed and existing solutions are shown in Cerutti 2015.
14 Cf. Chapter 10, in particular §3.

References

Acemoglu, Daron and Pierre Yared (2010) *Political Limits to Globalisation*, 'American Economic Review', 100(2), 83–88.

Anders, Günther (1956) *Die Antiquiertheit des Menschen/ The Antiquity of Man*, 5th edition, Munich: Beck, 1980.

Cerutti, Furio (2007) *Global Challenges for Leviathan: A Political Philosophy of Nuclear Weapons and Global Warming*, Lanham: Rowman & Littlefield.
Cerutti, Furio (2012) *Two Global Challenges to Global Governance*, 'Global Policy', III(3), September, 314–323.
Cerutti, Furio (2015) *Survival – Humankind's First Fundamental Right*, in 'Constellations', 22(1), 59–67.
Crouch, Colin (2004) *Post-Democracy*, Cambridge: Polity Press.
The Economist (2016), *Pocket World in Figures*, London: Profile Books.
The English Standard Version Bible, available at http://biblehub.com
Hobbes, Thomas (1651) *Leviathan*, ebook available at www.gutenberg.org/ebooks/3207
McCarthy, Cormac (2006) *The Road*, New York: Knopf.
Pogge, Thomas (1994) *An Egalitarian Law of Peoples*, 'Philosophy and Public Affairs', 23(3), 195–224.
Sagan, Scott D. and Kenneth Waltz (2003) *The Spread of Nuclear Weapons*, New York: Norton.
Schelling, Thomas (1962) *The Strategy of Conflict*, Cambridge: Harvard University Press.
Spengler, Oswald (1922) *Der Untergang des Abendlandes/ The Decline of the West*, ebook available at https://archive.org/details/Decline-Of-The-West-Oswald-Spengler
Strange, Susan (1996) *The Retreat of the State*, Cambridge: Cambridge University Press.
Θουκυδίδης/Thucydides (404 BCE) Περὶ τοῦ Πελοποννησίου πολέμου/ *The Pelopponesian War*, available at http://classics.mit.edu/Thucydides/pelopwar.1.first.html (404 BCE is Thucycides's presumtive year of death; title attributed in the Hellenistic era)

Further readings

On globalisation and politics:

Keohane, Robert (2002) *Power and Governance in a Partially Globalized World*, London: Routledge.

Diverging voices on globalisation:

Bhagwati, Jagdish (2007) *In Defense of Globalization*, Oxford: Oxford University Press.
Rodrik, Dani (2011) *The Globalization Paradox*, New York: Norton.
Stiglitz, Joseph (2007) *Making Globalization Work*, New York: Norton.

Two comprehensive readers on all facets of globalisation:

Held, David and Anthony McGrew (2003) *The Global Transformation Reader*, Cambridge: Polity.
Turner, Bryan, ed. (2010) *International Handbook of Globalization Studies*, London: Routledge.

On whether we have duties towards our posterity:

Tremmel, Joerg Chet, ed. (2006) *Handbook of Intergenerational Justice*, Cheltenham: Edward Elgar.

EXCURSUS 2
Politics and death

In this Excursus we want to peer still deeper into the subjective side of politics, raising more radical points about the *relevance of politics to the life of the individual human being*. This perspective must remain in the background of the study of politics, which deals primarily with communities, their order and their influence on the life of entire generations, with no particular attention to the lot of each of their members on the path from the cradle to the grave. Yet, at the end of the day, that is at the sunset of our journey on the earth (or perhaps on other planets in the future), what counts for each individual and gives meaning to their journey is the amount of satisfaction or happiness experienced or missed, as well as of sufferance avoided or inflicted by human action, most of which is coordinated or regulated by politics. Death remains the fundamental component of human life, the paramount constant defining the meaning of the existence of us mortal beings; but death is, at the same time, the principal destroyer of meaning, in the sense that it nullifies our life plans and bereaves of our presence the grid of social and emotional relations we may have built up during our life. This is even more true in the case of death prematurely and arbitrarily inflicted by political violence in warfare or under a tyrannical regime; and also when death is caused or not prevented by omission on the side of politicians and officials. Death is unavoidable, but when we die, how we die and how many of us must die, depends, among other factors, on politics – not just in the obvious case of war. This Excursus is dedicated to the main types of encounter between politics and death and is written looking at death from the venture point of secular Western culture, for which death is an event regarding the individual in her/his 'being thrown' (Heidegger's *Geworfenheit*, as conceived of in *Sein und Zeit/ Being and Time* 1927) into the world, with no assurance of life after death – neither as an individual nor in a cosmic perspective like in Oriental religions. On the other hand, and irrespective of the diverging metaphysics, for religious believers of most faiths causing the death of other humans is as problematic as for people of secular convictions.

Politics can impact on death *directly* or *indirectly*; let us see the several cases in this order. Direct impact occurs in war, civil war, terrorism, nuclear war.

In the contractarian account of the polity, which remains even now paradigmatic, the polity is established – at a price – in order to avoid for the citizens the loss of life and limbs, to put it with Thomas Hobbes. The price is not only the subjection to Leviathan's authority, which protects us from that loss in the realm of internal security, but also the obligation citizens incur if the state must ask for their lives in order to repel external threats. Military conscription used to be a 'sacred duty' to which generations and generations of young people (in Europe since the French Revolution) had to submit themselves. If political leaders fail to fulfil the polity's life-protecting mission, countries fight unnecessary wars such as the First World War, the result of which are the endless lists of dead soldiers we find in stone on the patriotic monuments adorning the main squares of Europe's towns. Or, for that matter, the 58,195 names of fallen Americans in the Vietnam Veterans Memorial in Washington, DC – just to mention another unnecessary, politically unreasonable war. It is up to the statesmen, politicians and public opinion to do all that is possible to avoid wars, and who does not follow this bottomline burdens oneself with heavy, blood-stained responsibility. To do all that is possible starts with keeping one's own head as free as it can go from conventional wisdom, prejudice, unverified misjudgement, hatred, fanaticism.

Wars are sometimes necessary, as in the case of the Second World War after the Third Reich attacked Poland in September 1939 or the UN-authorised operation that repealed the Iraqi invasion of Kuwait in 1990–1991. The Second World War might have been even shorter and less bloody if Germany had been attacked before, after Hitler remilitarized Rhineland in 1936 or as he invaded Czechoslovakia in March 1938. When a war results to be necessary in order to save a polity along with the values of freedom and self-government it embodies, the responsibility of statesmen and military leaders turns to containing the number of deaths, in particular of non-combatants. War is hell anyway, to put it with General William T. Sherman (1820–1891), who brought hell to the Confederate economy and society during the American Civil War; but hell can have a different intensity depending on how far the laws of war or *ius in bello* are respected by the warring parties, including foreign powers' interventions with or without UN Security Council authorisation.

Even in just wars, death can be unjustly distributed. The end of conscription was, for cultural reasons, mature and unavoidable, but should not be celebrated as the triumph of pacifism and humanity. Wars are still being fought, even if in a lesser and more fragmented scale, and the ones dying are – besides civilians – professional soldiers recruited among the less wealthy areas or social layers of a country (for example, ethnic minorities and working class in the USA, southern regions in Italy). Social inequality can translate, as it happened at almost any time, into *inequality of survival chances*.

Let us incidentally note that war and death in war has two faces. We are dealing with the political one, and diversify among just and unjust wars,[1] equally or unequally distributed survival chances. But even in the politically and morally best motivated war nothing can neutralise — for the victims and the people emotionally tied to them — the loss of the individual life and the bodily pain suffered (cf. Scarry 1985). This human or, philosophically spoken, phenomenological approach to death and suffering caused by politics cannot overwhelm and replace — as radical pacifists would like to have it — the political approach to them. The two approaches cannot be reconciled with each other, but if we are able to keep the both of them present to our mind, this can improve the intellectual and moral quality of our political philosophy of deadly conflicts. This same result can also be attained by looking at another fairly different point of contact between politics and death: the latter is sometimes accepted as a sacrifice of one's own life on behalf of civic and political values such as freedom or out of solidarity with fellow soldiers and countrymen (this solidarity or brotherhood is said to be a main component in the cohesion of combat units). But let us now come back to the main track of our review.

'Failed states', a journalistic but trenchant expression, are those polities that have failed their existential task to keep peace among citizens and given leeway to its opposite, *civil war*. As we saw in Chapter 6, civil war now comes mostly mixed with other types of war of the 'third type', which raises the percentage of prejudice and hatred among its motivations. Along with mass rape and ethnic cleansing, wanton killing is the regular tool of these armed conflicts, which hardly find any justification in national liberation or community protection. Those responsible for the outbreak of these, cruel as they are unnecessary, wars appoint themselves Masters of Death over adversaries and civilians, and deserve the harshest punishment at the hand of international peace-enforcers or national and international courts.

Death, as a principal if not exclusive element of power, attains its peak in terrorism, which is insofar the opposite of politics as temporary settler of conflicts and provider of some peaceful order. This remark holds for both *state terrorism* and group terrorism. The paramount example of the former remains the Nazi regime in Germany (1933–1945), whose principal activities were, on the one hand, the industrial killing of millions of Jews and other groups allegedly threatening the regime, and on the other hand, the death in the millions of its own soldiers and civilians in its desperate war against the rest of the world (except the few allies of the Third Reich). A regime in which the relationship of death and politics is set upside down, politics and the state becoming tools of a universal killing-and-dying policy,[2] is unique in the history of civilisation and remains an upsetting turning point in it. The other totalitarianisms of the twentieth century did not reach this qualitative peak, though Soviet communism in the time of Stalin came close and quantitatively outdid the Third Reich — not to speak of the Khmer Rouge regime in Cambodia (1975–1979). But even a just war with an acceptable distribution of burdens remains for the individual human beings an unacceptable source of death and suffering, which cannot be neutralised by political and historical justifications and explanations.

In *group terrorism* in the second half of the twentieth century, inflicting death on alleged enemies and 'culprits' or among civilians has been the political tool of choice, be it with an ethnic (IRA in Northern Ireland and Britain, ETA in the

Basque country and the rest of Spain) or an ideological (Red Brigades in Italy, RAF in Germany) motivation. What strikes most in this reduction of politics to giving death is the supreme self-righteousness with which terrorist leaders choose who has to be killed on the basis of their ideological frenzy.

A further step in this inverted relationship between politics and death is being achieved by Islamist terrorism, in itself a perversion of Islamic culture – not unlike Fascism and National Socialism when compared with European culture. This is said with regard not just to the spectacularization of the killing of 'infidels' and 'crusaders' shown on videos, but primarily to the suicidal killing of (mainly) civilians by people, even children, carrying explosive devices. It is as if politics had been blown out completely and all policies were restricted to the circle of death, inflicted upon others and oneself for God knows what delirious aims. Aims are indeed not relevant in these cases of fanaticism, it's rather the *triumph of death* (or rather of killing), an anthropological rather than political occurrence, and the overwhelming sensations of exerting an annihilating power upon others, as well as themselves, that move the suicidal assassins. Psychoanalytical and criminological categories seem to be more helpful in understanding this phenomenon than political ones.

This part on the direct intersection between politics and death closes with nuclear weapons. As the first, experimental atom bomb exploded in the desert of New Mexico in July 1945, its scientific creator, the theoretical physicist Robert J. Oppenheimer, was reminded of a verse spoken by Vishnu in the *Bhagavad Gita*: 'Now I am become Death, the destroyer of worlds.' The bombs dropped on Hiroshima and Nagasaki did not cause many more deaths than the conventional fire-bombing of Tokyo in 1945 with well over 100,000 dead. Vishnu's quote became more appropriate after the superpowers attained 'overkilling' capacity in the mid-fifties and 'mega death' (one million dead by nuclear explosion) became a unit commonly used in nuclear strategy – before being adapted to identifying a California heavy metal band. As results from Chapters 6 and 7, the power and security structure of our world, based on nuclear deterrence, implies the possibility of a failure leading to innumerable mega deaths up to the possibility, unlikely but not excluded by scientists, of the extinction of humankind. Where the relationship between politics, of which war is an element, and death is perverted up to this stage, a reflection over the path followed by human civilisation and a change of its course, as suggested in the previous chapter under the formula of 'Democracy Two', seem only appropriate, yes overdue.

★ ★ ★

Let us now examine cases of the *indirect impact* of politics on death, that is on processes that may have lethal even if involuntary outcomes and can be regulated by the state: health care maintenance, traffic and transportation laws, safety in the workplace, prevention of violent crimes particularly against those harming women and children, and, last but not least, climate policy or rather the lack of it. A related but distinct problem regards bioethical issues.

What we have called indirect impact results less from bad legislation than from the omission or the delay tolerated in legislating on new dangers and hazards brought in by technical advances (as on the road, in the sky or on the workplace) or new possibilities (as in health care) opened by scientific progress. The causes may range from resistance, exerted by groups that feel at a loss if their sector is newly regulated, to cultural prejudice that prevents decision-makers from recognising the new problem and the necessity to intervene. Omission or delay can occur on a local, national (for example, in the dismantling of asbestos-laden structures) or a global (no significant cuts in GHG-emissions by the big polluters) level. What keeps all these cases together is the eventuality, in many cases the certainty, that omission or delay allow for more people to die than would have happened if legislators and administrators had intervened immediately after the scientific ascertainment of the problem. This does not mean, as sometimes advocacy or protest groups say, that politicians and bureaucrats causing omission or delay commit murder and should be prosecuted as criminals. This would represent a problematic subjection of politics to jurisdiction, which at the end of the day would damage the constitutional balance existing between them. The appropriate location for highlighting the connection of wrong or omitted legislation with the unnecessary death of citizens is public debate, including parliamentary proceedings, which all too often deals with the protection of economic interests of smaller or larger groups and seldom with the incidence of legislation and its timing on the death or life of persons. Once again, it is not so much morality that is at stake; it is rather the universal (*erga omnes*) protecting mission of the state that should be remembered and reinstated with the main accent on the primacy of life preservation and death avoidance. In this context, the defining category is *responsibility*, not guilt, which can, in any case, hardly be assigned and punished because of the difficulty in determining the causal chain leading to harmful outcomes. The highlighting of political and moral responsibility towards death and suffering resulting from legislative and administrative omission can find its deterrent effect in the public assessment of the effective behaviour of politicians and in elections. Indifference and blindness towards the loss of human life contradicts the very constitutive mission of polity and politicians: protection – it does not take a special moral addition to politics to get this.

Life is not a once-for-all well-defined term, as we know from the debates concerning abortion, medically assisted suicide and euthanasia (death administered by a physician following an unequivocal expression of intention by the patient, released in normal mental conditions). Where does life begin? Is the question endlessly debated between so-called pro-life and pro-choice thinkers and activists? Even if we leave it open, in a pragmatically and less ideological sense, we must recognise that since abortion is practised anyway, its legal regulation has led to fewer deaths among women and fewer unwanted pregnancies, with fewer abortions resulting in the process.

Lastly, if one links the notion of life to that of *human dignity*, the wish to die expressed by persons hit by illnesses making daily life a meaningless ordeal becomes understandable; only ideological, in the first place religious rigidity and interference can oppose it. Legislation allowing for assisted suicide or euthanasia requested by the patient does not condemn anybody to die, it only opens a getaway to those to whom life has become unbearable because it has lost all dignity and meaning. This does by no means turn the relationship of politics and death upside down, it only makes politics protect our freedom of choice concerning our own life and death in exceptional conditions. Even the physician's mission to protect life cannot be misunderstood as an obligation to let us never die by technical devices and practises that cannot, however, make us immortal nor give us back a decent level of interaction with other humans and the environment.

Another – beyond war – common and much talked-about encounter between politics and death, the death penalty, is not discussed here because this was already done in Chapter 4, §6.

Notes

1 Some forty years after it was published, Michael Walzer's (1977) book on this matter remains unsurpassed.
2 A skull adorned the military hat and the honour ring (*Totenkopfring*) of the SS (*Schützstaffeln*), Hitler's own party militia.

References

Heidegger, Martin (1927) *Sein und Zeit/ Being and Time*, transated by Joan Stambaugh, Albany: State University of New York Press, 1996.
Scarry, Elaine (1985) *The Body in Pain*, New York: Oxford University Press.
Walzer, Michael (1977) *Just and Unjust Wars*, New York: Basic Books.

PART IV
Ethics and politics

This fourth and last part deals explicitly with normative political philosophy and examines its four fundamental categories: liberty, equality, justice, and solidarity. It does so in the light of the epistemological posture illustrated in Excursus 1, which entails two major differences from the mainstream literature in this field: political philosophy is not handled as a part of moral philosophy, as Isaiah Berlin still described their relationship. Practical philosophy, in the Aristotelian sense, is rather seen as comprising the two self-standing, but obviously not unrelated, spheres. Besides, in the present account normativity does not begin only when its main categories are laid on the table, as it happens in the present chapter, but has already shown up at more than one station of our journey: the legitimacy-identity-obligation complex highlighted the role values, principles and normative worldviews play in shaping the actors' subjectivity, while the theory of global/lethal challenges in Chapter 7 explicitly argued a new obligation to do our best in order to ensure humankind's survival. This obligation, which I call a meta-imperative, in the sense that it makes all other obligations possible and sensible, does not stem from a development of the categories we are going to examine in this chapter, though it has links to solidarity and justice. When normative problems involve our relationship to future generations and humankind against the background of our relationship to nature, we cannot expect the entire truth to come out of categories that over the course of centuries and in the context of one (Western) civilisation were devised with eyes focused on social relations among contemporaries.

In this part, however, it is not a task for a textbook to choose one normative doctrine out of many nor to give instructions and outline solutions to current problems such as those, say, raised by biotechnology or poverty or asymmetric warfare. It would be satisfactory enough if we were able to identify the problems, give them a name, and mark roadmaps that appear to be non-viable because they are too costly in material or ideal terms or laden with unacceptable consequences or unable to mean something for real political life.

8

LIBERTY, EQUALITY AND RIGHTS

Liberty and equality have turned out in the last hundred years or so to be twin concepts, building, however, a pair nearly as conflict-laden and possibly doomed – as in the case of 'real socialism' in the former Soviet bloc – as the Cain-Abel brotherhood. They have competed and still compete for primacy in liberalism and liberal democracy, with liberty in the forefront as long as liberation from the totalitarian regimes of the twentieth century was the leading theme in politics and later, since 1989, retreating because of two factors: the end of the Soviet Union with its liberating effects, which have made freedom something taken for granted and no longer exciting for more and more people around the world, and the involvement of freedom in neoliberalism, an ideology very effective in changing things in favour of a deregulated capitalism, but also passionately despised around the world because of the inequality it fostered. Stimulated by some new peak in inequality as well as by new scholarly inquiries into it, equality seems, at the time of writing, to be the temporary winner of the competition.

What we have just seen is a brief description of the *Zeitgeist* rather than a philosophical investigation of the two concepts, which we will first describe separately before looking into their relationships. Beginning with liberty we will first clarify this notion into its two fundamental meanings (§1), then deal with equality and its justification, egalitarianism (§2), while the subject of rights (§3) and specifically the problem of their universality (§4) will occupy the second half of this chapter.

1. Concepts of liberty

Some sixty years after first entering the philosophical stage through Isaiah Berlin's inaugural lecture at Oxford University, the odd couple negative and positive liberty still represents the most usual, though not necessarily the best approach to this field. I call them an odd couple in as much as the two poles seem at times to merge into one another, while at other times they look like irreconcilable extremes, making people doubtful about the wisdom of their distinction.

Negative liberty is easily understood as freedom *from* – while its twin comes with a different preposition: freedom *to*. Freedom from what? From *interference* within our own realm of action, is the plain answer. Interference can come from two sources: other persons in their private capacity or from public authorities. Other private persons could be the neighbours who are so noisy that they deprive me of sleep, thus interfering in my life activities; or they can be the owners of a heavily polluting plant that deprives me of clean air, thus interfering with my health. My liberty is, in these cases, protected by the ordinary (case or statutory) law of the country and the courts. Constitutional law instead is expected to protect my liberty against interference by public authority overpassing its competence and unlawfully limiting my freedom of speech or movement or ownership; on this level a dispute, whether or not my basic liberties have been violated, can come before a constitutional court, granted we are considering a country governed under the rule of law. In countries in which the rule of law is infringed upon, or nearly non-existent, interference or rather oppression by the ruling leader or bureaucracy or party threatens negative liberty on a daily basis, and the 'fight for freedom' is truly a fight for it. On the whole, the philosophy of negative liberty answers the question: *how much government should we accept?* This is a typical modern question, as room for it was opened first by Christianity, in particular by Augustine, then by the Lutheran Reformation, the Renaissance and the Enlightenment – disparate that these doctrines may have been, they shared a focus on subjectivity and interiority, the venture point from which government and politics are to be assessed.

Coming back to the conceptual level, it is clear that interference is a notion that needs differentiation: lawful and unlawful interference for example are opposite rather than different, while liberty is a concept that seeks qualification. It is indeed clear that unlimited liberty for all (as lack of both external constraints set by the law and internal prohibitions stemming from internalised norms) would unleash Hobbes's *bellum omnium contra omnes*, make the state of nature perpetual and civil coexistence impossible. Liberty must be limited, but by the force of what principle? We can exercise our liberty – is a first answer – only as far as its effects do not interfere with others' liberty, as the noisy neighbour or the polluting plant owner do with their behaviour. This reciprocity is the pillar not just of civilised relations among private people, but also of the range of state intervention in the field of those relationships: as long as they do not harm each other, the state should refrain from interfering in the web of relationships among them, and only step in for the sake of civil peace or the orderly execution of contracts, lest conflicts lead to private violence and revenge. This is not as uncontested as it may seem to be: it is easy to acknowledge the principle, but recognising the harm done and making public authorities act on this has, in many cases, required a long period of discussion and struggle. So was the case with polluting plants, or with the noxious interference of the excessive workday length on the workers' health in early capitalism, or more recently in sweatshops located in developing countries. More regulations and more trials in courts became necessary in this way. This has led neoliberals to lament the excessive interference of the state in the free private management of industries. Workers and unions have not been as energetic in making clear that at stake was and is also their liberty to not have their health and life conditions interfered with by the industrialists' less than responsible handling of noxious side effects or externalities of their business. This is not to justify all possible regulations issued by the public authority, since excessively detailed norms pretend too much (and can nonetheless hardly pre-figure all possible cases that may occur in the future) and successive negotiations between stakeholders can bring about more adequate solutions, once the principles are held firm. Administrative bodies have an innate tendency to overregulate, parliaments and governments are not sufficiently able and willing to correct this tendency, which can sometimes bring discredit to the principles. In a word, negative liberties are built upon acts of *abstention* to interfere (to legislate, to regulate, to intervene coercively) by the state, whenever interference is not essential to the preservation of the polity as framework for the citizens' peaceful coexistence – *ne cives ad arma veniant/*in order not to let citizens resort to arms, as the Romans said. This basic version of negative liberty is political liberalism's own view, and can live regardless of what actor makes the law – whether a democratic parliament or an enlightened prince, as Kant still saw it.

A further, specifically democratic development considers interference by the state to be justified only if the citizens themselves have made the law by universal suffrage and representative government. This is an advanced (Rousseauian) version of negative liberty as *autonomy*.[1] It opens up the question: is all democratic legislation, as such, respectful of our freedom? The liberal as well as the liberal-democratic answer is negative. Being passed by a democratic legislature does not guarantee the full preservation of freedom from interference; constitutional safeguards as enacted by constitutional courts and public opinion constitute a higher tribunal of liberty. This argument has analogy with the point made in Chapter 5, which held that so-called substantial democracy can by no means replace formal democracy.

From a democratic and also a socialist point of view, the priority and irreplaceable character of negative liberty has been criticised for noting that a person in a state or condition of poverty or destitution or illiteracy can draw no advantage from it because s/he is not able to make sense of her/his freedom of speech or right to vote, freedom from want being her/his first and foremost interest, which can be met not by having some formal rights recognised, but only by economic and social policies changing her/his life conditions. The truth contained in this criticism has been the presupposition for the shift from the liberal-democratic state to the liberal and social democracies of the mid twentieth century, whose present fiscal and financial crisis may therefore put at risk their attitude towards liberty as well. On the theoretical level, however, to say that negative liberties are nil without social policies making them enjoyable is different from – and less founded than – maintaining that those liberties remain essential as a principle, but need to be accompanied by conditions that make them effective. It must further be noted that freedom of speech, assembly and unionizing is the necessary condition for the social rights of the weaker members of society to be protected – as the history of workers' movements around the globe shows. By the way, 'to be a necessary condition for' is not identical with 'to be instrumental to': an instrumentalist justification of liberty would diminish and endanger it.

Some of these issues, such as democracy and the conditions for making liberty effective, lead us to liberty's second version: positive liberty, or liberty *to be* or *to become* something. In other words, to build a family with a decent standard of living, or to become a scientist, or to enter one's own country's Olympic team; in the political field, to build, along with others, a successful party or to make new legislation pass the parliamentary vote. It is the liberty to successfully develop one's own life plan, be it individual or collective in nature. This entails some problematic aspects, as the history of doctrines on liberty shows.

First, if *promoting positive liberty* is regarded as something society or the polity owes to its members, institutions are charged with the obligation to provide the conditions for life plans to be implemented. This is costly, the more those conditions are identified with policies enhancing the income of those interested – though there are other ways to act on the conditions, as we shall see in the equality section when speaking of equal opportunities. It can be as costly as to require raising heavily the level of public debt, to the detriment of future generations. Also, setting up a system of social rights, also known as entitlements, requires expanding the administrative apparatus and putting under its authority many aspects of the citizens' private life, which at the end of the day may lead to intrusion and infringe on their negative freedom. This is not to say that developing one's own positive liberty has well to remain in the hands of the individuals, according to their ability to score better than others in the social competition – as conservative liberalism would have it. Yet the public promotion of this liberty must carefully weigh the different interests at stake and find a balance between its own progressive intention and the perverse side effects. The first step is to discriminate between what can be acknowledged as a legitimate goal of self-realisation the state should contribute to (say, to go to university) and what it cannot (to be taught the art of origami).

Another doubt is linked to some doctrines of positive liberty that sees *self-realisation* as a process in which a better or authentic or spiritual Self determines the way to go, in opposition to its own lower levels such as those dominated by passions or shortsighted interests. As the individual problem of a split Self, this can be left to moral philosophy, but its translation into the political realm can become ugly. The French Jacobins wanted the people to learn how to live according to virtue, the Bolsheviks in the Russian Revolution or the Red Guards in China's Cultural Revolution or the genocidal Khmer Rouges in the Cambodia of the 1970s wanted to strip 'bourgeois' layers of the populace of their corrupt and egoistic traits – often eliminating peoples and bad traits alike. The effects of the translation range from paternalism to totalitarianism and terror. The opposite of it is to make the frustrated needs and life plans of the underprivileged layers of society interact with each other and the political leadership, in a reciprocal learning process that leads to public policies effectively freeing the energy of those layers towards the attainment of better life conditions and more political participation – as the workers' movement did in many countries, at best in Europe before the First and after the Second World War.

This is just a sketch of the complex relationship between negative and positive liberty. It is important to see their differences and not to let it bloat into an opposition or even dichotomy, in which the one pole rules out the presence of the other. Even interpreting positive liberty as the road to self-realisation, freedom from interference remains its presupposition, because self-realisation under guardianship, rather than autonomy, contradicts the very image of the Self, as this has developed in modern thought from the Renaissance's ideal of 'man' through the journey of *Selbstbewußtsein*/self-consciousness towards modernity in Hegel's *Phenomenology of Spirit* (Hegel 1807) down to important recent reconstructions of the Self's path (Habermas 1985; Taylor 1989).[2]

It only remains to note that, while this differentiated concept of liberty claims universal validity – wherever human rights and the rule of law are to be the foundation of the political community, both domestic and international – its philosophical roots lie in Western culture and the primacy it gives to the individual, as mentioned above. Where harmony, social cohesion around the family, and the cultivation of traditions are seen as paramount values, as in the debate of the 1990s on 'Asian values', liberty is given little leeway, and an anti-individualistic collectivism prevails. This cannot but weaken the defence of democratic regimes and parties against the authoritarian trends of a capitalism that was imported without passing through a liberal and democratic phase allowing for free debate on its regulation and the protection of workers' rights.

2. Equality and egalitarianism

Equality, which has the appearance of a simple notion, is no less complex than liberty, with which it is closely linked. This author sees little chance of reproducing on a small scale the intricacies of the intense debate that started with the publication of Rawls's *opus magnum* in 1971 and found a new peak with the publication of Ronald Dworkin's *Sovereign Virtue: The Theory and Practice of Equality* in 2002. It will be necessary to skip some philosophical developments while focusing on the aspects that can be seen as most relevant in a political perspective.

Equality makes its first appearance in the Greek *polis*, an anti-egalitarian, slave-owning society, in the shape of ἰσονομία/isonomy or equality before the law, a right for sure reserved to the citizens. The equality of all human beings before God, introduced by Christendom, but also present in Judaism and Islam, is a big cultural shift, though it remained socially and politically ineffective – except in Christian charities over the centuries and later in the Christian social movements of the nineteenth and twentieth century. As a social principle, equality pops up in modern revolutions, with radical turns represented by the Diggers in the English Revolution and Gracchus Babeuf's *conspiration pour l'égalité*/conspiracy for equality in the French Revolution. Marx was interested in unveiling the inequality hidden in the alleged equal and rightful exchange between capital and wage labour rather than in preaching equality in general; he believed that the equal exchange between compensation and amount of work provided by a single person, a principle characterising the first stage of communist society, would later make room for the formula 'from each according to his ability, to each according to his needs' – thus establishing an equal procedure respecting and promoting everybody's individuality (Marx 1875).

In modern history, inequality worldwide went down from its previous peaks after 1860 and particularly during the Great Depression of 1929, while gathering again momentum after 1977 as a likely side effect of globalisation, which can on the other hand be credited for bringing down inequality among countries. The recent and unmistakable growth of income inequality within countries as well as the disappearance of any alternative economic model like the socialist one may stay in the background of the growing philosophical attention on equality as an *ethical* (rather than political) guideline for course corrections inside capitalism. It could also be asked if the arguments in favour of equality and redistribution, such as Rawls's (1999, §11) second principle of justice (difference principle), are not to be seen as a *post-festum* justification of the social policies launched by the New Deal and heavily under attack since the rise of neoliberalism with all its rhetoric in favour of inequality as a path to wealth. As Hegel wrote in the Preface to his *Grundlinien der Philosophie des Rechts/Elements of the Philosophy of Right*, 'When philosophy paints its grey in grey, one form of life has become old, and by means of grey it cannot be rejuvenated, but only known. The owl of Minerva [*scil.* philosophy] takes its flight only when the shades of night are gathering' (1821, 8).

★ ★ ★

Of all the major differentiations the concept under examination allows for, we shall mention the following: substantive vs. procedural equality; equality of welfare/equality of opportunities/equality of capabilities. The two sets of notions overlap only partially.

Substantive equality places emphasis on the equality of the things that are a matter of redistribution, thus consisting of the possession of a nearly equal amount of the goods that are regarded as relevant to the actor's social condition. If it has to be exactly the same number, Aristotle at the outset (1301)[3] of Book 5, Part 1 of *Politics* calls it numeric equality in all things, as proposed – he adds – by democrats, while their extreme counterpart, the oligarchs, vow for a likewise complete inequality. Proportional equality means, on the contrary, to treat everybody according to a same principle of fairness such as 'treat like cases as like' or 'whatever the outcome in terms of goods, you will be treated not equally, but with equal respect for your dignity and concerns'.

In the triad mentioned above, the great divide lies between *equality of welfare* or positions and the other two. In the former, the goal of society and government is seen as providing everybody, or rather every citizen, with the same degree of well-being as based on a less and less unequal portion of material and relational goods. In its roughest version this takes the form of the state's monetary disbursements to the advantage of the worse-off. There is evidently a problem with the measurement of welfare, which can be done either authoritatively from the top, at the risk of infringing the individual's autonomy, or referring to preference satisfaction, which creates a delicate problem of either allowing chaos or filtering preferences according to a criterion almost impossible to reach by consensus.

Equality of opportunity presupposes a view of society as a competitive place in which a hierarchy is created according to the results attained by every member. Equality requires giving everybody equal chances of participation, regardless of the family, the place, the class and perhaps even the country one comes from. For this aim, the formal (legal) equality of access to positions in the social hierarchy is not sufficient; it must be made real by an equality of *resources* that allows for everybody to pursue her or his life plans and possibly climb up the social ladder. The opportunity to access the educational system is the first big equaliser that favours mobility beyond or against the (lesser) chances given by birth. Equal access to health care and social security for the elderly (once one has exited the competition) are – as we already know from the 'social' transformation of the state examined in Chapter 4 – the two other pillars of policy aimed at distributing equal opportunities to all citizens regardless of gender, race, ethnic origin, religion and sexual orientation.[4] This may include proactive policies targeting discrimination (affirmative action).

This is equality of opportunity in a meritocratic market society as differentiated from, say, a feudal or caste society. Equality can, however, be pushed one or two steps forward, in a shift from moderate to reinforced egalitarianism. The first step imposes on the state and society a duty to correct the inequalities resulting from unfavourable/conditions created by nature (birth defects, genetic diseases, being born in a malarial swamp), especially when compounded by exceptional innate gifts at the other end of the spectrum; the persons hit by cases of 'brute luck' are by no means responsible for it, and the attitude to compensate them is called *luck egalitarianism*. In a second, more radical step, some theorists think that a compensation is due to the worst-off also when their condition results from the choices they made or omitted because these choices were based on unequally distributed skills, for instance cognitive or cultural ones. This background inequality is believed to limit the responsibility for choices connected to it. This can lead in the stronger case to a legal duty for the state to provide aid or in the weaker case to a moral motivation for societal organisations to act benevolently. Behind these perspectives lies the notion of human dignity, which we should never allow to be diminished, and/or the Kantian principle (second formulation of the categorical imperative [1785, 29]) telling us to treat all other human beings as ends in themselves and never as means; both principles sever the recognition of somebody as moral personality from her/his performances in social life.[5]

Equality of capabilities, granting everybody the freedom to 'function' according to one's own ends, replaces for Amartya Sen (1999) the equality of resources because the latter does not take into account the diversity of the starting conditions among persons, which rather requires unequal resources to be allotted for compensation. Focusing on resources is said to be fetishist, as things (the resources) are believed to possess the social quality of letting people realise their life plans. On the other hand, reconciling public policy decisions with a myriad of individual aims seems to contain the risk of generating, along with a chaotic multiplicity, unbearable costs for public finance.

As with the choice between negative and positive liberty, this book is not arguing towards which of the three main road maps to equality the balance should tip, nor if any of the numerous variations to them can be regarded as an alternative. Let us remark that the equality these doctrines have been talking about is equality inside a standardised highly developed society, and let us add that models of equality, if they are to be taken seriously as compass for policy making, should be thought of in conjunction with their economic and financial feasibility – lest they remain a futile exercise in wishful thinking. It need not be feasible under the presently given circumstances of poorly regulated capitalism; yet normative models targeting inequality should also say which economic and social reforms are capable of making them viable – this happens rarely. In any case, inequality in developing countries – both domestically and in the comparison of GDP (Gross Domestic Product) or HDI (Human Development Index) *per capita* between poor and rich countries – seems to be a bigger intellectual and moral challenge than, say, choosing between the resources and capabilities approach in highly developed societies. Economists have devoted to this challenge much more attention and research than political philosophers, with more sense of the international dimension and real world dynamics.[6] On another count, equality among present and future generations is a question almost completely unknown to the literature, in which only recently this complex of problems has been examined under the heading of intergenerational justice and in the narrow terms of analytical ethics, with little sense for the political context.

But why should we choose equality over inequality? This is far from self-evident, as witnessed by the persistent existence of both doctrines praising the advantages of inequality (to which we will come back later) and practical attitudes favouring inequality such as tax cuts for the rich. Nature, with its very unequal distribution of luck and gifts, does not seem to be a champion for equality; nor does it suggest gender equality, since it gives women the chance of an experience, maternity, that divides them from men. Gender equality has been only recently established by law, which means that its proper venue is not nature but the polity, though many existing polities fail to enforce and even to acknowledge gender equality. Nonetheless, nature contains a basic equalising factor for all human beings: the *vulnerability* to death and bodily or mental suffering, (we are all equally mortal, even if the actual – not the possible – degree of exposure to suffering is unequal). This, rather than than the ability to form a conception of the good and to shape a life plan as rational beings (Rawls's fairly thick criterion for being a moral person) seems to be the only – thin but robust – unifying feature of humankind that includes its most destitute members too; an anthropological basis on whose grounds arguments for promoting more equality can develop. If we do not keep the criteria for being recognised as a human being thin, we may be forced by our own standards to exclude people who, handicapped by hunger, poverty and lack of any education, cannot satisfy our 'civilised' criteria for rationality and morality.

Among these many arguments, what concerns us most here are the political ones. Preventing inequality from surpassing certain limits (which limits depends on the prevailing culture at any given moment) has two effects: it also prevents dissatisfaction, resentment, frustration and hatred from building up to levels engendering civil strife and social conflict from becoming violent or leading to exit behaviour. Yet it also creates better conditions for economic growth, for which high inequality is known to be an obstacle, while under favourable political conditions sustained growth is a factor of social peace and democratic development.

★ ★ ★

Underlying all these considerations are two questions that the reader may want to apply as tools capable of clarifying what is contained within doctrines about equality:

- *equality of what* (outcomes, resources, capabilities or something else)?
- *equality for whom*?

This second question, already mentioned in this book with reference to humankind at large or future generations, is becoming again very significant because of a number of factors, from regional instability and war to climate change, which have unleashed mass migrations that are predicted to become a stable factor in future world politics. Most of the principles and proposals mentioned above are indeed focused on the citizens of the rich or relatively rich host countries and need to be rethought in light of the circumstances of mass migration. Otherwise, the notion of citizenship, so far somehow overburdened with the rhetoric of rights and empowerment, risks losing its shine and becoming a keyword of exclusion and division. Its destiny is also overshadowed by its polysemic nature: it means the trove of rights, entitlements and duties connected with being in general citizen of a polity, but also owning the national and exclusive citizenship of a specific country. Finally, in this case globalisation and lethal challenges question or even debunk doctrines that were conceived within the framework of the nation state without paying attention to the limited truth of statements made under this condition.

Equality, we saw, is not an uncontested value, and is for sure more contested than liberty, also because it can, in certain circumstances, collide with liberty. To take it for incontestable while not taking the doubters' points seriously is a sectarian attitude that does not reinforce the credibility of egalitarianism. Outright opposition to equality is expressed only by Nietzsche and other elitist thinkers who are contrary to it, to democracy and socialism.[7] Fascist ideologies built on this elitism, particularly with the cult for the almost superhuman Chief (*Duce* in Italy, *Führer* in Germany, *Conducator* in Romania); racism is one of its sub-types. More influential today is an instrumental *defence of inequality* as means to produce higher economic efficiency, allegedly to everybody's advantage: higher wages motivate workers to more productivity, higher profits encourage business owners to more risk-taking and innovation, while more wealth stimulates more investment and job creation in a trickle-down effect – a link rather dissolved by the extreme financialization of the economy. Another, less ideological argument, is concerned with the political and economic *costs of egalitarianism:* public policies aimed at fostering more equality not just of income, but also in the access to health care and education require the build-up of huge welfare bureaucracies that take much of the citizens' private life under administrative control and spread uniformity into the tissue of society – though this old-liberal point 'equality vs. liberty' has been less and less debated in the last two decades. Yet the economic cost of egalitarian policies remains a crucial issue: the way they have been managed after 1945 have often produced either too many entitlements or too expensive administrations or both, has been increasingly inefficient and has created new inequalities, for example disfavouring the unemployed or uninsured youth. Combined with the fiscal crisis of the state and the rise of public debt, due to the costs of egalitarianism being covered by huge borrowing by the state rather than redistributive policies, these developments have engendered a nearly perfect storm in many countries, particularly in those with unfavourable demographic trends. Does all this announce the end of egalitarianism?

Not necessarily. Once again, the concept must be disassembled into its main versions, which have only one feature in common, that is a preference for equality rather than inequality. Radical egalitarianism, in the sense of pursuing a general equalisation of incomes and positions, a posture that has largely disappeared from literature and politics, is very different from the attitude aimed at containing a further rise in inequality and compensating for the peak already reached. Likewise important in rethinking egalitarianism is the attention to new forms of inequality (say, the digital divide) and the perverse effects of some former measures of equalisation.[8]

In any of its versions, equality belongs within the field of positive liberty. The moderate version which we briefly sketched avoids the danger of the pervasive, paternalist shape of positive liberty. Another notable characteristic is that equality, the leading value of democracy, is not necessarily in harmony – as frequently mentioned in this book – with liberty, the main virtue of liberalism, and can even collide with it – a tension reproducing the tension that inhabits the very notion of liberty, between its negative and positive versions. Reconciling these several values with each other in the institutions of liberal democracy has been neither an easy task nor a short journey, as it took some 150 years; also the achieved balance is not warranted to stand under the new strains and constraints that are recently (2016–2017) emerging as an unexpected backlash to globalisation. This knowledge seems to be unknown or uninteresting to the populist detractors of present-day democracy.

3. Rights

Humans may struggle and die for freedom, but they never encounter it in their daily lives, in which they have to do with the concrete forms freedom can take: liberties. Liberties, however, are relevant to the citizen's life if they are not only collectively asserted, but also translated into legal institutions: rights, of which a core set is regarded as pertaining to all human beings. When acknowledged in the Constitution and implemented in ordinary law, we speak of fundamental rather than human rights. The latter are good for theory, mobilisation and rhetoric, while the former are the politically significant format of rights, the cornerstone of the polity. We are now going to briefly see the history, the conceptual structure and the function of *fundamental rights*; in the next section their origin and validity will be questioned, their enumeration discussed, then closing with the question of a right to survival for humankind.

Their rise in the eighteenth century was a Copernican revolution in European and American politics, as the view on politics *ex parte principis*/from the side of the prince or ruler was reversed into a view *ex parte civium*/from the side of the citizens. The individual and her/his rights substituted the state and the duties it imposed legitimately on the citizens. Modern liberty, as liberty of the individual, replaced ancient liberty, as liberty and sovereignty of the polity, only acting as a member of which the citizen can realise his liberty (women were not citizens).[9] Since the American Bill of Rights[10] and the French *Déclaration des droits de l'homme et du citoyen*/Declaration of the Rights of Man and of the Citizen, both issued in 1789, similar normative texts stating the fundamental rights of the citizens have been incorporated into the Constitutions of most states, including the People's Republic of China and the Democratic People's Republic of Korea – cases in which one is reminded that words are not always deeds. While the rights of the citizens remain limited to each nation state's members, with the exception of the European Charter of Fundamental Rights, which is legally binding since 2009 for all EU member states, the rights of man – or human rights, as they are now called in a wording deemed to be less sexist – are only partially enshrined in international treaties and conventions and remain otherwise heralded and supported, but not protected in a legally binding way by the Universal Declaration of Human Rights (UDHR) of 1948 – though this protection was later anchored in the 1967 International Covenant on Civil and Political Rights and the International Covenant on Economic, Social and Cultural Rights (1966).

Of the several distinctions made in the literature on rights, the most important seems to be the one regarding *claim rights* and *liberty rights*. Liberty rights give a person permission to do something: to speak in full freedom, to buy or sell property, to travel wherever s/he likes to. Claim rights allow a person to enjoin another person or body not to do something that can limit her/his/its liberty. In an ideal liberal world, liberty rights (also called privileges) are limited only by the obligation not to infringe upon other people's liberties. These concepts are a better analytical tool than the usual pair negative vs. positive rights. It must be also noted that in Latin, Romance languages and German, which do not have two different words for right and law, and the collective singular *ius/le droit/il diritto/el derecho/das Recht* also indicates the totality of norms (the law), both liberty and claim rights are regarded as 'subjective' rights, which only in its modern evolution does the legal system acknowledge as belonging to the individual as such.

This last feature is important in order to deny the legitimacy of group rights: the group counts only as a gathering of individuals who share certain characteristics, for example being an ethnic minority and making use of the right of such minorities to be taught also in their native tongue. Granting rights to the group as such would mean depriving members of their autonomy and making them dependent on the will and the whims of the group leaders.[11]

What is the *function* of rights? The so-called will theorists intend that they affirm the citizen's sovereignty over her/his course of action and – in case of claim rights – the duties another citizen or an institution has against her/him (s/he can request them to be implemented or waive them). The background idea is that in exercising one's own rights, one sees her/his own human dignity, a Kantian concept, respected and realised. In a consequentialist key, interest theorists believe that rights are good for furthering a person's interest in wellbeing. The two schools of thought differ in their moral philosophy, deontological and utilitarian. In both cases rights are, in legal or political arguments, 'trump cards', as Ronald Dworkin (1977) dubbed them, which can overwhelm any other consideration because of their prescriptive strength.

We have now seen that a discourse on rights implies contaminations between moral, legal and political theory; by no means, however, a transportation belt on which rights, dictated by morals, are first found and then go on to shape the law and eventually their execution by political means. The relationships between the single branches of practical philosophy is a little more complex. Rights remain a primarily legal and political concept; and the very notion of *moral rights* is questionable and should be used with caution or left in the drawer – even if this remark does not imply sharing the outright opposition to the notion of rights found in utilitarianism. For things we as moral agents believe to have ground to claim, this word 'claim' seems more appropriate than 'right'. What normative morality focuses upon are otherwise obligations.

4. Rights: universal or not?

Where do rights come from? From nature, from the culture that formulated them, from the very logic of the legal system? Could there be a legal system, or the sheer existence of the law be in place if rights, that is the dignity and autonomy of the agents, were not acknowledged? Each of these explanations can contribute something, but we can neither develop all implications nor be conclusive. Suffice it to say that early modernity's belief in natural rights has almost completely vanished, though some relationship to nature cannot be dropped outright. As mentioned above, the natural vulnerability of any human being to suffering and death, particularly when inflicted by other humans, remains an undeniable lasting fact that requires protection by the polity, if the polity is to make any sense. This holds even more so in the time of man-made lethal challenges, as we will soon see.

This explanation, granted we accept it, covers, however, only the right to life and the right not be hurt, while all other civil, political and social rights cannot be explained but as evolutionary acquisitions achieved by humankind, or parts of it, along the path it has gone down in its development – another development could have generated different rights or even done without them. Given the journey of the West through Christianity, the Renaissance, the Enlightenment, the market economy and capitalism, the role acquired in it by the individual is well understandable. Does this acknowledgement give leeway to a relativism according to which each culture has its own system of rights and principles, which are not transferable except by (colonial, imperial) imposition? The answer is no, for two reasons. First, the market economy supported by highly developed technology is now shaping life in nearly all corners of the planet; it seems therefore only consequential that the institutions born to regulate them and to shield the individual from their misuse find universal expansion, which allows for their adaptation to national circumstances – provided adaptation is not emasculation of the regulations and protections deriving from fundamental rights. It can also be adaptation to new values and requirements within the same culture, as it happened in the West with the critical reinterpretation of fundamental rights by theorists of the emancipation of women and later liberation movements. Second, the particular (Western) origin of a concept or institutions does not, as such, justify a judgement of limited, exclusively particular validity for the values and principles it entails, the merging of origin (or genesis) and validity being a historicist error. This approach sounds as parochial as rejecting any universal significance of Gandhi's notion of non-violent struggle because it originated in India. On the whole, the universal validity of fundamental rights originated in the legal and political cultures of the West should neither be systematically denied nor blindly accepted, but rather rethought in the framework of a comparison with proposals and requirements stemming from other cultures. The diversity that can now be seen on the benches of international courts should be complemented by a much more intense worldwide conversation among philosophers and legal theorists.

Lastly, we have to briefly remember how to classify human or fundamental rights, though the reader is advised to look at their list and the specifics in the legal system best known to her/him.

For the conceptualization of politics we prefer to speak of:

- civil rights, including the right to life, the rights known as *habeas corpus* and the right to due process of law, the right to privacy, freedom of movement, thought, religion and conscience, free speech, the freedom of the press and the (qualified) freedom to have property
- political rights: freedom of association, the right to assemble, the right to petition, the right of civil disobedience and, last but not least, the right to vote
- social rights: the rights to work, health, education, housing and protection in their elderly years
- among the 'fourth generation rights', whose list is open-ended and questionable, let us mention the right to a clean environment.

All these rights are – it is almost needless to say – subject to a non-discrimination clause, maintaining that they are recognised irrespective of gender, race, ethnicity, religion, sexual orientation. Civil rights all imply non-interference by the state, political rights its limited activity (mainly to convene and organise elections), social and environmental rights require an intense and costly engagement by the state, that is by the generality of tax payers, and imply – as we know – bureaucratic enmeshing by public authorities – though its degree can be limited and many people would be worse off without this interference. They are peculiar claim rights, which imply a proactive behaviour rather than abstention on the side of the state. For all these reasons they are mostly seen as not generating obligations for the state that are as binding as civil and political rights; the right to work represents a policy indication in the direction of favouring job creation strategies, but it does not mean that the public authority has to create a job for every unemployed citizen, who has rather to be protected by social security from the consequences of her/his condition. Things are, however, in the midst of change as, for example, lawsuits based on environmental rights for omitted climate policies are now becoming possible in the US with the support of the public trust doctrine, according to which environmental goods are held 'in trust' for present and future generations by the government.

This remark leads to a final point that is particularly highlighted in this author's own research: if it is true that lethal challenges endanger the life of present and future generations, the proclamation of human rights is incomplete or rather lacks foundation if they are not preceded by the recognition of the *right of humankind to survival* against man-made threats.[12] This is a meta-right rather than a right among others because it makes all other rights possible in both senses: it aims at keeping – a not-so-obvious precondition – the future bearers of rights physically alive, and it constitutes the founding act of respect for human dignity, in the absence of which all particular rights would not make morally sense. This right, born out of a new threat, should not simply be declared as a human right, but constitutionalized as a fundamental one, in a procedure that cannot be analysed here. It would thus give more strength to legislation and jurisdiction on climate change.

This last proposal should be seen as an attempt to give human rights a more basic and sturdier foundation as a meta-right rather than as an expansion of the already long list. Inflationary expansion can depreciate the existing rights, as inflation does with the existing currency. Not all legitimate or sensible aspirations or 'moral rights' fulfil the requirements for becoming rights. For moral aspirations or obligations to become rights, it takes social or political conflict, with actors willing and capable of engaging in it with a political rather than moral logic. The flood, in the last decades, of human rights argued for in philosophical debates rather than born as an object of political and cultural struggles involving their potential bearers and creating a tissue of solidarity between them, is a step away from politics into a region of uncertain solidity.

Notes

1 Only in this specific meaning can autonomy be associated with negative liberty. In a more common version autonomy is tied to self-realisation, hence to positive liberty.

2 On another, social-psychological key, a fundamental contribution to the theory of the Self was given by George Herbert Mead (1863–1931), in the framework of the so-called Chicago School.
3 What these otherwise mysterious numbers mean in quotations from Aristotle is explained at https://en.wikipedia.org/wiki/Bekker_numbering.
4 Deepening the full philosophical range of these questions should start at Rawls's concept of 'primary goods', cf. Rawls 1999, §11.
5 In this sense, the article by Bernard Williams, *The Idea of Equality* (1962) remains seminal.
6 For evidence, put 'international inequality' in a search engine and visit the websites of the World Bank and the International Monetary Fund, among others.
7 Friedrich Nietzsche (1844–1900) regarded equality as a lie concocted under the influence of Christianity by inferior people, who organise themselves in herds in order to overpower those who are naturally superior to them. Elite theories in political science (Vilfredo Pareto 1848–1923, Gaetano Mosca 1885–1941, Roberto Michels 1876–1936 and Joseph Schumpeter 1883–1950) have little or nothing in common with this attitude.
8 For example, in countries where most universities are funded by the state, the seemingly egalitarian free tuition favours students from affluent families, who could easily come up for it, while making all tax payers, even the less well-off, pay for the education of both well-situated and low-income students.
9 This is the core view Benjamin Constant advanced in his famous speech (1819) *De la liberté des Anciens comparée à celle des Modernes/ The Liberty of the Ancients Compared with That of the Moderns.*
10 The pre-history of this document goes back to the Magna Carta of 1215 and the English Bill of Rights of 1689.
11 Whether or not related to the issue of group rights, the so-called political correctness – particularly as developed in some American universities – appears to be a distortion or even a caricature of human rights protection.
12 See Cerutti 2015, in which the constitutional questions mentioned below are also discussed. It is clear that humankind, the community of present and future human beings characterised by being threatened by lethal challenges as seen in Chapter 7, has nothing to do with the notion of a particular, self-confining group, whose rights I have denied above.

References

Aristotle (350 BCE) *Nicomachean Ethics*, ebook available at http://classics.mit.edu/Aristotle/nicomachaen.html

Cerutti, Furio (2015) *Survival – Humankind's First Fundamental Right*, in 'Constellations', 22(1), March, 59–67.

Constant, Benjamin (1819) *De la liberté des Anciens comparée à celle des Modernes/ The Liberty of the Ancients Compared with that of the Moderns*, e-book available at http://oll.libertyfund.org/titles/constant-the-liberty-of-ancients-compared-with-that-of-moderns- 1819

Dworkin, Ronald (1977) *Taking Rights Seriously*, Cambridge: Harvard University Press.

Dworkin, Ronald (2002) *Sovereign Virtue: The Theory and Practice of Equality*, Cambridge: Harvard University Press.

Habermas, Jürgen (1981) *Theorie des kommunikativen Handelns/ Theory of Communicative Action*, Boston: Beacon Press, 1984–1987.

Habermas, Jürgen (1985) *Der philosophische Diskurs der Moderne/ The Philosophical Discourse of Modernity*, Cambridge: The MIT Press, 1987.

Hegel, Georg Wilhelm Friedrich (1807) *Phänomenologie des Geistes/ Phenomenology of Spirit*, translated by A.V. Miller, Oxford: Oxford University Press, 1977.

Hegel, Georg Wilhelm Friedrich (1821) *Grundlinien der Philosophie des Rechts/Elements of the Philosophy of Right*, available at www.marxists.org/reference/archive/hegel/works/pr/philosophy-of-right.pdf (*Recht* includes both law and right).
Kant, Immanuel (1785) *Grundlegung der Metaphysik der Sitten/Groundwork for the Metaphysic of Morals*, available at www.earlymoderntexts.com/assets/pdfs/kant1785.pdf
Marx, Karl (1875) *Critique of the Gotha Programme*, e-book available at www.marxists.org/archive/marx/works/1875/gotha/ch01.htm
Rawls, John (1999) *A Theory of Justice*, revised edition, Cambridge: Harvard University Press.
Sen, Amartya (1999) *Development as Freedom*. Oxford: Oxford University Press.
Taylor, Charles (1989) *Sources of the Self*, Cambridge: Harvard University Press.
Williams, Bernard (1962) *The Idea of Equality*, in *Problems of the Self*, Cambridge: Cambridge University Press, 1973, 230–249.

Further readings

Along with the chapters on liberty (by Mario Ricciardi, 149–160) and equality (by Ian Carter, 161–170) in Besussi, Antonella, ed. (2012) *A Companion to Political Philosophy*, Farnham: Ashgate, a critical contribution to the two concepts of liberty is:

Carter, Ian (2012) *Positive and Negative Liberty*, in *Stanford Encyclopedia of Philosophy*, 2003, available at http://plato.stanford.edu. Updated, 2007, 2012.

9
JUSTICE AND SOLIDARITY

The two categories we are dealing with in this chapter are much less intertwined than liberty and equality in the previous chapter. Justice is usually seen as the queen (*Iustitia* in Latin) of normative political philosophy and is not expected to have a good neighbouring relationship with solidarity. Solidarity may stand up as a critic, if not an opponent, of justice: the 'and' between the two terms is sometimes replaced with 'vs.' In mainstream textbooks of political philosophy, solidarity has no business, whereas justice reigns like emperor Charles V (1500–1558) of the Holy Roman Empire, on whose lands, which included the bi-continental Spanish Empire, 'the sun never set'.[1]

The centrality of justice is partly due to its position as a meta-category. We can speak of liberty, equality and solidarity in descriptive terms by saying that a country has the highest degree of freedom, a society has a low degree of equality, or the population of a town shows a remarkable degree of internal solidarity. This leaves open to choice and debate whether or not we appreciate freedom in full measure or think it should be subjected to conditions, or believe that a higher level of equality would compromise the economic efficiency of a country. On the contrary, if we say that a society or regime or institution is just, we cannot but issue an axiological statement that is attributing a certain moral or political value to it according to our value system. Moreover, the axiological charge of statements of justice easily translates into prescription: what is recognised as just, must be enacted by agents. The *predicate just/unjust* can never be descriptive, as it is, by its nature, evaluative. What we, according to our particular value system, recognise as just or unjust remains to be seen: for racists it is just to exclude people with another skin colour from societal life and government; for other people this is utterly unjust and despicable. Justice is not by itself a magic word that guarantees universal respect and recognition.

In §1 a grid of possible meanings of justice is offered, while in §2 we look into the most popular example of distributive justice together with its most refined theorist, John Rawls, as well as some of his critics. What solidarity means and why it is worth being taken seriously is explained in §3.

1. Versions of justice

In the history of Western political philosophy, justice started her brilliant career in Plato's *Republic*, in which δικαιοσύνη/*dikaiosune*[2] is argued by Socrates not to be 'what is useful to the strongest' (Plato BCE 380, Book 2, 338c), as the Sophist Trasimachos in his scepticism or nihilism would have had it, but rather to consist of 'giving to each what is owed to him'. This very same principle 'unicuique suum tribuere' will be crucial in Roman law, in particular as highlighted by the jurist Ulpian (AD 170–228), along with the other principle 'naeminem laedere'/do not inflict harm on anyone. Starting with Plato, s/he who raises the question of justice looks at the existing power structure with critical eyes and asks it to justify itself with regard to criteria that are neither self-centred nor utilitarian or opportunistic – yet modern utilitarianism is itself a theory of justice having the wellbeing of the greatest possible numbers of persons as target. Questioning power in the name of justice (but also liberty or equality or solidarity) means putting its legitimacy to the test, as we anticipated in Chapter 2, though we cannot here unfold in its entirety the connection between political legitimacy and normative categories.

Now, a first criterion useful to put order to the many versions of justice is to distinguish *substantive* from *procedural* versions. The former understand justice as the conformity of our acts, laws, political regimes to substantive values such as equality in one of its several meanings or to those enshrined in a cosmic order or belonging to what we regard as natural order – as is the case with natural law theories. In common parlance, particularly in Europe, 'just' is often by default merged with 'equal' or 'egalitarian'.

Procedural versions avoid the identification with substantive, hence controversial and evolving values, and strive for a higher degree of generality by seeing justice realised in the application of a rule of behaviour that is applicable to all concrete cases. The drawback with these versions lies in the often empty abstractness and fungibility of some formulas such as *unicuique suum*, which leaves open which rule (and which value system) should be followed in order to identify what is owed to each. This found a macabre confirmation in the German version of this principle *Jedem das Seine* being used by the Nazis as a menacing maxim engraved on the iron gate of the Buchenwald death camp.

A different story regards another procedural principle we have already met back in Chapter 7 where we discussed our normative attitude towards global/lethal challenges: the Golden Rule. In the Old Testament this principle is formulated negatively 'and what you hate, do not do to any one' (Tobit 4:15); from the Gospels let us choose the positive formulation given in Luke 6:31 'and as you wish that men would do to you, do so to them'. The transcultural nature of this rule is proven by its likely origin in India and its presence in Confucianism; its interpretations range between *do ut des* reciprocity (a favour for a favour, or the other way around: do not excite others to perform tit-for-tat) and universal respect for every person's dignity.

In this second reading, it comes closer to Kant's categorical imperative in its second formulation, as quoted in the previous chapter (cf. Kant 1785, 36). Let us note that, properly understood, these principles regard relations between individual persons, not communities or polities. It is therefore an unduly simplification to apply them directly to political relationships, except we are determined to deny any autonomy to politics and want it to be – as Kant wanted – an application of moral laws to a field whose nature can however be deemed to be very different from morality.

Let us now look at another classification of justice: *commutative/retributive* and *distributive*. The first elements of this distinction were laid down by Aristotle in Book V of *Nicomachean Ethics*. *Commutative justice* tells us to burden people (with a fine, or a prison term) in a way proportional to their wrongdoing; or to compensate them for the harm they suffered or the commendable acts they performed in a measure that matches their loss or performance. This type of justice is aimed at regulating the exchange between evils or goods. As such, it does not entail an entire scheme of political cooperation for society, but addresses primarily two cases of such an exchange: civil and criminal justice (tort law and penal law) and the wage system. In the first case we speak of retributive justice if the justice system focuses on the retribution for the wrong done that can be claimed by both victims and the state. It is, however, known that a justice system based only or primarily on retribution fills prisons to the utter limit, as in the USA since the mid 1990s, but is unlikely to lead to a permanent crime reduction; re-education – or rehabilitative justice – as the primary aim of the sentence works better.

As to the wage system, the point rather regards the capitalist system as presumably the cause of an unjust distribution of the goods produced by social cooperation, or exploitation. This used to be, and still is, a widespread feeling, but its classical formulation was given some 150 years ago by Karl Marx (1867) in the first book of *Das Kapital*, Chapter 4, §3. What appears to be a fair exchange between the wage-labourers offering their labour-power and the capitalist rewarding them with an amount of money corresponding to what the labourers and their family need to survive is only illusion, because, in fact, the capitalist lets the workforce toil for a much longer time and makes a profit out of this. In the sphere of production, in the factory, the illusion of a fair exchange born in the sphere of circulation on the job market vanishes. This classical explanation, meanwhile abandoned by most economists, was presented by Marx as a further development within the labour theory of value initiated by Adam Smith (1723–1790) and David Ricardo (1772–1823). It found an extension in Arghiri Emmanuel's (1911–2001) theory of the *unequal exchange* between developed and developing countries in the capitalist world economy. The political outcome of these theories of social and international injustice were revolutionary and anti-imperialistic movements.

2. Distributive justice

Distributive justice regards the rules of how to organise the distribution of material and immaterial goods to actors (persons, classes, countries) seen as members of a group of a given dimension (citizens of a country, countries of the world). Plain examples of the rules are distribution proportional to the personal merits in meritocracy, to the hours worked on the workplace, to everybody's needs and/or skills in an ideal society. Some of these topics are known to us from our reflections on equality, but now the corresponding models come provisioned explicitly with the predicate 'just'.

From Plato onwards philosophers have theorised several models of polity based on increasingly elaborate conceptions of justice. The most sophisticated and, at the same time, the most interested in a *political* model of justice, 'the first virtue of social institutions' (Rawls 1999a, 3), remains John Rawls's theory of justice as developed in 1971 (now Rawls 1999a, 1993 and 1999b). The purpose of Rawls's research is how to ideally set up a polity or 'well-ordered society' whose institutions are based on justice as fairness; he understands this model of a constitutional democracy to be an alternative to utilitarianism, which is, in his view, unfit to secure the basis of such a regime because it gives the 'calculus of social interests' (Rawls 1999a, 4) priority over the liberties of equal citizenship. While rerunning the basics of the contractarian tradition, from Locke to Rousseau and most importantly to Kant, Rawls designs an 'original position' in which citizens find out what the best principles of a just society are expected to look like. In doing so, their impartiality is assured by a 'veil of ignorance' that prevents them from knowing their social status, their possession of natural assets and abilities, the conception of the good they may adhere to, the generation of which they are a part (Rawls 1999a, 118–123). They are thus enabled to determine the best principles of society removed from particular interests and ideologies they would otherwise tend to let prevail. The outcome consists of the principle of greatest equal liberty for all and of a second principle, called the difference principle; they are both developments of a more general conception of justice:

> All social values – liberty and opportunity, income and wealth, and the social bases of self respect – are to be distributed equally unless an unequal distribution of any, or all, of these values is to everybody's advantage.
> (Rawls 1999a, 54)

The difference principle is contained in the qualification 'unless . . .' and is further specified in §46 of *A Theory of Justice* in the sense that social and economic inequalities are to be arranged so that they 'are to the greatest benefit of the least advantaged' (Rawls 1999a, 266). This can, for example, justify fiscal policies that redistribute income in favour of the less advantaged layers of society, but also a rejection of radical egalitarianism, which would cancel the stimuli given to the efficiency of national economy by individual aspirations to higher income, to be attained by business creation and higher productivity. In Rawls's order of priority, efficiency ranks, in any case, after equal liberty and welfare. The priority given to a 'system of equal basic liberties compatible with a similar system of liberty for all' (from the First principle as formulated in §46) explains why Rawls's conception has been seen as the peak of (left-leaning) liberalism in the American sense of the word. In *Political Liberalism* (1993) Rawls corrected his own previous view of justice based on liberalism as a 'comprehensive doctrine' (including a theory of moral values and metaphysics) and focused on the political character of democratic liberalism. This stance is deemed to facilitate reaching an 'overlapping consensus' (another key item in Rawls's vocabulary) among different conceptions of justice, provided the debate is regulated by 'public reason', which acknowledges only rules that can be justified in front of those to whom the rules apply; for example, civic rules deriving from a particular religion are not of this sort, since among the citizens to whom they are expected to apply some or many are no believers and are not ready to accept religious justifications of those rules.

Of the innumerable debates ignited by Rawls's philosophy since 1971 I shall name only a few here: first the dissent about international justice that unfolded within his own followers; then, in the last part of the section, follows a brief account of the critique launched by what we could dub the opposition (Nozick's libertarianism, communitarianism, Derrida). Only later on we will deal with the existential question as to how far general normative theory or 'ideal theory' makes sense in political philosophy.

Rawls conceives of international society as a society of peoples (*scil*. countries), not free and equal individuals; remaining far away of any cosmopolitan egalitarianism, he sees for wealthier countries only a duty of 'assistance' to 'burdened' societies, helping them attain decent and stable domestic institutions that respect human rights; this does not include a duty to narrow the gap between rich and poor. This is, with various arguments, criticised by cosmopolitan theorists of justice such as Charles Beitz (2000) and Thomas Pogge (2001), and this discussion has given birth to a current of studies and suggestions called 'global justice' that issues and assesses policy proposals concerning problems such as poverty, the reduction of illiteracy, the promotion of gender equality, a better food production and distribution, but also issues of international criminal justice, particularly after the creation of the International Criminal Court. Contrary to this tendency, David Miller (2000) has argued that, as nation states are ethical communities, we owe to our fellow-nationals duties that are not only different from, but also more extensive than, the duties we owe to human beings as such.

My thoughts in Chapter 7 on how to treat with respect and fairness the people of the far future may seem to come closer to this current, except that they differ from 'global justice' for two reasons: first, my proposal results from a political philosophy of man-made lethal challenges, not from elaborating on general normative principles. Second, the time universalism I propose finds correspondence neither in Rawls's principle of the 'just savings' for future generations nor in the global justice literature, focused as it is almost exclusively on space universalism. A further difference lies in the political (as different from moral) reflection that reducing inequality and promoting retributive justice for human rights violations worldwide is not only a normative issue of justice, but also an issue of stability and peace. Egalitarian steps, for example, allowing more and more immigration from less wealthy countries because all human beings have a right to what Rawls dubs primary goods, cannot be undertaken simply out of their rightness, but must find the consent of the hosting populations, which cannot be expected to flow from discourses of charity or justice, but as the result of a well-designed political process, in which the interests of both guests and hosts are both taken into consideration. Large-scale and efficient development aid delivered in the emigration countries (side-stepping if necessary their rogue regimes) can prevent mass emigration, which is unavoidably tied to human suffering. In any case, the category of solidarity fits these problems better than that of justice, as we shall see.

★ ★ ★

Opposition to Rawls's theory of justice came up vigorously three years after its publication with Nozick's minarchism or theory of the *minimal state* (Nozick 1974), in which freedom, rather than distributive justice, is the leading principle and 'end-state theories', so-called because the final distribution is normatively fixed once and for all, are rejected. Nozick favours a historical theory of distribution, which respects property as it was originally distributed or later acquired, though a rectification procedure for past injustices is also foreseen. In his utopia people who disagree with the state of affairs in their own society can leave and found another one. In this extreme case of ideal theory (see below), the relationship between liberty and equality is brought back to the radical opposition that marked the original tension between liberalism and democracy.

A more systemic and less otherworldly opposition to the theory of justice and liberalism altogether is represented by *communitarianism*, a wide field including philosophers of quite diverse orientation such as: Alisdair MacIntyre (1981), Michael Sandel (1982),[3] Charles Taylor (1989), Michael Walzer (1983). The landscape here is totally different: not the isolated, atomized, unencumbered individuals of liberalism, who in this communitarian description are all driven by self-interest, but the community with its traditions and customs. In it alone can individuals achieve a sense of their associate existence in a mindset that is guided by the search for meaningful ends rather than the enacting of abstract rights. The good is more important and a better motivating force than the right, as the communitarians believe in a shift backwards from a deontological to a teleological posture.[4]

In the communitarian rejection of liberal individualism themes come up which were all anticipated in Hegel's critique of Kant's moral philosophy; this was sort of inevitable, since Rawls himself presents his theory as a rerunning of Kant undertaken after (and against) the utilitarian wave that went through (Anglo-American) thought in the last two centuries. Kant reborn could not but evoke a renewed Hegelian wave, though communitarians lack Hegel's view on world history. They do rather echo the anti-liberal and anti-capitalist, in a word anti-modern, stance of Romanticism and recall to mind the conception of community/*Gemeinschaft* examined in Chapter 4. Though not without influence on the philosophical debate in Europe, communitarianism has been almost exclusively an American phenomenon, and the 'community' it intends can only be fully understood by keeping in mind American social history and the particular aura this word is surrounded with in American political and religious language.

A critical comment on the liberal notion of justice has been formulated in France by Jacques Derrida (1930–2004), the philosopher of the now popular deconstructionism. He has pointed out the amount of force and willful decision that lies at the origin of whatever system of justice, which must therefore remain self-contradictory and impossible; his philosophy of democracy is, rather, centred on the notion of hospitality, along with the tension between the unconditional and the conditional versions of it.

3. Solidarity

We are now turning to a category that enjoys little recognition in political philosophy and is subject to misunderstanding, partly because of its binary status, analytical and normative. Its analytical version is best known through the work of Émile Durkheim (1858–1917), who along with Max Weber is regarded as the (French) founder of sociology. For him, solidarity is the force that keeps human beings together in society and consists of two sub-types corresponding to different structures of society. In traditional societies, mechanical solidarity prevails, often enforced by punitive law and violence, among individuals that are very similar to each other and live in communities with a low degree of integration, but strong common values. Organic solidarity develops in modern society, in which the division of labour creates differentiation and interdependency among individuals.

Durkheim's solidarity concept remains objectivistic, inasmuch as it focuses upon the driving forces, resulting from the evolutionary stage of society, that keep it together; while we are rather interested in solidarity as a piece of the subjective side of politics (solidarity felt as such is a layer of political identity). We are better served by the definition found in the Oxford Dictionaries:[5]

> Unity or agreement of feeling or action, especially among individuals with a common interest; mutual support within a group.

This wording rightly moves the focus to a 'feeling', though in the philosophical language we cannot say solidarity to be just an emotion. Also, this definition expresses a phenomenology of solidarity, but makes no hint at its normative element: the solidarity we are talking about here, taking place in an 'organic' Durkheimian context, brings together feelings and a sense of obligation, though this obligation does not result from a higher principle, but is rather felt and enlivened as a known condition of the group's (in our case, the polity's) survival, while the individual can only find in group support and meaning for one's own life. This explains my suggestion to understand *solidarity as a self-imposed obligation to and a feeling of mutual support and sympathy between equals*. Self-imposed out of the knowledge that without mutual support of its members the polity is likely to dissolve, while none of the other normative categories can nourish the cohesion it needs to survive and perhaps flourish – cohesion is necessary also in order to let liberty, equality and justice develop. Sympathy, which is here introduced without a chance to discuss its relationship to David Hume's (1711–1776) conception of it, is the moral sentiment accompanying the readiness to mutual support, and means the ability to put oneself in somebody's else shoes, sharing imaginatively her/his pains and problems.

'Between equals' requires a more differentiated explanation. The equality meant here is not matter-of-fact, but normative: I lend my support to others because I recognise them as equal in rights and dignity with myself, even if they are presently unequal in the enjoyment of freedom and life chances. This is what distinguishes solidarity, which is horizontal, from charity and philanthropy, which rather evoke verticality. Also, solidarity as the fundamental category we are talking about cannot be downsized to its meanings in social aid groups or in Catholic social thought. Lastly and consequently, solidarity is seen here as a political virtue to be implemented by the state, not merely as a relationship between individuals.

Another question regards how to determine the perimeter of the equals: equal in the local community, in the region or province, in the nation, in a civilisation, or among humankind? To date, the current definitions of solidarity have pointed at the (however defined) particular group as the sphere within which solidarity can sensibly be expected to develop. This is well-known from its social history in the West: the Freemasons in the Enlightenment, the clubs of the French revolutionaries (before they started to send each other to the guillotine), the movements and later the parties of the working class, including their pledge to the international solidarity of the proletarians, who, however, could not but massacre each other in the trenches of the Great War. Yet can there be, contrary to this factual limitation, a solidarity extended to the *whole of humankind*, as it has been suggested over time by humanists, pacifists and religious leaders? With an eye towards religious cleavages and the upsurge of nations, this suggestion or appeal was, with good reason, regarded as politically ineffective. Things are now changing, as we have learned in Chapter 7: with respect to its chances to survive global and lethal threats, and only in this respect, humankind is becoming the dimension in which men and women can experience solidarity with each other and the fellow humans of future generations.[6] This has normative relevance, but also – as explained above – an analytical profile: without assuming that an initial form of the solidarity of humankind is at work, especially with regard to future humanity, it is difficult to explain the progress made, for example, by a more reasonable climate policy at both a national and international level. Self-interest or security considerations do not explain everything that is going on in politics, as we shall see in the Epilogue.

The relevance I am giving to solidarity comes from, among other things, the puzzlement about the disappearance of its predecessor *fraternité* from the glorious triad 'liberté égalité fraternité' of the 'ideas of '89' (*scil.* 1789) – the brilliant career of the two first partners notwithstanding. It looks like solidarity had been dismissed or pushed to the sidelines due to three adverse and illusionary beliefs:

A. Social and political cohesion is not a political issue, but a side effect of market relationships.
B. Abstract deontological guidelines provided by ethics such as justice create enough of political unity.
C. Cohesion is important, but it is entirely provided by living together in the nation.

Justice and solidarity **183**

FIGURE 9.1 In this French etching of 1793 *fraternité*, the predecessor of solidarity, is embedded within other political values of the Republic and dramatically highlighted by the pledge of preferring otherwise to die.

The disruptive effects of the market (A) on the social fabric when it is not shaped by rules chosen by political decision have showed up time and again in early and then again in postwar capitalism. The 2008 financial crisis was the definitive proof of unchained neoliberalism's failure in making the economy work to the general benefit and to preserve the society in good health, instead of preaching a limitless possessive individualism. The consequences for political cohesion, such as populism and the perversion of direct democracy have been also described above in

Chapter 5. Justice theory (B) does not seem to be on its way to influencing politics as the 'ideas of '89' once did and remains an academic business (more on ideal theory in the next chapter). The cohesion furnished by nations (C) and their degeneration into nationalism has largely vanished after 1945, all attempts (post-Soviet and post-Yugoslavia politics in the 1990s, Euroscepticism paired with national pride in EU-member states, Arab nationalism) to reinstate it could not but fail and have sometimes shown poisonous side effects.

It is against this backdrop that solidarity needs to be rethought as both a normative category (from which duties of solidarity derive for policy-making actors) and a sense of belonging together that survives any defensive closing of the borders, both geographic and mental. Since solidarity is a word coming up more and more with regard to migrants, it is perhaps useful to be explicit on this matter: solidarity does not mean admitting all migrants for whatever reason they migrate from all possible corners, but taking care of them wherever they are, instead of leaving them in the hands of traffickers or violent governments. On the other hand, reinstating solidarity as a self-imposed obligation is not a normative indication that can go without a measure of political wisdom, for at least two reasons. First, solidaristic or welfare policies – if not well-carved and provisioned with safety mechanisms – can be easily misused by people who end up using them as a permanent instead of a temporary source of outcome, and acting as a lobby of welfare receivers. Second, the difficulties of states overburdened by tasks and not receiving enough tax money are likely to last for an entire epoch until a new wave of (sustainable) growth takes effect or the economy is reformed in a more efficient and more just way – a model for this combination is, however, not in sight.

In the light of these two considerations, a problem that comes up again is our stance towards future generations, this time however not in the framework of lethal problems affecting people of the far future. Though support cannot be mutual between generations if their life-spans do not partially overlap,[7] here too time universalism applies: there is no reason why future generations should not deserve our solidarity like our contemporaries, particularly with reference to public debt and the pension system. Also, generous solidarity towards contemporaries is wrong if it compromises or spoils in advance the financial premises of similar policies to be implemented in 50 or 75 years. Let us also remark that in countries with declining birth rate, two aspects of solidarity policies – the acceptance and integration of migrants and the care for future generations – converge; the first can reveal itself to be instrumental in keeping the social security system afloat to the benefit of the posterity.

Finally, my reintroduction of solidarity as a self-standing category in the family of normative concepts accompanying politics is due to the intention to complement this family with a neglected member, by no means to counterpose it to the other, more celebrated partners. Rather than rejecting liberal political thinking altogether, as communitarians do, solidarity as a category in the company of the three others appears to be able to give answers to the questions liberalism leaves open with regard to social and political cohesion as well as the interconnectedness of individuals, who remain the fundamental agents.

How liberty and equality, justice and solidarity can interplay is not up to a textbook to determine, but is rather left to citizens, polities and thinkers reflecting and acting within specific configurations of problems and conditions. The tools that may be useful to them have been presented in the last two chapters, while in the next one suggestions and warnings as to how to use those tools will follow.

Notes

1 Titles of books and articles are nowadays flooded with 'justice', added as a sort of universal operator (as they say in logic) to the most various topics, both in general and applied political philosophy of normative obedience. In Cerutti (2016) this approach is criticised with specific reference to climate ethics as the wrong way to develop a political philosophy of climate change.
2 This word means both 'justice' and 'righteousness'. As with other words relevant to political philosophy, the semantic of justice is not homogeneous across languages.
3 Sandel is also the author of the famous online course (MOOC) *Justice*, available on the Harvard-MIT edx.platform at http://www.justiceharvard.org/.
4 For this terminology see the next chapter, §1.
5 www.oxforddictionaries.com/definition/english/solidarity
6 With regard to them, I have used in Chapter 7 the notion of empathy, which is related to sympathy, though being by no means its namesake.
7 This is true for support, but not in the same measure for sympathy: if we cannot know if our posterity will look back upon us with sympathy, we can, nonetheless, act in a way that we can reasonably expect it will induce them to do so.

References

Aristotle, Ἠθικὰ Νικομάχεια/*Nicomachean Ethics*, e-book available at http://classics.mit.edu/Aristotle/nicomachaen.html
Beitz, Charles (2000) *Rawls's Law of Peoples*, in 'Ethics', July, 669–696.
Cerutti, Furio (2016) *Climate Ethics and the Failures of 'Normative Political Philosophy'*, in 'Philosophy and Social Criticism', 42(7), 707–726.
The English Standard Version Bible, e-book available at: http://biblehub.com
Kant, Immanuel (1785) *Grundlegung der Metaphysik der Sitten/Grounding for the Metaphysics of Morals*, Cambridge: Hackett, 1993.
MacIntyre, Alasdair (1981) *After Virtue*, Notre Dame: University of Notre Dame Press.
Marx, Karl (1867) *Das Kapital/Capital*, Book I, e-book available at www.marxists.org/archive/marx/works/download/epub/
Miller, David (2000) *Citizenship and National Identity*, Cambridge: Polity Press.
Nozick, Robert (1974) *Anarchy, State, and Utopia*, New York: Basic Books.
The Oxford Dictionaries, available at www.oxforddictionaries.com/definition/english/
Plato (380 BCE) Πολιτεία/*The Republic*, Book 2, available at http://classics.mit.edu/Plato/republic.3.ii.html
Pogge, Thomas (2001) *Priorities of Global Justice*, in *Global Justice*, Oxford: Blackwell, 6–23.
Rawls, John (1993) *Political Liberalism*, New York: Columbia University Press.
Rawls, John (1999a) *A Theory of Justice*, revised edition, Cambridge: Harvard University Press.
Rawls, John (1999b) *The Law of People*, Cambridge: Harvard University Press.
Sandel, Michael (1982) *Liberalism and the Limits of Justice*, Cambridge: Cambridge University Press.

Taylor, Charles (1989) *Sources of the Self: The Making of the Modern Identity*, New York: Harvard University Press.
Walzer, Michael (1983) *Spheres of Justice*, New York: Basic Books.

Further readings

Reading Rawls:

Freeman, Samuel (2002) *The Cambridge Companion to Rawls*, Cambridge: Cambridge University Press.
Mandle, John and David A. Reidy, eds. (2014) *A Companion to Rawls*, Oxford: Wiley Blackwell.

Materials on solidarity:

Bayertz, Kurt, ed. (1999) *Solidarity*, Dordrecht: Kluwer Academic Publishers.
Boyd, Scott and Mary Ann Walter (2014) *Cultural Difference and Social Solidarity: Solidarities and Social Function*, Newcastle upon Tyne: Cambridge Scholars Publishing.

10
ETHICS, PHILOSOPHY AND POLITICS

In this conclusive chapter of Part IV, we want to explore questions and perspectives that have come up in previous chapters but have not yet been specifically addressed. First comes what, since the outset of modernity, has been the thorny relationship between morality and politics, along with the issue of political realism (§1). The question of the ethics that should guide politicians is next (§2). Only partially overlapping with this complex is the question now known as the relationship of ideal and non-ideal theory, which touches once again upon the status and definition of political philosophy (§3). The so-called Critical Theory presents an arrangement of philosophy, ethics and politics that is different in more than one respect from what we have seen thus far; this is why we are going to briefly deal with it in §4.

1. Ethics and politics

Politicians and political theorists, along with clergymen and essayists, do often evoke this relationship, but mostly leave its first pole fuzzy in appearance, which is why we need first a short interlude in order to bring some order to the field. In the following, I shall restrict the use of the common wording 'ethics and politics' and replace the first term with 'morality', the attitude based on the moral point of view, that is the attitude to act on principles, to reject egoism, to regard what is good for other people as having equal dignity with what is good for me.[1] Whatever the specific attitude and doctrine, morality is clearly opposed to a self-centred stance, aimed at an opportunistic evaluation of what is best in the given circumstances for oneself or one's own community. This stance has sometimes been called *prudence*, in a last twist to the history (already mentioned in Chapter 1) of this word, far removed from Aristotle's original understanding of φρόνησις/phronesis.

Moral theories, giving shape and justification to human acting, can treat the question of 'what is right?' (normative theories, assessing the morality of single acts or principles/rules of acting) or the very different problem of 'how to achieve the (moral) good'. Normative theories can be deontological, assessing the rightness of acts from the point of view of principles allowing or prohibiting certain acts, such: as killing or lying; but they can also look at our acts from the point of view of their consequences (consequentialist theories). Kant's morality is the paramount case of deontologism,[2] the categorical imperative in its two formulas, its typical expressions. He who speaks of ethics (or morality) and politics with little philosophical differentiation usually intends 'deontological ethics and politics' – while a decent pluralism would require the examination of how other types of morality relate to politics. With utilitarianism, the main version of consequentialism and, since Jeremy Bentham (1748–1832), a major current in the Anglo-Saxon cultures, the main political difficulty is the impossibility to lay a foundation for human rights, sidelined by the principle that right is what best contributes to the happiness or wellbeing (philosophical welfarism) of the greatest number of peoples. A very different relationship to politics can be found in the theories of the good, also called teleological because they assess our contribution to the good according to the overall balance of our moral life as seen from its end, the achievement, to put it with Aristotle, of the 'good life'. Moral teleologism tends to converge with political communitarianism, but this is not a stringent link.

Back to the relationship of politics to morality in its, as it were, default version: deontologism. We have already reported Kant's indication to re-establish harmony between the two by bringing politics back again under the auspices of morality or rather of the law as descending from Reason's moral commands. This is a monistic solution that recognises only one principle as justified, but another monism with a different content can lead to the opposite conclusion: in Hobbes's conception of human coexistence within the state, there is no room left for an individual morality that may differ from or contradict the laws established by the *recta ratio*/right reason that underpins the Leviathanic commonwealth, the only source of protection for individuals.

Hobbes represents one leading position in the wide field of *political realism*. In philosophical language, heeding a very 'realistic' view on all things politic – as it sounds in ordinary language – is only a marginal component of realism in the political sense. Essential to this are two tenets:

1. Politics can be better understood and better managed if taken according to the laws and patterns its real course offers to our observation. Consequently, politics cannot be ruled by morality in either of its versions.
2. Crucial to any politics, domestic as well as foreign, is humankind's search for security and protection, which makes its main provider, the state, the central actor. In international politics, which is played between separate units, the states, power relationships matter first, and the forefather of realism, Thucydides, explains the outbreak of the Peloponnesian war with the fear caused to the Spartans by the increase in Athens' territorial and military strength (Thucydides BCE 404, Book I, XXIII, 6).[3]

Within these coordinates variations have come up. The most significant is Machiavelli's understanding of politics as being guided by principles no less imperative than morality is; but principles of different nature and enshrined in the Roman motto *salus reipublicae suprema lex esto* /the safety of the commonwealth has to be the ultimate law. The good of the commonwealth or country, its liberty and greatness, is seen as a universal good, no less so than the goods upheld by individual morality, and likewise worthy of personal sacrifice including that of one's own life – as witnessed by many examples from antiquity, first of all Pericles's obituary for the fallen Athenian soldiers quoted in Chapter 5.[4] It would indeed be good, Machiavelli (1532) concedes, if a prince were to keep faith under any circumstance; but since men are evil (an anthropological statement) and do not act in this way, he who does not break faith would go down whenever keeping it would give him a disadvantage, yes, lead him to ruin – the 'sexist' language is in the original, though the former Florentine Secretary of state considers ruling princesses as well (Machiavelli 1532, Chapter 18).

This position confers politics a universalistic normative status not inferior to that of (deontological) morality and marks the birth of politics as an *autonomous sphere of action* – and, moreover, of political philosophy as not being a branch of moral thought. This 'Machiavellian moment' became crucial for the 'republican' current in modern political thought.[5] But the legitimacy deficit of nation states after 1945, the universalism of worldwide human rights and the emergence of global challenges have largely modified the terrain on which classical republicanism flourished, so that the relaunch of it, recently attempted, seems to underrate the characteristics of our post-modern (in the sense defined in Chapter 7) time.

Another strain, among the attempts at recombining politics and morality, was the tradition of the 'reason of state', which took its name from the Jesuit Giovanni Botero's work (Botero 1589). It pledges, dissimilarly and in opposition to Machiavelli, to respect the canons of morality, but with the exceptions made necessary in order to preserve the state. This tradition has long since extinguished in philosophy, but not at all in real politics, given the fact that, especially but not only in dictatorships, rulers have resorted to that same 'reason' in order to justify the brutal use of force. The issue of lying and deception in politics seems to belong to the question of what is morally allowed or prohibited, but does rather refer to a political normativity concerned with the health of the polity rather than to individual morality.[6]

Still on the side that disentangles politics from morals, but on a higher philosophical level, we find Hegel's condemnation of the formal and abstract character of Kantian morality along with his celebration of the state as the dimension in which the substantial destiny of peoples and individuals is shaped in epochs whose succession represents the ascent of the Spirit (*Geist*) to full self-awareness and self-realisation (Hegel 1821). On this path, abstract morality of the Kantian type remains on a stair lower than the full *Sittlichkeit* (concrete ethical sphere) of the state in which the life of the individuals is comprised. Hegel has been much criticized, first by Marx because of his identification with Prussia's oppressive and bureaucratic state, later by Karl Popper, who saw in him a precursor of totalitarianism and an enemy of the 'open society' along with Plato and Marx (Popper 1945). Nonetheless, his philosophy of individual, state and society – as it emerges also from the *Phenomenology of Spirit* (1807), and once it is read disregarding its systematic ambition – remains a rich, indispensable contribution to the understanding of modern politics; though not in the sense still present today among some German philosophers, who still believe – as it was the case 200 or 100 years ago – the fundamental choice political philosophy is confronted with in our days to be the same choice between Kant and Hegel.

2. Which ethics for politicians?

The mapping of the positions regarding politics and ethics ends with a bipolar formula that, though a hundred years old, still preserves its grasp on the matter we are discussing and has not lost popularity in political and media debate. This is Max Weber's idea that, in order to prove one person's *vocation to politics*, s/he has to think and act according to two ethical principles that are in principle opposed to each other and must nonetheless both be practised in a balance.[7] One is called by Weber 'ethics of conviction' (Weber 1919a), that is the attitude to act on principles and ideologies, anchored in one's own deep beliefs, and regardless of the practical consequences; this was a much practised orientation in 1919, after the Great War, the Russian Revolution and the attempted revolutions and coups in the rest of Europe, but has never ceased to move masses and individuals up to our time and will probably not cease to do so in the future. The 'ethics of responsibility', on the contrary, directs us towards actions whose consequences we can stand up to, aware as we are that we cannot assume other humans are by nature as good as to do the best of our own intentions and acts. The underlying problem for both ethical orientations is that their own terrain, politics, is where even the best intentions are confronted with the inevitable, basic component of any politics: violence. This essential presence of violence lets Weber, himself a realist, acknowledge that politics is an ethically sensible business, which causes suffering and death – as we saw in Excursus 2. Against this background the danger for those following the ethics of conviction is thoughtless agitation and fanaticism, that is the proclamation of splendid, but unattainable ends, followed by the inability to stand up to one's own responsibility, because the failure with its costs is entirely burdened on others' shoulders (by evoking the evil allegedly essential to humankind, or the unreasonableness of fellow citizens). On the other hand, an orientation led exclusively by a sense of responsibility can lead to a political behaviour devoid of ideas and ideals, ending up in cynicism, barring any change and innovation.

The bipolarity found in Weber's two forms of ethics is to be understood as an alternative to the sheer and unbridgeable dualism of other configurations given by philosophers and theologians to the relationship of politics and morality – though Weber's two poles do not overlap with their traditional counterposition, as in Machiavelli's or Kant's design. Weber's image denotes a tension between the two terms that can and should give way – he maintains – to a balance; this is never easy to find and can never be expected to last, because the vagaries of politics (as summary to those of society, economy, technology and culture), continuously upset and redefine the balance we believe to have found.

It is left to the readers to assess whether today's politicians, worldwide or in a specific country, meet Weber's criteria for being found endowed with a vocation to politics and enough professionalism as to decently practise it – this is the twin meaning (vocation and profession) of the German word *Beruf*. They should also find out if those criteria still express the requirements set by political reality in a globalised world, constrained by those nuclear weapons that make resorting to violence so absurdly suicidal, and in which international governance matters more than national parliaments and executives, the addressees of Weber's argument. In the period between the World Wars, and still during the Cold War, the world risked to drown in a stormy sea of 'convictions', including, as a follow-up episode after its end, the ideological neocons rule during the presidency of George W. Bush in the USA; its political blunders (the Iraq war, the dissolution of the Iraqi army, the treatment of Iraqi Sunnis) contributed to the ignition of the horrors perpetrated by jihadism and lately an Islamist 'state' based on an illusionary 'ethics of conviction'. On the other hand, the 'responsibility' (in the sense of business-as-usual policies) practised by politicians over the last three decades, particularly in Western countries, has shown little understanding of the under-the-surface processes going on in the middle-long run, such as: rising inequality, youth unemployment and youth disaffection, problems of the ageing population, environmental downsides of 'progress'. In other words, to be 'responsible' without analysing the long-term trends or having a strategy, flexible though it may be, can also erode the basis of democratic governance. Even a political realist can agree on this. The fear of resuscitating big ideological convictions, such as the *grand récits*/great narratives on progress and/or classless society put to rest by postmodernists,[8] has unfortunately led to the bloating of so-called pragmatism, as if being smart and flexible in the political business were only possible in the absence of deeper ideas and designs.

Let us now draw a more general conclusion. In its absolute version, the opposition of realism and idealism which we have some times alluded to shows ample signs of obsolescence and, furthermore, was never fully real. Plenty of thinkers, religious or secular, upheld idealism, but hardly any real political entity ever acted according to it. Look at the revolutionary regimes, such as the French one after 1789 and the Soviet-Russian after October 1917: the more they proclaimed to act on idealistic principles of liberty and equality, the more they used the bloodiest tools justified by realists in order to impose themselves, survive civil wars, eradicate the opposition. Politics is neither a gala dinner nor a religious service and mostly consists of a difficult *entanglement of principled and selfish behaviours*. The best we can hope to achieve as people of good will is to move weights inside this mix in favour of the former, also by manoeuvring the latter to the former's advantage.[9] In order to do so, a theoretical framework for 'reading' political events that is less rough than realism vs. idealism is helpful.

There is another reason why that opposition was never fully real or properly designed. Idealism or normativism, which is in my view the more adequate term, used to be, and still is, a purely normative doctrine, telling people and countries how they should ideally behave in order to uphold certain values. A realist approach to politics is, first of all, a privileged way to understand it and to make predictions, at least conditional ('if A acts like that, B will be likely to react in this other way'); as such, it made the birth of political science possible, which would have never materialised if politics had always been looked at with normativist lenses. On the other hand, realism was and is not just an academic discipline or school, but also a practical intention of directing politics on its own terms. This was essential in *Il Principe*, much less in the (implicitly realist) political science of the twentieth century. Here methodological realism is paired with different political orientations, and not always on the right wing of the spectrum.[10] The association of realism with figures, such as Carl Schmitt or Henry Kissinger has been misread as a necessary link between it and conservative or imperialist positions, as if progressive politics were only possible on the fragile and erratic shoulders of idealistic prescriptions.

There is more to say on the evolution of realism. Kenneth Waltz (1959) tried to disengage it from its questionable anthropological roots (the moral good is not possible in politics because, in humankind, evil and aggressive tendencies prevail) and to re-found it on systemic grounds (international anarchy between sovereign states makes war always a possibility, or Waltz's third image, cf. above Chapter 6). It was wise to detach the realist pattern of explanation from philosophical views on human nature; on the other hand, this last issue cannot be excluded from debates on ethics and politics. It is unavoidable to question the hidden anthropological assumptions of normativism (the openness of human beings and – what is more doubtful – political communities to behave according to an universalistic legislation deriving from a reasonable top principle). Yet let us look at the realism of the systemic type: its substantive basis, international anarchy, has been significantly eroded in the sixty years after *Man, the State and War* was published. Nuclear weapons have made the world less immediately anarchical and the resort to war much less likely than it used to be; climate change has moved the entire international society to at least try to find a solution in favour of future generations; and human rights have become talked about more frequently and fought for more energically than it used to be before 1948, the year of the Universal Declaration of Human Rights (UDHR).[11] In the second and third case, normativity based on worldwide shared concern, fear and solidarity, is directly playing a role in politics, even in its darkest corner: international politics, in which, unfortunately, many actors keep behaving like Machiavelli's beasts, the fox and the lion, or worse. In the case of climate change and nuclear weapons, we have seen in Chapter 7 how these man-made challenges raise in the very heart of politics issues of universalistic normativity that include future generations. This shows that, along with problems regarding the regulation of biotechnology, moral questions now arise in the middle of politics, and their separation is a tale from other eras. While moral pluralism (implying different moral approaches to different spheres of action or types of relationships) seems to take the stage in moral philosophy, also on the side of realism things are no longer so clear-cut, as if the world still consisted of only the likes of either St. Francis or of

Cesare Borgia, the cruel prince much praised in *Il Principe* (clones of the latter do however abound).

3. For and against ideal theory

What is ideal theory? Why are we discussing its justification and usefulness?

According to John Rawls, ideal theory 'develops the conception of perfectly just basic structure and the corresponding duties and obligations of persons under the fixed constraints of human life and favourable circumstances' (Rawls 1999a, 216). Non-ideal theory deals with the principles that are to be adopted 'under less happy conditions' and in the case of non-compliance to the norms issued by ideal theory, which assumes instead strict compliance with the principles of justice.

This sounds like a commonsensical stance, but Hegel warned us that what is called common sense contains plenty of metaphysical assumptions. In this case, it is the assumption that life, political life in a democracy in particular, will be better if we redesign it thinking that people have in mind high values that are rationally established and can build institutions perfectly adequate to them, except that the latter are to be reconciled with people not always compliant with the models, or with circumstances that are not exactly favourable to them. We know, however, that those perfect people never existed in history or were a tiny minority of losers or fanatics, sometimes with blood on their hands. We also know that models of justice or liberty or solidarity are effective only inasmuch as they are born from conflicts and movements in a particular country or area at a particular time, hence they are very much marked by history and anthropology; not as specification or readaptation of a systematic ideal honed by philosophers. Also, to become politically effective, the values we pursue, the concrete models of better institutions we may have in mind must be to a certain extent able to accommodate the less ideal and rather self-centred interests of the groups who are to support the movement aspiring to realise the model. Innovative policy shifts can be performed not by a company of the stainless, but rather by *coalitions* in which angels are ready to walk for a while hand-in-hand with less noble creatures, if not with devils.

The idea that political philosophy deals with perfect institutions that all citizens are loyal to, while non-compliance with those institutions is a matter for non-ideal theory as a sort of B-theory goes against this book's basic view that politics is first of all about conflicts, in which by no means the parties are a priori on the right or the wrong side, because a perfectly just solution rarely exists, while the first and foremost problem is to develop institutions and policies that prevent conflicts from degenerating into war and disruption. The notion of ideal theory does not lack a certain naiveté paired with the philosopher's arrogance: on the one hand, the belief that possessing the perfect model is prior and conditional to redesigning reality ignores how the reality of political and social life comes about, in a way very distant from conceptual engineering. A whiff of arrogance is, on the other hand, undeniable in the pretence to find criteria capable of reordering to the best problem-laden areas of human life by philosophical deduction from principles, doing better than the actors themselves and ignoring other types of knowledge, collaboration with which, rather, should be attempted. This unhappy complex is what makes 'normative political philosophy', both in general and applied to a specific sector, futile and boring every single time it does not even attempt at preserving in the theory the fullness of the stuff it pretends to ideally regulate.[12] What is missing in this mental attitude is the *sense of the obstacle* one should keep alive and bring to bear when looking for theoretical formulas concerned with human life in politics and society; otherwise those formulas seem to be borne by solipsistic parthenogenesis.

Another trouble with ideal theory is that its very idea fails to recognise politics as the sphere in which ideas matter, but only do so if they can find cultural, social and political forces endorsing them and translating them into policy decisions. The great ideas that in the far or recent past moved the world had each a bearer or protagonist, whom theorists identified as the principal agent of their ideas: the monarchy for absolutism, the bourgeoisie for constitutionalism and liberalism, the working class and sections of the middle class for European socialism and the New Deal, peasants and intellectuals in the liberation movements of the 'Third World'. The attempt at locating this agent is lacking in the recent, pale appearances of ideal theory; the need to provide, along with speculative formulas, a *Zeitdiagnose*/diagnosis of the times as their complement is disregarded and possibly felt as unphilosophical. With its two foci – ideal theory of communication and democracy as well as *Zeitdiagnose* – Habermas's work displays a refreshing difference in perspective from this attitude. On the other hand, all this is not to deny the heuristic value of ideal theory whenever it contributes to defining concepts and alternatives without fully renouncing a more or less explicit tie to real political phenomena and anthropological or cultural components.

All of this can also be looked at from an evolutionary point of view. European modernity has already experienced a powerful endeavour to rethink the polity in the light of a morality shaped by the idea of Reason. This happened in the Enlightenment up to its philosophical culmination in Kant's thought, but had hardly any influence on real politics, which continued to be better understood and managed on a realist path. Even the timid and for a long while (until the creation of the United Nations in 1945) ineffective efforts to build a collective security system were due to the reaction to the unprecedented bloodletting of 1914–1918 rather than to the teachings of the idealist tradition, though this helped formulate the theory of a new international order.[13] After this evolution, something different from an updated and refined rerunning of Kant's normativism, such as Rawls's work in the substance is, was to be expected, for example a normative theory capable of integrating into its method the awareness of the real behaviour of actors and the role of the historical context, rather than throwing all that differs from the speculation called 'ideal theory' into the dustbin of 'non-ideal theory'. All of this with full knowledge of the obsolescence of the ossified counterposition idealism vs. realism, as discussed above. Yet things have, so far, not moved forward in this direction.

Another notion that may seem to have some similarity with ideal theory, though it should by no means be mistaken for it, must be discussed here: *utopia*. Rawls himself resorted to this term when he spoke of the "Society of liberal and decent[14] Peoples as a 'realistic utopia'" (Rawls 1999b, 5–9); he did, not, however specify the meaning of 'utopia'. This word comes from Greek οὐ-τόπος (no place), indicating the venue for an ideal polity as the one described by Thomas More (1478–1535) and located on the island of Utopia (More 1516). In the English pronunciation, this word is indistinguishable from Eutopia, which derives from εὖ-τόπος (good place), while in other languages one is able to distinguish eutopia and utopia. A further member of this word family is dystopia, which means a bad place that is better to be avoided, or a negative utopia such as the *Brave New World* described by Aldous Huxley (Huxley 1932) and the society of *Nineteen Eighty-Four* depicted by George Orwell (Orwell 1949).

The utopian current in political philosophy is rich and can be said to culminate in the work of the French writer Charles Fourier (1772–1837). Marx and Engels intended their socialism to be based on scientific knowledge, in opposition to the rather literary or rhetorical 'utopian socialism' of their predecessors and contemporaries; but critics maintain that Marx's own theory is not free from ties to utopian elements of the Jewish tradition. 'Utopian' has very often been the damning word thrown at socialist and communist reform projects by conservative adversaries. As a reaction, the protest movement of the 1960s reloaded this term with a positive value, as for example in the writings of Herbert Marcuse (Marcuse 1967). In the warm and fuzzy version of 'whatever is against the existing state-of-affairs and in favour of a better world' this is still the (now rather seldom) use of the word in Western political rhetoric, yet it is deprived of any theoretical foundation, and found on the mouth of ideologues and literati rather than on that of the people who really need a change for the better. They – the poor of any age, destitute families, low-wage workers, migrants and more – do indeed deserve better than appeals to believing in utopia: well-carved programmes of economic and social reform, political strategies for gathering consensus behind them and implementing them, the upsurge of an appropriate leadership.

4. Critical Theory

What we are going to talk about in this section is one of the paths followed by the thinkers who do not recognise the primacy or the legitimacy of ideal theory and also try to escape the frontal opposition realism-idealism. 'Critical Theory' comprises a thick and precise, as well as a thin and vague version. In the first one, it was institutionalised in the Institut für Sozialforschung, established by mostly Jewish academics of Marxist orientation in 1923 at the University of Frankfurt am Main, where it is still active; it was renamed as the Institute of Social Research during the Nazi years, in which the Institute was hosted by Columbia University in New York City. The leading figure of this interdisciplinary group was Max Horkheimer, who in the 1930s defined the idea of 'critical theory' in opposition to the traditional one and redefined philosophical materialism; he was supported by the economist Friedrich Pollock and later by Herbert Marcuse, Theodor W. Adorno, Leo Löwenthal and others. 'Critical theory of society' was the heading they used for their own view,[15] while the more popular label 'the Frankfurt School' came up much later and was never endorsed by the founders – although being embedded in the liberal spirit of the city of Frankfurt am Main was an aspect of the group's identity.[16] Horkheimer and Adorno wrote around 1944 the already mentioned *Dialektik der Aufklärung/Dialectics of Enlightenment*, the major philosophical foundation of Critical Theory. From the 1960s onwards, the leading figure has been Jürgen Habermas. Endorsing Critical Theory in the thinner sense, often without connecting it to the founding period, means acknowledging his thought as defining. In a still thinner sense, 'critical' has become a fairly fuzzy adjective, applied to whatever is or pretends to be against the mainstream in philosophy or politics or literary criticism; this attitude has thus become itself a part of the mainstream on the market of ideas.

The old Critical Theory has been relevant to social movements, being a large part of the background for the student and protest movement in the 1960s in Europe and North America, here mainly in the wake of Marcuse's radical theory of civilisation as formulated in *Eros and Civilization* (Marcuse 1955) and *The One-Dimensional Man* (Marcuse 1963). Being a theory of society based on Marx's critique of political economy, it did not acknowledge the specificity of politics and gave nearly no contribution to political theory, except for the work of Otto Kirchheimer (1905–1965) and Franz Neumann.[17] Starting in the early 1960s, this changed to some extent with Habermas, even if one does not take into account his prolific writing, lasting decades, on Germany and the European Union, which has made him the most respected public figure inside and outside Germany. The following is a brief account of Critical Theory as redefined in Habermas's thought.

His main contributions regard a binary view (lifeworld vs. system) on society and politics (Habermas 1981) and a philosophy of law and democracy (Habermas 1999). In the first one Habermas, though being a critic of Luhmann's holistic system theory of society, comes to regard as irreversible the rationalization, following an impersonal system logic, of the lifeworld[18] into societal sectors such as the economy (regulator: money) and politics (regulator: *Macht*/power). The expectation of early Critical Theory for a revolutionary renewal of the whole society is thus abandoned. On the other hand, the sectors of life concerned with the cultural reproduction of society, the social integration among citizens and education must and can be shielded against imperatives coming from the sub-systems (economy and political-bureaucratic realm), which tend to 'colonise' spheres of interaction that are entrusted to the power-free communication among persons mediated by language. It's the structures of language, as detected by the speech acts theory, that encapsulate the chance of a reasonable understanding among actors, far from manipulation and reciprocal instrumentalisation. In Western countries this attitude of Habermas has partly mirrored, partly itself fostered or at least justified the shift of democratic politics from income (in)equality and class conflict to questions of cultural or principled nature such as human rights and gender.[19] It's the so-called shift towards postmaterialistic values,[20] though in the years following the economic crisis of 2008 the 'old' class-based discontents seem to have regained importance – now often immersed in a populist ideology – in the sections of the electorate that have suffered most from globalisation. A balance is still missing.

In *Faktizität und Geltung/Between Facts and Norms*, Habermas (1993) focuses on law because of its contribution to social integration in a centrifugal society in which neither religion nor metaphysics give the people enough motivation to sticking together. In law, normative validity or legitimacy is as important as its legal facticity and formal correctness, which are the core of the positivist view of law. For Habermas's discourse theory of the law, 'only those norms are valid to which all persons possibly affected could agree as participants in rational discourses' (Habermas 1999, 940). The legitimacy of the law in allocating liberties to individuals does not stem from morality; on the contrary law complements the weak post-traditional morality of late-modern societies. Though still in a normative terrain, we are, in this communicative conception of social interaction, far from the monistic rule of a single principle (of justice).

Habermas's discourse theory consistently gives deliberation priority over decision by majority voting. He sees democracy and human rights as interdependent, and declares the insufficiency of both dominating traditions, the liberal (politics as compromise between self-interested actors) and the republican (ethical foundation of politics in justification and exaltation of the commonwealth) one; his design for an ideal procedure for deliberation claims to integrate elements from both traditions. That design is where Habermas comes closer to an ideal theory that should be a benchmark for the real interaction among diverging positions; alone, politics is almost never a cooperative and sober dialogue in search of a better understanding, akin to that between the four instrumental voices in the classical era of string quartets, from Haydn and Mozart to Beethoven and Brahms (and Hugo Wolf).

With this proceduralist view of democracy, Habermas's Critical Theory tries to respond to the quest for its normative foundation after the break-down of its original roots in the Marxian philosophy of history: if you have such a philosophy telling you how history came about and, what is more, how it will go on or end, you do not need to find out which principles of justice should govern your actions, because they are already inscribed in past and present history (hence Marx's contempt for 'modern mythology with its goddesses of Justice, Freedom, Equality and Fraternity' worshipped by liberals and utopian socialists).[21] How far Habermas's turn towards a normative theory that is proceduralist in nature answers the questions raised by the more substantive old Critical Theory, in particular Horkheimer's, cannot be discussed here. On the other hand, his theory marks a different path from the unreflected normativism of the theory of justice.

Notes

1 Cf. Baier 1958. I shall however resort to the more common 'ethics and politics' whenever the specific meaning of morality is not in play. The Greek root of ethics, ἦθος/ethos, means character or behaviour, and ethics includes a course of action that can be, but is not necessarily guided by morality.
2 From the Greek δέον: regarding what ought to be done or the obligation.
3 This relational structure, the security dilemma (see Chapter 7, §5), is a central notion in political realism.
4 This example is not quoted by Machiavelli, and we do not know how far his knowledge of Thucydides's text in the Latin translation by Lorenzo Valla (completed in 1452) went.

5 The republican tradition has been in the past half century investigated by historians such as J.G.A. Pocock (1975) and Quentin Skinner (1978).
6 A major example of this literature remains Arendt's essay *Lying in Politics* in Arendt 1972, 1–47. Politics that is indifferent to the (argumentatively verifiable) truth, hence often hostile to it, seems to represent a very new chapter, which *The Economist* of 10 September 2016 has dubbed 'post-truth politics'. Also, a philosophical inquiry into this complex under the conditions of the digital age would be welcome.
7 Weber's main text in this respect is *Politik als Beruf/Politics as a Vocation* a talk given in Munich at the end of 1919, a few months before Weber died, at the age of fifty-six, of the Spanish flu pandemic that ravaged the world immediately after the Great War; it has been already quoted several times in this volume (Weber 1919a).
8 The original move in this direction was made by Lyotard (1979).
9 A superb example of both these moves was Dr. Martin Luther King's ability to force or persuade President Lyndon B. Johnson to use his own clout as President and his shrewdness as former Democratic majority leader in the Senate in order to forward the passage of the Civil Rights Act and the Voting Rights Act in the US Congress back in 1964–65, cf. Kotz 2005.
10 For reformist realism see Scheuerman 2011.
11 Eleanor Roosevelt (1884–1962), who as First Lady of the United States had acted against racial and gender discrimination, was the driving force behind the drafting of UDHR, see https://en.wikipedia.org/wiki/File:EleanorRooseveltHumanRights.png.
12 I have examined these aspects of 'normative political philosophy' in the case of climate ethics (see Cerutti 2016).
13 The key figure, in this sense, was US President Woodrow Wilson (1856–1924, in office from 1913 through 1921), whose interventionist 'democratic idealism' as a tenet of foreign policy continues to build one of the recurrent strains in US diplomatic history.
14 The term 'decent' describes 'nonliberal societies whose basic institutions meet certain specified conditions of political right and justice' (Rawls 1999b, 3n2).
15 This label also had the advantage of not making explicit any reference to Marxism, suspicious to public authorities both in Germany and the USA in the Thirties.
16 Walther Benjamin, a close friend Adorno's, was never a member of the Institute, even if he was supported by them; nor can his thought be labelled as belonging to Critical Theory.
17 See above Chapter 3, §2, note 3, Neumann also wrote *Behemoth*, an early political conceptualization of the National Socialist regime (1942).
18 'German *Lebenswelt*, . . . the world as immediately or directly experienced in the subjectivity of everyday life, as sharply distinguished from the objective "worlds" of the sciences, which employ the methods of the mathematical sciences of nature' (from https://www.britannica.com/topic/life-world). The term was introduced in philosophy by Edmund Husserl (1859–1938) and developed in the phenomenological sociology of Alfred Schütz (1899–1959).
19 In Marx's vocabulary, this means giving a higher relevance to *Überbau*/superstructure in comparison to the economic basis of society and politics; for this terminology see Marx 1859.
20 The now popular concept of postmaterialism was introduced by the American sociologist Ronald Inglehart (Inglehart 1977).
21 As Marx wrote to F.A. Sorge (Marx 1877).

References

Arendt, Hannah (1972) *Lying in Politics*, in *Crises of the Republic*, San Diego: Harcourt Brace, 1–47.
Baier, Kurt (1958) *The Moral Point of View*, New York: Random House, 1965.

Botero, Giovanni (1589) *Della ragion di Stato/ The Reason of State*, New Haven: Yale University Press, 1956.
Cerutti, Furio (2016) *Climate Ethics and the Failures of 'Normative Political Philosophy'* in 'Philosophy and Social Criticism', 42(7), 707–726.
Habermas, Jürgen (1981) *Theorie des kommunikativen Handelns/ The Theory of Communicative Action*, Boston: Beacon, 1984–87.
Habermas, Jürgen (1993) *Faktizität und Geltung/ Between Facts and Norms*, Boston: Blackwell, 1996.
Habermas, Jürgen (1999) *Between Facts and Norms: An Author's Reflections*, 76 Denv.U.L. Rev. 937 1998–1999.
Hegel, Georg Wilhelm Friedrich (1807) *Phänomenologie des Geistes/ Phenomenology of Spirit*, translated by A.V. Miller, Oxford: Oxford University Press, 1977.
Hegel, Georg Wilhelm Friedrich (1821) *Grundlinien der Philosophie des Rechts/ Elements of the Philosophy of Right*, e-book available at www.inp.uw.edu.pl/mdsie/Political_Thought/Hegel%20Phil%20of%20Right.pdf
Huxley, Aldous (1932) *Brave New World*, New York: HarperCollins, 1998.
Inglehart, Ronald (1977) *The Silent Revolution: Changing Values and Political Styles Among Western Publics*, Princeton: Princeton University Press.
Kotz, Nick (2005) *Judgment Days. Lyndon Baines Johnson, Martin Luther King Jr., and the Laws That Changed America*, Boston: Houghton Mifflin.
Lyotard, Jean-François (1979) *La condition post-moderne/ The Postmodern Condition*, Minneapolis: University of Minnesota Press, 1984.
Machiavelli, Niccolò (1532) *Il Principe/ The Prince*, New York: Cambridge University Press, 1988.
Marcuse, Herbert (1955) *Eros and Civilization*, New York: Beacon Press, 1966.
Marcuse, Herbert (1963) *The One-Dimensional Man*, e-book available at www.marcuse.org/herbert/pubs/64onedim/odmcontents.html
Marcuse, Herbert (1967) *The End of Utopia*, e-book available at www.marxists.org/reference/archive/marcuse/works/1967/end-utopia.htm
Marx Karl (1859) *Zur Kritik der politischen Ökonomie. Vorwort/A Contribution to the Critique of Political Economy. Preface*, available at www.marxists.org/archive/marx/works/1859/critique-pol-economy/preface.htm.
Marx, Karl (1877) *Marx-Engels Correspondence – Marx to Friedrich Adolph Sorge*, available at www.marxists.org/archive/marx/works/1877/letters/77_10_19.htm
More, Thomas (1516) *Utopia*, New York: New American Library, 1967.
Neumann, Franz Leopold (1942) *Behemoth: The Structure and Practice of National Socialism*, New York: Reprint Octagon, 1983 (based on the expanded edition of 1944).
Orwell, George (1949) *Nineteen Eighty-Four*, e-book available at https://openlibrary.org/works/OL1168091W/Nineteen_Eighty-Four
Pocock, J. G. A. (1975) *The Machiavellian Moment: Florentine Political Thought and the Atlantic Republican Tradition*, Princeton: Princeton University Press.
Popper, Karl (1945) *The Open Society and Its Enemies*, Princeton: Princeton University Press, 2013.
Rawls, John (1999a) *A Theory of Justice*, revised edition, Cambridge: Harvard University Press.
Rawls, John (1999b) *The Law of People*, Cambridge: Harvard University Press.
Scheuerman, William E. (2011) *The Realist Case for Global Reform*, Oxford: Polity Press.
Skinner, Quentin (1978) *The Foundations of Modern Political Thought*, Cambridge: Cambridge University Press, 1998.

Θουκυδίδης/Thucydides (404 BCE) Περὶ τοῦ Πελοποννησίου πολέμου/ *The Peloponnesian War* available at http://classics.mit.edu/Thucydides/pelopwar.1.first.html (404 BCE is Thucycides's presumtive year of death; title attributed in the Hellenistic era)

Waltz, Kenneth (1959) *Man, the State, and War*, New York: Columbia University Press.

Weber, Max (1919a) *Politik als Beruf/ Politics as a Vocation*, in Hans Gerth and Charles Wright Mills, eds., *From Max Weber: Essays in Sociology*, Abingdon: Routledge, 2009, 77–128.

Weber, Max (1919b) *Wissenschaft als Beruf/ Science as a Vocation*, in Hans Gerth and Charles Wright Mills, eds., *From Max Weber: Essays in Sociology*, Abingdon: Routledge, 2009, 129–158.

Further readings

On philosophy and politics:

Geuss, Raymond (2008) *Philosophy and Real Politics*, Princeton: Princeton University Press.

On the original Critical Theory:

Wiggershaus, Rolf (1994) *The Frankfurt School*, Cambridge: Polity.

On Habermas:

Rasmussen, David and James Swindal, eds. (2010) *Habermas II*, London: Sage, in particular Vol. 3.

EPILOGUE

What drives people to politics

This is not a Conclusion, nor can a textbook really have a conclusion, since it is not written in order to prove and expand a substantive position upheld by the author, even if his views do not remain hidden – adherence to rigid neutrality whenever facing a controversial set of problems would be hypocritical and not credible.

This book started with the question 'What is politics?', and went on to examine how politics works and what it sets out both within political units and among them or globally; it also examined how politics interacts or should interact with other attitudes in human action such as morality. It ends now with the attempt to answer in an orderly, though succinct way, a question that has already peeped out somewhere: what drives people when they act politically, be they states, (wo)men or voters, followers or protesters? In this inquiry, which is clearly not limited to professional politicians, reconstructive political philosophy works with elements of knowledge deriving from philosophical anthropology and theoretical sociology.

We can identify four major driving moments of political behaviour, four basic types that only rarely come up alone, as they mostly make an impact in a mix that can be discerned only analysing single cases. We are now going to present them in an order that is not an order of priority; there is no recognisable general rule regulating their intertwinement in the concrete actions of men, women and groups. They are

- *self-interest* for one's own preservation, which includes the enhancement of one's own power as the best shield under which self-interest can be pursued. Jumping from this Hobbesian vocabulary to the contemporary, economy-dominated one, we can speak of maximization of one's own utility, achieved by prudential behaviour (classical language, as mentioned in Chapters 1 and 10) or instrumental/strategic action. These patterns apply to the hedgefund administrator as well as to the labourer going on strike to improve her/his wage, and are the patterns assumed by rational choice theory and related theories, which have the fully informed and rationally choosing *homo oeconomicus*/economic man as their protagonist.

On the one hand, this type of action is almost always present in political behaviour, even where other types of motivation prevail. There can be honest and wise men and women in politics, but – to reconnect to Madison's dictum quoted in Chapter 1, §1 – hardly or very rarely any angels disregarding all self-interest and never acting based on calculation. On the other hand, the unilateral and oversimplifying attitude considering the latter to be the predominant or sole paradigmatic mode of political behaviour integrating all others, has blinded political science and made it unable to use a more complex and differentiated grid, as required by a business as murky as politics. Moreover, self-interest as a general formula is not what effectively drives people to act in this or that way: roughly defined, basic interests are *interpreted* by the actors in any given situation, in a way that is largely shaped by cultural and ideological factors of many kinds. Frequent is the case in which layers of the electorate vote and make choices in a way that is disadvantageous to their interest and will bring them, say, fewer jobs and higher taxes, or even war; and they do so under the influence of what the English philosopher Francis Bacon (1561–1626) called *idola fori*/idols (or prejudices) of the marketplace (or more generally of social exchange).

- *passions*, to put it again with the words of Hobbes, or emotions – both disruptive and destructive (daughters of Thanatos/Death, such as: hatred, despise for other groups, envy and resentment, both very relevant to social dynamics) or nourishing and strenghtening the ties among individuals and groups (such as: sympathy and empathy, helpfulness, all daughters of Eros/Love, to speak in the terms of Sigmund Freud. The first ones are those that in common parlance are said to require containment, discipline or outright denial, because they 'inflame the minds' and have been indeed, as objects of skilful manipulation and propaganda, pillars of the totalitarian regimes in the twentieth century, while they now play a large role in the populist movements of the twenty-first. The other type of passions is an indispensable element not just of societal bonds, but collective political action as well – how could polities, parties, communities stick together without including this emotional cement?
- *universalistic motivations*, inspired by morality or religion or a worldview or by 'civil religion', the set of solidaristic and inspiring beliefs holding a community, especially a nation, together – as Rousseau first saw under this formula in Book IV, Chapter 8 of *The Social Contract*. These motivations strive to redefine the purpose of politics and the life of the body politic in a less self-centred direction, against the disrupting effects that a mere instrumental or strategic behaviour and destructive passions have on the polity. A political identity filled with ideal motivations of moral or civic nature can be a powerful driver of political action, though there are hardly any Kantian or Rawlsian politicians.

The identity of a democratic community with its openness and integrative force belongs primarily here. Yet it is also true that a democratic identity cannot remain an intellectual argument, if it is to drive people, and is best embedded in positive emotions of solidarity and equal respect.

- remembering Chapter 3, a fourth driving element must be acknowledged: *institutional* (in the sense of institution-driven) *action*. Individuals, as well as groups, (administrative or political bodies, parties and more) do not every single day reinvent their course of action driven by strategy, passion or ideal: in normal times, a major component of their actions is the conformity to (or the endeavour to reinterpret or change) the grid of rules that allow for the existence and continuity of the polity, which is also the venue in which to enact the life plans of individuals and groups. Only in the now seldom revolutionary times this type of action loses terrain, but does not disappear, waiting for new institutions to start working. Institution-driven behaviour should not be mistaken for proneness to apply rules whatever their justification or however based one's own assessment; it only implies the acknowledgement that at the end of the day interests, ideals and identities must find expression in rules embodied in institutions, both informal and formal. The predominance of the latter bears witness to the crucial, though not exclusive role of the law – already seen in Chapter 4, §5 and again in Chapter 10 with regard to Habermas – in shaping and upholding the old and new arrangements in which we manage the business of life.

A major examination of the four-tiered grid, and in particular, of all the intertwinements between the four elements would require more space than is given in an Epilogue. The grid is little more than a stub, in the hope it is useful to put some order to hints found all across the book. It also has the task to stress the distinctive nature of the four driving moments, which become very much intermingled within the concrete actors' behaviour, but must be mentally kept from each other. Any attempt to explain an event or process on the basis of just one of these drivers must fail, given the mix of high and low, reasonable and murky of which our behaviour as individuals and groups consist. Against all reductionism, for example, it would be wrong to subsume acting on universalistic, principle-driven motivations under strategic, self-centred behaviour, as the less refined realist writers, modern followers of the Sophist Trasimachos remembered in Chapter 9, §1, do with the pretension to unmask the hoax – as they say – perpetrated by idealistic actors who claim to act for the sake of humanity or the law while pursuing their own interest. This attitude does not have more truth than the conventional wisdom heeded by the people for whom 'all politics is a dirty business'. The truth regarding such a multilayered being as a human and such a contradictory business as politics is more articulated than what can be unveiled by simplifications and alleged 'cynical lucidity'.

Twin cases of reductionism can also be found with regard to passions. The older one wants passions to be altogether a factor of corruption for politics, leading to irrational and destructive results, and calls for having them chastised by reason. We have already argued that even the best political life does not develop without an emotional component, while passions do not build a compact bunch and a differentiation must be drawn between them. The younger step into reductionism goes in the opposite direction: politics was always icy and dull, far from the hearts of the people, women in particular, and should finally be put in the flow of positive, community-building emotions. This proposal forgets about the obstacle represented by the fact that, left alone, without the company of reason (both as calculus and moral reason), emotions cannot be easily discerned into positive or negative and can wreak havoc; while, along with motivation and purpose, politics also includes policy making and controlling public administration, all tasks in which emotions can replace reasoning and bargaining as little as, say, the much praised 'gift economy' can replace the market and the money in advanced societies – the problem being rather how far the two economies can coexist.

★ ★ ★

This book ends with a warning that is at the same time an invitation.

Politics as represented here is politics looked at through the lenses of concepts, an irreplaceable instrument – a political philosopher tends to believe – to understand it and also to find a firmer ground to orient oneself in political action. Yet it's a long way from the concept to the understanding, let alone the handling of any concrete political situation in which we can get involved as participants or observers. On this long path it is not political philosophy that can provide food for thought, though expansion and refinement of the concepts explained here would help. Armed with the tools offered in this book, the reader is rather invited to plunge into a wealth of documents that are closer to the flesh and blood of real politics: history books primarily, about general history as well as, say, social or military history. Then come biographies and autobiographies: the well-written ones give a vivid picture of how policy making and consensus seeking, the two main components of concrete politics, come about or end in failure and omission. They also give the reader the advantage of getting the sense of a dimension that has not been discussed in this book because it is highly elusive and almost impossible to conceptualize: the role of *personality* in politics, once a popular theme among ancient writers of politics, first of all Plutarch.

Another invitation is to read sociological (first of all from economic sociology) and anthropological literature that can give a fresh and well-documented image of how things are evolving in society and politics, thus helping readapt or discard concepts that have lost currency in a changing reality. A further fascinating source, dull that their language may sound, are sentences issued by high courts – national such as the US Supreme Court or the German *Bundesverfassungsgericht* as well as international such as the European Court of Human Rights – in cases of political and ethical relevance. This kind of attention must now extend to the books based on hard science concerned with the events in nature (or rather in the human handling of it) that challenge the responsibility of politics (in the sense of Democracy Two, as explained in Chapter 7, §6). Climate change, energy resources, human and non-human biotechnologies and neuroscience are among the present cases.

Political philosophy deals with categories, both reconstructive and normative. Yet categories are better investigated and with more intellectual fun if we keep in our sights the lifeforms they are supposed to help understand, while also providing actors with some reasoned practical orientation in political life.

INDEX

Endnotes are indexed; References and Further Readings, as well as front matter, are not. Latin words are registered; Arab, Chinese, Greek (with exceptions), and Russian are not. Only occurrences of conceptual significance are taken into account.

1984 195

absolutism, absolutist 52, 61, 70, 99, 194
Acemoglu, Daron 131
Achaemenids 48
Aden 63
Adenauer, Konrad 120
Adorno, Theodor W. 195–6, 198n16
Afghanistan 7
Africa 7, 116, 122; dictatorships 130
agenda, agenda-setting 12, 15, 53, 67, 135, 137, 148
Ahuramazda 34
AIDS 135
Al-Andaluz 60
Alighieri, Dante 63, 76n13
Allende, Salvador 35n7
All the President's Men 22n27
Almond, Gabriel 65
analytical, analytically 24, 31, 36, 41, 43n3, 92, 112, 118, 131, 146, 166, 169, 181–2
Anarchical Society (The) 123n4
anarchy, anarchical 108, 110–12; anarchism 37, 56n10; international 108–9, 114; society 107, 109–12, 114, 122, 123n4, 131–2, 192
Anders, Günther 137, 149n12
Anthony, Marc (Marcus Antonius) 55n1
anthropogenic 126, 134–5, 138

anthropology, anthropological 5–7, 34–6, 38, 43, 75, 134–6, 138, 154, 166, 189, 192, 194, 201, 204; cultural 42, 58, 124; pessimism 20; philosophical 42, 48
Antigone 18
Aquinas, Thomas 7, 17
Arabia, Arab(ic) 63, 76n12, 82, 184; Saudi 34n2, 73
Arendt, Hannah 10, 101n3, 198n6
Argentina 101n16; Argentinian dictatorship 21n3
Aristotle 7, 21n11, 38, 64, 76n17, 79, 88, 164, 173n3, 177, 187–8; Aristotelianism 9
armed forces, army *see* military
Art of War (The) 123n7
Asia, Asian 97; East Asia 97, 100, 163; South-East 98
association 33, 65, 76n15, 149n5; freedom of 192; non-voluntary 145
asymmetry, asymmetric 10, 18–19, 88, 113, 130–1, 157
Athena (Pallas) 145
Athens, Athenian 9, 34, 81, 84, 101n12, 101n16, 188–9
Augustine (St.) 64, 116, 160
Aurelius, Marcus (Marcus Aurelius Antoninus Augustus) 55n1
Auschwitz 31
Austria, Austrian 95, 100, 110

authoritarianism, authoritarian 26, 31, 48, 51, 71, 80, 86, 94, 97, 101n3, 137, 149n6
authority, authoritative 18, 25, 33, 57, 60, 62, 65, 70, 172; internationally 137, 140
autonomy 63, 82–3, 100, 101n15, 107–8, 161, 163, 165, 170, 173, 177; and negative liberty 161, 172

Babeuf, Gracchus 163
Bacon, Francis 202
Baier, Kurt 197n1
balance(s): checks-and 9, 88; of power 110–11; of terror 115, 129, 136, 147
Baltic states 110
Bangkok Declaration 97
Baroque period 61
Basic Elements of the Philosophy of Law 76n7
Basque country 154
battle: Lepanto 63; of Poitiers 76n12; Tours 63; Vienna 63
Bauer, Otto 101n6
Beethoven, Ludwig van 197
behaviour, behavioural 25–6, 33, 43n4, 49; and ethos 197n1; norm-driven 123, 201; selfish 191, 203
Behemoth 112; *Behemoth* 123n6 (Hobbes)
Behistun 34
Beijing 31, 98
Being and Time 151
Beitz, Charles 179
Belgium 121
bellum omnium contra omnes 52, 112, 160
Benjamin, Walther 198n16
Bentham, Jeremy 68, 188
Berlin 111, 140; Wall 31
Berlin, Isaiah 157, 159
Bernstein, Eduard 53
Beruf see vocation
Betrothed (The) 123n3
Between Facts and Norms 197
Beveridge, William 53, 62; Report 62
Bhagavad Gita 18, 154
Bismarck, Otto von 55n6
Bobbio, Norberto 38, 43n3, 93, 101n7, 137
Böckenförde, Ernst-Wolfgang 30–1
Bohemia 110
Bolsheviks 162
Bond, James 75n3
Borgia, Cesare 193
Borís Godunóv 13
Botero, Giovanni 189
bourgeoisie, bourgeois 14, 39, 54, 60–1, 67–9, 76n18, 102n18, 162, 194

Brahms, Johannes 197
Braudel, Fernand 149n1
Brave New World 195
Bretton Woods 128
Brexit 90, 101n17
Britain, British 29, 53, 66, 68, 83, 89, 122, 123n11, 153
Britannicus 18
Brühl, Marie von 112
Brussels 101n14, 120–2
Brutus (Marcus Iunius Brutus) 34
Budapest 95
Buddhism, Buddhist 30, 73–4, 119
Bull, Hedley 123n4
bureaucracy 19, 55, 61, 76n10, 82, 84, 94, 160; Euro 121
Burke, Edmund 84
Burma 82
Bush, George W. 118, 123, 191

Caesar (Gaius Julius Caesar) 76n16; Caesarism 91
Caliphate 108
Calvin, Jean 88
Cambodia 64, 153, 162
Canada 53
Capital 54, 56n12, 177
capitalism, capitalistic 15, 53, 61–3, 67, 89, 95, 100, 128, 132, 163–4, 171; anarcho 54; definitions of 98; and democracy 80, 89, 99–100, 102n21; deregulated 159, 166; early 39, 147, 160; financial 132; postwar 183; ultra 95
capital punishment *see* death penalty
Carr, Edward H. 17, 124n19
Cassius (Gaius Cassius Longinus) 34
Castilian 71
Catalonyan 60
Catherine of Aragon 76n4
Catholic 60, 74, 182
Cerutti, Furio 34n2, 134, 149n4, 149n7, 149n11, 149n13, 173n12, 185n1, 198n12
change: in international relations 38, 115; motivations for 141; and order 48; political 72, 80
Charlemagne 60
Charles the Fifth (Holy Roman Emperor) 74, 110, 175
Chicago School 173n2
Chile 35n7
China, Chinese 16, 21n21, 55, 57, 59, 63, 73, 75, 81, 91, 95, 97–100, 123n7, 128, 130; ancient 60, 109; Cultural

Revolution 162; Deng's 100; People's Republic of 57, 69, 97, 169; post-Maoist 28; Republic of 58; Standing Committee of the Central Committee of the Communist Party of 25
Christ, Christian, Christianity, Christendom 30, 53, 60, 62, 64, 73, 95, 117, 130, 160, 163, 171, 173n7; Judeo- 95
Church 43n9, 95; Eastern Orthodox Church of Constantinople 60; of England 76n4; Orthodox 73; Roman Catholic 60, 108
Churchill, Winston 122, 124n18
Cicero (Marcus Tullius Cicero) 33, 37, 64, 70, 76n15, 79, 101n9, 102n19
citizenship 32, 86, 167, 178
civilization 30, 98, 140, 143, 196; clash of 98; European 63, 116; history of 113, 153; Islamic 108, 117; survival of/threats to 134–8, 144, 153, 157, 182, 196; Western 34, 35n6, 116–17, 157
Civil Rights Act 101n5, 198n9
Clark, Christopher 77n26
class 12, 14–15, 21n18, 25, 54, 60–1, 72, 81; middle 73, 96, 98–9, 129; struggle 9, 54, 66, 196; working 6, 15, 54, 61, 94, 152, 182, 194
Clausewitz, Carl von, Clausewitzian 112–13
climate: agreements 107, 118, 138, 144–5; change 25, 51, 67, 107, 118, 126, 129, 135, 137–8, 141–8, 154, 167, 172, 182, 192, 205; ethics 185n1, 198n12; governance/policy 142, 154, 172, 182
Clinton, Bill (William J.) 122
colony, colonialism, colonial 6, 27, 56, 63, 116, 123, 140, 171; post 69, 72, 76n14, 86
combatant, non-combatant 113, 116, 152
Commission on Global Governance 132
common good 3, 17, 92
communication 67, 91, 127, 134, 146–7; and democracy 194, 196; and symbol 32
communism, communist 15, 54, 69, 113, 195; economy 95; post- 69; society 9, 54, 164; Soviet 7, 15
community, communitarian 61, 66–8, 73; communitarianism 179–80; epistemic 107; European 114; imagined 85; international 111; political 76, 105
Community and Society 67
Comte, Auguste 9
confederation 53, 122, 152; Confederate 152
conflict, conflictual, conflicting 4–7, 9, 15–16, 18–19, 21n4, 21n11, 33–4, 70, 77n30, 80, 86, 88–9, 97, 99–100, 111–13, 117, 119, 122, 129, 140, 147, 149n2, 172, 193, 196; identity 5–7; ideological 5–7, 69; of interest 5–7, 15
Confucianism 143, 176
Confucius, Confucian 52, 55, 98
Congress of Vienna 111
conscription 10, 58, 69, 113, 152
consensus 16, 19, 25, 69, 74, 118–19, 141, 165, 179; and contract 65; and democracy 89; and legitimacy 26; Washington 128
Constant, Benjamin 101n12, 173n9
Constantin (Flavius Valerius Aurelius Constantinus) 43n9
constitution, constitutional 13, 16, 29, 42, 53, 61–2, 70–2, 74–5, 76n1, 114, 178; of China 169; court 84, 88, 101n11; of Iran 34n1; law 43, 160; of North Korea 169; and *polis* 79–80; protection of humankind 172, 173n12; of Saudi Arabia 34n1; of the USA 9, 75, 88
contract, contractarianism, contractarian 18, 20, 37, 49–53, 72, 152, 178; and public law 65, 67, 160; *The Social Contract* 202
cooperation, cooperative 30–1, 33, 96, 107–8, 110–11, 122–3, 135, 145, 177
Copernican revolution 169
corporatist, neo-corporatist 16, 62
Corpus iuris civilis 70
corruption 60, 66, 97, 99, 203
cosmopolitanism, cosmopolitan 118–19, 137, 179
Council of Regions (EU) 121
covenant *see* pact
Critical Theory 187, 195–7, 198n16
Critique of the Gotha Programme 56n13
Croce, Benedetto 55n7
Crouch, Colin 133
Cuba, Cuban 75, 130; missile crisis 136, 144
Cubeddu, Raimondo 100
Czechoslovakia 152

Dahl, Robert 96, 100
Darius I the Great 34
Davos, Switzerland 128
death 50, 55n2, 110, 119, 151n2, 166, 170; megadeath 154; and terrorism 153–4
death penalty 34, 58, 74–5, 156; abolition of 58, 75
debt (public) 8, 16, 69, 76n5, 84, 129, 162
decision, decision-making 12, 15–16, 19, 27, 50, 64, 74, 97n3, 100, 145, 197; in the global dimension 118, 142, 147–8; and the market 188
Declaration of the Rights of Man and of the Citizen 169

De Gasperi, Alcide 120
deliberation 16, 20, 92, 101n13, 102, 197
democracy, democratic 9, 20, 35n7, 43,
    54–5, 61, 75, 79–80, 89, 115, 168;
    authoritarian 26; and capitalism 99–100;
    Chinese alternative to 98; and conflicts
    9, 129; deliberative 16, 92, 102n7; direct
    100n1, 183; downsides of 92; and *ethnos*
    85; framework conditions of 95; and
    globalisation 132–3; and human rights
    98, 197; legitimacy of 148; and liberalism
    62, 67, 69, 130, 161; mass 19–20, 67;
    and nation 69; and order 48, 53; origin
    of 85–6; post 133; preconditions of
    87–9; as a procedure 63, 81, 86, 93; and
    representative government 83, 86; and
    Rousseau 83; social 53, 56; substantial
    94–5, 130; under lethal challenges 147–8
Democracy in America (Of) 91
demos 53, 68; and *ethnos* 85–6, 147
Deng Hsiao Ping 97–8, 100
Denmark 121
deontological 170, 180, 182, 189
Derrida, Jacques 179–80
despotism 80, 119
Deutsch, Karl 65
Dialectics of Enlightenment 196
dictator, dictatorship 21n3, 32, 51, 54–5, 61,
    70, 72, 80–1, 87, 95, 148
Diet of Worms 74
dignity 25, 113, 142, 155, 164–5, 170, 172,
    176, 182, 187
diplomacy, diplomatic 57, 61, 108–10, 114,
    120–1
discrimination, non-discrimination 165,
    171, 198n11
Divina Commedia (La) – Inferno 63, 76n13
Doktor Faustus 18
domination 12, 15, 21n17, 32, 74
Dostoyevsky, Fyodor 18
Dresden 140
Durkheim, Émile, Durkheimian 180–1
Dworkin, Ronald 163, 170

Easton, David 4, 65
Economist (The) 149n6, 198n6
economy 14, 55, 62, 64, 95–7, 100, 112,
    127, 147, 168, 171, 177–8; gift 214;
    market 64, 96, 100; political 40–1, 53,
    196
Economy and Society 26
Edelman, Murray 32
egalitarianism, egalitarian 20, 54, 61, 163,
    167, 173n8, 176; luck 86, 165; radical
    168, 178
Egypt 68

Einaudi, Luigi 55n7
Einstein, Albert 119
Eisenstein, Sergej Michajlovič 22n27
electorate, elections 7, 51, 60, 72, 82, 87–8,
    92, 94–5, 147, 172, 202; and draw 84;
    and participation 85
Elements of the Philosophy of Right 164
Emirate of Granada 60
Emmanuel, Arghiri 177
emotion, emotional 39, 66, 68, 112, 147,
    149n12, 151, 181; and solidarity 202–4
empire: British 123n11; Charles the
    Great's 60; Communist 130; Hapsburg
    59; Holy Roman 108, 110, 175; Mongol
    63; Ottoman 73; Persian 48; Roman
    55n1, 59–60, 108; Soviet 121; Spanish
    175
ends-rational (*zweckrational*) 77n25
Engels, Friedrich 9, 12, 14, 21n18, 36, 43n2,
    54, 56n13, 195
English 16, 21n21, 55n3, 59, 77n35, 121,
    123n2, 123n4, 123nn6–7, 195, 202; Bill
    of Rights 173n10; Enlightenment 53;
    Revolution 163; School of International
    Relations 123n4
Enlightenment 40, 53, 61, 73–4, 95–6, 117,
    120, 160, 171, 182, 194
Entlastung see relief
equality/inequality 7, 18, 91, 95–6, 108,
    115, 129, 152, 159, 191, 196; gender
    30, 74, 95, 179; as isonomy 71, 163; and
    liberty 168, 175; and Marx 197; as a
    normative notion 73, 93, 164–7, 173n7;
    political 19, 81–2, 86, 88, 163, 182
Eros and Civilization 196
ETA (Euskadi Ta Askatasuna) 153
ethics 14, 36–7, 40, 43n4, 74, 166, 177, 182,
    187–8, 190–1, 197n1
Ethiopia (Kingdom of) 111, 123n11
ethnos, ethnic 29–30, 59, 68, 85–6, 113, 147,
    153, 170
Europe, European 15, 29, 33, 37, 51, 53,
    57–63, 67–8, 71, 73, 74n12, 74n21,
    75n32, 81, 92, 96, 107, 116–21, 121n3,
    126, 128, 130, 147n9, 150, 161, 174, 178,
    188, 194; Atomic Energy Commission
    118; Central Bank 121; Charter of
    Fundamental Rights 167; Coal and Steel
    Community 118; Commission 121;
    countries 11, 28, 83–4, 144; Court of
    Auditors 121; Court of Human Rights
    202; Court of Justice 121; cultural
    identity 27, 33; culture 152; Eastern 66;
    Enlightenment 72; Eurobureaucracy
    121; history 27, 99n15; institutions
    46; integration 105; meaning 53n5;

Mediterranean area 106; Middle Ages 7, 62, 108, 128; model of democracy 52; modernity 55, 192; parliament 82, 121; people 27, 29; socialism 192; social model 27; South Eastern 71; state 11, 55, 57–9; system 108; university system 41; Western 14, 57–9, 97, 114

European Union (EU) 25, 27, 48, 66–7, 75n32, 112, 114, 116–21, 194

exchange: fair or unequal 177

Fabian Society 53
failed state(s) 14, 20, 33, 64, 122, 153
fanaticism, fanatic 6–7, 53, 72, 74, 96, 117, 123n11, 130, 154
Fascism, Fascist, Fascists 6, 15, 32, 51, 53, 76n11, 86, 97, 111, 113, 116, 154; fanaticism 117; ideologies 167; Italian 101n3, 101n16
fear 47, 50–1, 55nn2–3, 146–7, 149n10, 188
Fear and Politics 55
Federalist (The) 5, 9, 53, 88
federalists 120
federation, federal 28, 40, 53; federative 115, 118, 120
Ferguson, Adam 65
feudal 12, 60–1, 84, 165
Feuerbach, Ludwig 43n2
Fichte, Johann Gottlieb 35n5
Fifteenth Amendment 101n5
Fischer, Ernst 95
force (as guarantee of power) 4, 10–13, 18, 45, 189; military 109–10, 114, 119; monopoly of 28, 57
Foucault, Michel, Foucauldians 15, 18, 133
Fourier, Charles 195
France, French 6, 13, 16, 28, 59–64, 68, 71–3, 77n23, 85, 88, 99, 101n12, 110–12, 120–1, 140, 149n1, 180–1, 191, 195; Declaration of the Rights of Man and of the Citizen 169; democracy 85; Jacobins 162; literature 77n25; people 85; *poujadisme* 101n16; Revolution 25, 29, 68, 73, 85, 152, 163; revolutionaries 181
Frankfurt am Main 195–6; Frankfurt School 55n3, 196
fraternité 62, 73, 182–3
freedom 9, 25, 30, 37, 40, 42, 48–9, 52–3, 72–3, 81, 88–9, 93, 115, 119, 140, 149n6, 152–3, 156, 180, 191, 197; and equality 167–8, 178, 180; modern 169, 173n9; negative 160–1; positive 162–3, 168, 172n1; (specific freedoms of) 53, 56n9, 67, 161, 171

Freud, Sigmund, Freudian 119, 202
Friedrich II (Holy Roman Emperor) 60
Frost/Nixon 22n27
fundamentalism 29, 88, 100, 117, 130
future generations 16, 25, 90, 136, 138, 140, 42–4, 46, 48, 162, 166–7, 179, 192; solidarity with 182, 184

G7, G8, G20 132
Galtung, Johan 117
game 11, 88, 92–3, 120; win-win 16; zero-sum game 16, 123
Gandhi, Mahatma 119, 124n14, 171
gays 7, 113
Gehlen, Arnold 22n28
gender 7, 76n14, 138, 165, 171, 196; equality 30, 74, 95, 166, 179
General Agreement on Trade and Tariffs (GATT) 128
Geneva Conventions 116
genocide 64, 119, 122, 123n11, 143, 162
Germanic 59; -Roman 70
German Ideology (The) 43n2
Germany, German 6, 16, 22n28, 27, 30, 32, 43n2, 43n9, 55n3, 55n6, 56nn12–13, 60, 67–8, 70–1, 76nn10–11, 76n18, 76nn22–3, 77n29, 82, 96, 100, 101n8, 110, 116, 120–1, 123n3, 123n11, 124n14, 136, 149n6, 152–4, 167, 169, 176, 190–1, 196, 198n15; Bundestag 25; *Bundesverfassungsgericht* 204; *Bürgerliches Gesetzbuch* 59; Democratic Republic 94; Federal Republic 25; Germans 66n7, 86; *Lebenswelt* 198n18; literature 77n25; National Socialism 72; Reich 72, 76n11; social-democracy 53; West 62
Gettysburg Address 81
Gini coefficient 129
globalisation, global 69, 99–100, 126–7, 130; challenges 105, 109, 134–6, 139–40, 176, 189; commons 142–5; and democracy 147; governance 131–3, 144; warming
God 76n15, 88, 163
Goethe, Johann Wolfgang von 29
Golden Rule 143, 176
Gospels 143, 176
government 9, 14, 19, 48, 53, 56n9, 95, 100n1, 115, 131, 152, 160; art of 4–5, 69, 97; and democracy 86–8; e- 101; forms of 79–83, 89, 101n9; good 28, 98; mixed 88, 120; representative 20, 83, 85, 161; world 118–19, 122, 132, 137
Gramsci, Antonio 12
Grand Duchy of Tuscany 74–5
Great Depression 62, 164

Great Recession 83, 100, 132
Greece, Greek, Greeks 9, 17, 20n1, 34, 56n10, 64, 67, 71–2, 80, 88, 91, 100n1, 109, 119, 163, 195, 197nn1–2
Greenhouse Gases (GHG) 138, 146, 148, 155

Habermas, Jürgen 43n3, 43n7, 76n22, 92–3, 163, 194, 196–7, 203
Hamilton, Alexander 5, 53
Hamlet 39, 43n8
happiness 7, 17, 25, 53, 188
Haydn, Franz Joseph 197
health care 53, 63, 129, 154–5, 165, 168
Hegel, Hegelian, Hegelianism 32, 35n5, 36, 42, 43n6, 54, 65–6, 76n7, 105, 149, 163–4, 180, 189–90, 193; -Marxian 98, 180
hegemony, hegemonic: (in Gramsci's lexicon) 12; in IR 110, 115, 129
Heidegger, Martin 151
Heisenberg, Werner Karl 40
Henry VIII (of England) 76n4
Heraclitus of Ephesus 5
Herero 123n11
Hiroshima 113, 140, 154
Hirschman, Albert O. 76n23
historia magistra vitae 42, 102n19
history: philosophy of 42, 54, 66, 131, 197; and political philosophy 38, 41–2, 101n2, 101n15, 162
History of the Peloponnesian War 81
Hitler, Adolf 32, 77n34, 113, 120, 124n14, 152, 156n2
Hobbes, Thomas, Hobbesian 9–10, 17, 21n11, 22n26, 40, 42, 50, 52, 55n2, 55n4, 59, 83, 105, 109, 111–12, 114, 117, 123n6, 123n12, 144, 152, 160, 188, 201–2
Hoffmann, Stanley 124n19
Holocaust *see* Shoah
Holsti, Kalevi J. 123n9
Holy Alliance 111
Holy See 34n1, 73
Horkheimer, Max 101n3, 195–7
House of Cards 22n27
House of Lords 76n8, 88
Human Development Index (HDI) 166
Hume, David 181
Hungary 68–9
Huntington, Samuel 28, 98, 102n21
Hussein, Saddam 111
Husserl, Edmund 198n18
Huxley, Aldous 195

Iberian peninsula, countries 59, 121
ideal: theory 141, 179, 187, 193–5, 197; types 6, 39

idealism: practical 112, 123; theoretical 35
ideals 3, 26, 55, 65, 69, 81, 87, 163
Idea of Equality (The) 173n5
ideas: (role of) 12, 18, 21n18, 34, 99
identity 28, 31; conflict 6, 57, 140; cultural 29; cultural and social 32; in democracy 32, 148, 203; disruption of 74, 91; humankind 147; and legitimacy 29, 157; mirror and wall 29, 31; not citizenship 32; pathologies of 28–9, 34n4, 74; political 6, 24, 27–32, 37, 40, 73, 181, 202–3; politics of 28, 30, 32; shifts in 40, 74; social 29; and symbols 32
ideology, ideological 13, 43, 54, 62, 94, 111, 113, 118, 154, 159, 191; conflict 5–7; definition of 36, 38
immigration *see* migration
India, Indian 69, 73, 85, 119, 123n11, 128, 143, 171, 176; Ocean 63
influence 3, 11–13, 16, 89
Inglehart, Ronald 198n20
Institute of Social Research 55n3, 195
institution(s), institutional 9, 11, 20, 22, 28, 35, 45, 47, 65, 92; action 203; Bretton Woods 128; definition of 49–50; history of 52, 88, 91, 93, 101n2, 168; innovation 148, 193; international 107, 118–19, 122–3, 124n19, 129, 137, 162; and legitimacy 25, 30, 77, 147; market 170
integration, integrationist 7, 9, 21n11, 30, 107, 118, 122, 181, 196
interdependence 127, 129
interest 3, 5, 10, 15, 37, 50, 65, 85, 110, 121, 146, 170, 178, 181; national 132, 141
intergovernmental 120–1, 132, 137
international 6, 11, 17, 24, 38, 48, 50, 63, 67–8, 90, 97, 105, 107–9, 115, 126, 130–1, 140–1, 173n6, 182, 189; anarchy 110, 112, 114, 122, 192; covenants 169; Criminal Court 179; institutions 100, 111, 118, 129, 132, 147, 149n5; International Relations 5, 41, 123n3; justice 177, 179; law 68, 71, 108–9, 116, 169, 171, 179; Monetary Fund (IMF) 128, 173n6; order 58, 112–13; peace 91, 98, 116, 153
IPCC (Intergovernmental Panel on Climate Change) 107
IRA (Irish Republican Army) 153
Iran, Iranian 34, 73, 75, 82, 97, 136; Republic of 34n1
Iraq, Iraqi 111, 152, 191
irrationalism, irrationalist, irrational 31, 51, 77n25, 147, 204

Islam, Islamic 6–7, 21n10, 30, 35n6, 55n4, 73–4, 108, 163; civilization 117; culture 130, 154; religion 130; Republic of Iran 34n1
Islamism, Islamist 7, 21n10, 117; fanaticism 116–17, 130; fundamentalism 29, 88; jihadism 74; 'state' 191; terrorism 92, 154
Italy, Italian 16, 32, 43n9, 53, 55n7, 59–60, 62, 71, 76n10, 82, 85–6, 96, 101n3, 101n8, 110–11, 120–1, 123n11, 152, 154, 167; fascism 101n16; literature 77n25; *Risorgimento* 69
ius: *ad bellum* 116; *gentium* 68; *in bello* 110, 113, 116–17, 152
iustum potentiae equilibrium 110
Ivan the Terrible I–II 22n27

Jacobins 162
Japan, Japanese 12, 59, 63, 123n8
Jaspers, Karl 137
Jay, John 53
Jefferson, Thomas 29, 61
Jehovah's Witnesses 113
Jews, Jewish 30, 84, 102n18, 113, 124n14, 153, 195
jihadism 7, 74, 191
Johnson, Lyndon B. 101n5, 198n9
Johnson, Samuel 86
Joyce, James 76n13
Judaism 21n21, 73, 163
Julius Caesar (tragedy) 18
justice, just/unjust 20n2, 37–8, 110, 143, 175–82, 185nn1–2, 193, 197; global 115–32; international criminal 108, 177, 179; theory of 143, 176, 178, 180, 197; war 115–16, 152–3

Kant, Immanuel, Kantian 22n26, 42, 48, 53, 105, 111–12, 115, 117–19, 143, 161, 165, 170, 177–8, 180, 188–90, 194, 202; morality 189
Kelsen, Hans 93
Keohane, Robert 124n19
Kermanshah 34
Keynesian deficit 129
KGB (Komitet gosudarstvennoy bezopasnosti) 75n3
Khmer Rouge regime 64, 153, 162
King, Martin Luther, Jr. 101n5, 198n9
Kirchheimer, Otto 196
Kissinger, Henry 122–3, 192
Kongzi (Confucius) 52
Koselleck, Reinhart 21n16, 43n11, 102n19
Kotz, Nick 198n9
Kramer, Stanley 142

Kuwait 111, 116, 152
Kyoto Protocol 138, 144

Labour government 53, 62
laissez-faire 53, 55n12
Lasswell, Harold 32
Latin 16, 21n14, 50, 58–9, 76n15, 76n17, 169, 175, 197n4
Latin America 68, 99
law 11, 14, 18, 24, 26, 30, 33–4, 43, 52, 58, 64–5, 70–1, 74, 77, 81–2, 160, 169, 181; Basic Law for the Federal Republic of Germany/*Grundgesetz* 25; constitutional/fundamental 49, 70, 160, 189; international 68, 108–9, 116; in Kant's view 115; and liberty 161; philosophy of 65, 196; Roman 12, 176; tort 142, 177; universality of 71
Law of Peoples (The) 43n5, 68
League of Nations (Society of Nations) 111
Lebanon 20, 111
legitimacy, legitimate 11, 17, 19, 21n17, 57, 60, 71, 176, 197; democratic 148; international 110, 114–15, 132, 147; and legitimation 24–8; and obligation 33–4; types of 80
Lenin (Vladimir Il'ič Ul'janov) 54, 90
Les Trente Glorieuses 128
Leviathan 55n2, 123n12
Leviathan, Leviathanic 21n11, 50, 52, 112, 144, 188; Super- 144, 152
Lexington 72
lex sub rege 70
LGBT (lesbian, gay, bisexual, transgender) people 7
liberal-democratic 29–30, 48, 51, 63, 69, 72–3, 82, 88, 94, 159, 178
liberalism, liberal 31–2, 53–4, 55n5, 55n7, 61–3, 67, 90, 162, 168, 197; and communitarianism 76n21, 180, 184; economic 39, 100; and war 115
libertarianism 54, 56n9, 179
liberty *see* freedom
Liberty of the Ancients Compared with That of the Moderns (The) 173n9
Libya 20, 123n11
life: and dignity 155–8; form 15, 68, 164, 205; plan 3, 162, 165–6, 203; right to 171; world (*Lebenswelt*) 196, 198n18
Lijphart, Arend 89
Lincoln, Abraham 81
Livy (Titus Livius): Commentary on 9
Locke, John 22n26, 40, 53, 83, 178
Löwenthal, Leo 195
Luhmann, Niklas 196

Lukács, György 15
Luke (Gospel) 176
Lukes, Steven Michael 15, 21n22
Luther, Martin, Lutheran 60, 74, 160
Luxembourg 121
Lying in Politics 198n6
Lyotard, Jean-François 198n7

Macbeth (tragedy) 18
McCarthy, Cormac 142
Machiavelli, Niccolò, Machiavellian 9–11, 17, 40, 42, 59, 79–80, 88, 149n9, 189–90, 192, 197n4
MacIntyre, Alisdair 180
Madison, James 5, 53, 202
Magna Carta 173n10
Malaysia 97
Man, the State and War 124n19, 192
Manchesterian liberals 120
Manhattan Project 147
Manifesto of the Communist Party 14, 54
Mann, Thomas 18
Manzoni, Alessandro 123n3
Mao, Zedong (Chairman Mao), Maoist 31, 98; post- 28
Marcuse, Herbert 195–6
market 62, 96, 100, 147, 165, 171; effects of 182–3; myth of 132; *vs.* plan 100; *vs.* state 53–4, 55n5; world 128
Marx, Groucho 146
Marx, Karl, Marxian 9, 12, 14, 21n18, 21n20, 36, 54, 56nn12–13, 65–6, 76nn18–19, 99, 102n18, 163–4, 177, 189–90, 195, 197, 198n19, 198n21
Marxism, Marxist 5, 14–15, 39, 42, 43n2, 54, 72, 198n15; *Austromarxismus* 101n6; critical Western 15; orientation 195
mass, masses 32, 55, 62, 91, 97; democracy 19, 82; and political life 62
Massachusetts 72
Matthew (Gospel) 76n16
Mazzini, Giuseppe 69, 101n6
Mead, George Herbert 173n2
meaning 3, 50, 63, 116, 155, 180; death as destroyer of 151
meritocracy 81, 97, 165, 178
metus legis 51
Michels, Roberto 173n7
Middle Ages 7, 38, 64, 68, 76n17, 108, 110, 128, 130
Middle East 7, 117–18
migration, emigration, immigration, migrant 30, 51, 59, 73, 86, 92, 118, 122, 127, 133, 138, 146–7, 167, 179–80, 184, 195
Milan 123n3

military 5, 11, 13, 57, 59, 61–2, 74, 82, 109–14, 116, 146, 152
Mill, John Stuart 83
Millennium Development Goals 118, 132
Miller, David 179
Ming dynasty 64
Minimal State (The) 180
MIRVs (Multiple Independently targetable Reentry Vehicles) 146
Missile Technology Control Regime (MTCR) 149n5
MNCs (multinational corporations) 107, 133
modernity 40, 57–8, 63, 68, 74, 80, 90, 109–10, 113, 117, 130, 140, 163, 170, 187; modernisation 20, 59, 63, 67, 100
Monnet, Jean 120
Montesquieu (Jean-Louis de Secondat, Baron de) 53, 80
moral 30, 33, 37, 49, 52, 88, 95, 140, 142, 165, 172, 177–81; morality 40, 74, 142, 155, 166, 187–92, 194, 197n1, 202; moral philosophy 38, 43n4, 75, 86, 143, 157, 162, 170
More, Thomas 195
Morgenthau, Hans 17, 77n24, 124n19
Mosca, Gaetano 173n7
movement: Chinese protest 81; democratic 82; Enlightenment 73; freedom of 171; *indignados* 101n17; Iranian Green 82; mass 55, 72; national liberation 72; Peron's 101n16; populist 91, 202; *Poujadisme* 101n16; protest 58, 128–9, 195; totalitarian 96; *Uomo Qualunque* 101n16; women's 62; workers 69, 162–3; youth 98
Mozart, Wolfgang Amadeus 197
Muhammad (the Prophet) 55n4
Mussolini, Benito 32
Mussorgsky, Modest Petrovič 13, 29
myth 32, 51, 55, 71, 91, 100, 132; demythologise 80, 93; mythology 9, 197

naeminem laedere 176
Nagasaki 113, 154
Namaqua 123n11
Namibia 123n11
Napoleon, Bonaparte, Napoleonic 60, 70, 111, 120; anti- 112
nation, nation state, national 59–60, 67–9, 71–2, 101n6, 129, 132, 167, 179, 182, 184; and democracy 84–6, 97, 133, 147; in the EU 102–1; postnational 29, 50, 67, 121; supranational 121, 137
nationalism, nationalistic 6, 29, 55, 68–9, 122, 184

Native Americans 109
NATO (North Atlantic Treaty Organization) 111, 117, 123n5
Natural History of Civil Society (A) 65
Nazism, Nazi 12, 54, 77n34, 88, 101n3, 116, 153–4, 176, 195; fanaticism 117
ne cives ad arma veniant 161
Neo-Aristotelians 17
neo-conservative, neocon 118, 123, 191
neo-institutionalism 122, 124n19
neoliberalism, neoliberal 54, 100, 102n23, 128–9, 132, 159, 161, 164, 183
Netherlands, the 110, 121
Neumann, Franz 55n3, 196, 198n17
New Deal 62, 77n31, 100, 164, 194
New England 74
New York City 55n3, 100
NGOs (Non-Governmental Organisations) 65
Nicomachean Ethics 177
Niebuhr, Reinhold 124n19
Nietzsche, Friedrich 167, 173n7
Nieuwenhuis, Domela 21n20
non-violence, non-violent 5, 72, 171
norm(s) 33, 70–1, 81, 109–10, 116, 123, 160–1, 169
normative, normativity 27, 157, 179, 182–4, 187–9, 191–2; and Critical Theory 197; and democracy 92, 98; and history 42, 66; and ideal theory 193–4, 148; internationally 115, 118, 132, 142–3; and political philosophy 36, 39, 73, 79, 89
North America 39, 63, 196
Northern Ireland 153
North Korea 55, 111, 130; Democratic People's Republic of 80, 94, 169
Nozick, Robert 54, 179–80
Nye, Joseph 124n19

Obama, Barack 137, 146
obedience 49, 52–3, 171
obligation 24, 33, 38, 87, 142–3, 146, 157, 162, 169–70, 181, 192
Octavian (later Caesar Divi Filius Augustus) 55n1
Of War 112
Old Testament 143, 176
ombudsman 148
omission(s) 16, 142–3, 148, 151, 155
One-Dimensional Man (The) 196
On the Beach 142
On the Jewish Question 102n18
order 7, 12; cosmic 23, 176; democratic 53; imperial 48; international 58, 110–12, 114; just 48; legal 71–2; models of 54–5;

as pattern of regularity 47; peaceful 153; political 34, 48–50, 52–3, 110; world 31
Oriental 151
Orwell, George 195

pacifism 117–21, 124n14, 152–3
pact(s) 21n11, 38, 48, 70, 110, 114, 169
pacta sunt servanda 48
Pakistan 7, 69
Pareto, Vilfredo 173n7
Paris 72, 111; *Commune* 14; Congresses of Paris 111; Paris (Climate) Agreement 118, 138, 144–5, 148; Treaty of Paris (1951) 120
Parsons, Talcott 9, 21n21
Parthenon 9
passion 50, 55n2, 87, 162, 202–3; and ideas 34
peace: *pax augustea* 55n1; of Westphalia 60, 109–10
peace, peaceful 31, 48, 50, 55nn1–2, 88, 108–9, 111, 114, 117, 119, 123n10; democratic 91, 115; domestic/internal 97, 100, 160; enforcement 153; and EU 120–3; and globalisation 129; international 91, 116; and nuclear weapons 136; perpetual 112, 117–18; world 122
pension system 62, 92, 184
Pericles 81, 189
Perpetual Peace 115, 119
Persepolis 48
Persia, Persian 34, 48
Phenomenology of Spirit 163, 190
philosophy 20, 34, 40, 42, 50, 65, 137, 146, 170, 187; history of 33, 42, 176; moral 43–4, 86–7, 162, 180, 192; political 15, 17, 19, 21, 28, 36–9, 41, 43, 50, 52, 73, 112, 135, 148, 153, 181, 185n1, 189, 194, 201, 204–5; social 39
physics 25, 40, 100, 135
Pizzorno, Alessandro 21n8
Plato 48, 79, 100n1, 176, 178, 190
Plutarch 204
Pocock, J.G.A. 198n5
Pogge, Thomas 149n11, 179
Poland 68–9, 152
policy, policy making 15–16, 19, 25, 90, 99, 105, 127, 166; analysis 41; symbolic 32
polis, poleis 3, 5, 34, 52, 79, 109, 123n1, 163
politheism 9, 21n13, 42, 88, 96
Political Liberalism 178
political science 24, 27, 32, 40–2, 75, 173n7, 192, 202
political theory 7, 41, 66, 79, 131, 170, 196

Politics 164
Politics Among Nations 77n24
Politics as a Profession 18
Pollock, Friedrich 195
polyarchy 96, 109, 146
Polybius 88
Pope Francis 146
Pope Leo III 60
Popper, Karl 189–90
Popular Front 21n9
populism, populist 19, 51, 84, 86, 91–2, 101nn14–16, 115, 122, 129, 133, 148, 183, 196, 202
Porto Alegre, Brazil 128
positivism, positivist 4, 40, 71, 197
posterity *see* future generations
postmaterialistic 196, 198n20
postmodern, postmodernism 32, 51, 140, 191
post-modernity, post-modern 120, 140, 144–5, 189
Poujade, Pierre 101n16
poverty 81–2, 86, 97, 100, 107, 128–9, 157, 161, 179
Prague 95, 137
Prince (The) 11, 59
Profession and Vocation of Politics (The) 22n25
progress, progressive 31, 42, 54, 140–1, 162, 191–2
proletariat *see* class, working
property 47, 53, 56n9, 61, 79, 169, 171, 180
Protestant 21n21, 74
Protestant Ethic and the Spirit of Capitalism (The) 21n21
prudence (*phronesis*) 4, 187
Prussia, Prussian 59, 112, 189
Przeworski, Adam 82
Pushkin, Aleksandr Sergeevič 29
Putnam, Robert 92

Québec 32

Racine, Jean 18
racism 28, 34n4, 51, 69, 86, 123n11, 167, 175
RAF (Rote Armee Fraktion) 154
rationality, rational-irrational, rationalised 6, 20, 26, 31, 51, 55, 116, 130, 136, 147, 166, 196–7; choice 40–1, 202; ends-rational (*zweckrational*) and value-rational (*wertrational*) 77n25
Rawls, John, Rawlsian 17, 21n23, 38, 43n7, 54, 68, 72, 97, 112, 163–4, 166, 173n4, 176, 178–80, 193–5, 198n14, 202
Reagan, Ronald 54, 55n5

realism, realist: *vs.* idealism 191, 194–5; neo 122–3, 124n19; political 10, 17, 28, 40, 93, 124n19, 136, 187–8, 190–1, 197n3, 203
Reason 61, 141, 188, 194
reason: public 179; of state 18, 189
recognition, recognising 6, 26, 28, 30, 58, 60–1, 96, 110, 161, 165, 175; among states 107–8
Red Brigades 154
Red Guards 162
reductionism 5, 32, 203–4
Reformation 43n9, 60, 160
region, regionalism 29, 85, 101n15, 111, 114, 118, 145, 167; in the EU 121–2
relief 20, 22n28
religion 6, 14, 30, 34, 60, 64, 73–4, 83, 88, 144, 151, 171–2; civil 202; and war 60, 110, 119
Renaissance 40, 61, 96, 149n9, 160, 163, 171
Renan, Ernest 86
representation, representative 20, 83–5, 87, 89–90, 92, 97, 102n17, 122; external 61
Republic 100n1, 176
resources 4–5, 21, 24–6, 63, 138, 143; equality of 165
res publica 33, 60, 64, 75n2, 76n15
revolution 11, 14, 28, 54, 71–2, 85, 109, 149; American 25, 72, 85; bourgeois 102n18; China's Cultural 162; Copernican 169; 'enemies of the' 88; English 163; Fourth Industrial 92; French 25, 29, 68, 72, 152, 163, 182; proletarian 66; Russian (October Revolution) 21n9, 25, 90, 162, 190
revolutionary 26, 99, 111–12, 177, 191, 203; anti-revolutionary 111; post-revolutionary 28, 54
rex sub lege 70
Rhineland 152
Ricardo, David 177
Richard III (tragedy) 18
right(s) 6, 32, 83, 87, 94, 96, 142, 148, 161, 167, 182; to bear arms 75n1; civil 88, 171–2; claim 169–71; divine 68; environmental 172; fourth generation of 171; fundamental 70, 91, 96, 169, 171; to go to war (*ius ad bellum*) 116; human 71, 73, 97–8, 117, 130, 163, 169, 172, 173n11, 179, 188–9, 192, 196–7; liberty 169; to life 25, 63, 170; meta 172; moral 170, 188; political 94, 169, 171–2, 198n14; social 53, 99, 162, 170–2; to survival 172; universalization of 86; of women 93, 130

Rio de Janeiro 138
Risorgimento 69
Robespierre, Maximilien 25
Roma 113
Romania 167
Romanticism 180
Rome, Roman, Romans 9, 43, 59–60, 64, 67–8, 76n4, 108–10, 128, 140, 161, 176, 189; ancient 19, 67–8, 114; Church 60; empire 55n1, 59–60; Germanic-Roman 70; Holy Roman Empire 108, 110, 175; law 12; mythology 9; Napoleonic-Roman 70; *Pax Romana* 48, 114; Senate 9, 70; Treaty of 120
Roosevelt, Eleanor 198n11
Roosevelt, Franklin Delano 53, 55n5, 62, 77n31
Rosselli, Carlo 53
Rothbard, Murray N. 54
Rousseau, Jean Jacques, Rousseauian 22n26, 49, 53, 83, 161, 178, 202
Ruggie, John 124n19
rule of law 20, 48, 53, 64, 71, 77, 80, 82, 91, 160, 163
Russell, Bertrand 137
Russia, Russian 29, 55, 59, 69, 91, 122, 136, 191; Federation 69–70, 75; Revolution 25, 90, 162, 190

Sagan, Scott D. 136, 149n3
salus: humani generis 141; *reipublicae* 140–1, 189
salus reipublicae suprema lex esto 140, 189
Sandel, Michael 180, 185n3
Sartori, Giovanni 91
Saudi Arabia 34n1, 73, 75
Scandinavian countries 149n6
Scarry, Elaine 153
Scharpf, Fritz 27
Schelling, Friedrich Wilhelm Joseph von 32, 35n5
Schelling, Thomas 136, 149n9
Schengen countries 124n16
Scheuerman, William E. 198n10
Schiller, Friedrich 123n2
Schmidt, Vivien 102n23
Schmitt, Carl 9, 17, 21n12, 72, 77nn34–5, 192
Schuman, Maurice 120
Schumpeter, Joseph, Schumpeterian 93, 132, 173n7
Schütz, Alfred 198n18
Scotland, Scottish 53, 61, 65, 76n8
security 27, 47, 72, 92; dilemma 141, 197n3; in the EU 121; external/international 53, 109, 111, 115–16, 118, 123n10, 140, 146, 194; social 62, 100, 165, 172, 184
self 19, 52, 162; centred 48, 73, 144; defence 58, 73, 116; destruction 138, 143; identification 6, 28–9; interest 5–6, 33, 40, 66, 90, 92, 108, 123, 141–4, 180, 182, 193, 197, 201–2; realization 9, 162–3, 172n1; rule 19–20, 27, 108, 152
Sen, Amartya 165
Shakespeare, William 18, 34, 43n8
Sherman, William T. 152
Shia 74
Shoah 69, 77n27, 113
Sieyès, Emmanuel-Joseph 68
silent inter arma leges 109
Singapore 97
Sinti 113
slavery, slaves, enslavement 52, 61, 163; of women 7, 74, 116, 130
social democracy, social-democratic 15, 54, 56, 133
socialism, socialist 72, 167, 194–5; liberal 53; Soviet 21, 72, 94–5, 99, 159
society 9, 14–15, 30, 65, 90, 95, 168, 177–8, 181, 183, 190; civil 65–6, 99; classless/communist 9, 54, 72, 164; knowledge 66, 82; and politics 4, 15, 27, 39, 54, 196, 198n19; world 66, 130; *see also* anarchy
sociology, sociologism, sociological 32, 39–40, 67, 181, 198n18, 201, 204
solidarity 66, 73, 86, 135, 153, 172, 175–6, 179–84, 203
sovereignty, sovereign 58, 85, 89, 116, 118, 133, 137, 160–70; external 107–8, 110; national 114, 147; popular 61–2, 68, 91, 93
Spirit (*logos, Geist*) 54, 66, 163, 189–90
stability 27, 30, 91, 110, 114, 147; Financial Stability Board 132
state(s) (*only occurrences with specific links to the main entry are considered*): and bureaucracy 54, 66; and death penalty 74–5; failed 14, 20, 33, 64, 122, 153; and international politics 96, 100, 123, 129, 136–7, 140, 160–1, 188; liberal and liberal-democratic 30, 62–3, 81, 132; modern 60–2, 141; and the monopoly of force 10, 57, 75n1; nation 29, 67, 132, 179, 189; and rights 169–72; social/welfare 19, 31, 55n5, 59, 66, 94, 161, 165; sovereign 58, 107–8; terrorism 12, 54, 80, 153; and war 118, 137, 145
strategy, strategic 5, 68, 73, 101n13, 122, 149n9, 201–3
suffrage 53, 67, 91, 95, 161
suicide, suicidal 113, 130, 138, 154–6, 191

survival of: civilization 134; group 181; humankind 108, 113, 144, 149n9, 157, 169, 172; individuals 52, 144, 152
symbol, symbolism, symbolic 28, 30–2, 51, 146
sympathy 181, 185nn6–7, 202
system theory, systemic 64, 66, 192, 196

tax, taxes 10–11, 57, 61, 64, 129, 166, 173n18, 202
teleology, teleological 3, 17, 48, 52, 180, 188
terrorism 51, 92, 118, 130, 135–6, 149n3, 152–4; state 12, 54, 80
time (as element of politics) 16, 25, 28–30, 49, 90–1, 117, 143, 145, 151; universalism 38, 142, 148, 179, 184
totalitarianism, totalitarian 21n10, 62, 71, 74, 80, 83, 88, 96, 115, 140, 159, 202
tradition, traditional 25–6, 29–30, 68, 181, 195, 197
truth, post-truth 6, 51, 88, 101n16, 198n6

unicuique suum 176
universalism, universalistic, universality 3, 6, 12, 20n2, 38, 69, 85; universalization 86, 98
utilitarianism, utilitarian 75, 170, 176, 178, 180, 188

value(s) 28, 30–1, 50, 68, 81, 83, 85, 152, 175–6, 181, 183, 193; Asian 97, 163; freedom (*Wertfreiheit*) 40–1; labour theory of 177; laden 15, 40; politheism of 9, 42, 47–8; post-materialistic 83, 196; rational (*wertrational*) 77; state and 72–4
veil of ignorance 138, 178

violence 7, 11, 48, 71–2, 75n1, 110, 112, 117, 119, 151, 160, 181
virtue 25, 162, 178
vocation (*Beruf*) 20, 190–1, 198n7
vulnerability 143, 166, 170

wage 99, 127, 163, 167, 177, 202
war 5, 7, 18, 31, 52, 58, 60–1, 71–3, 85–6, 105, 107–20, 122–3, 123n2, 123n7, 123n11, 124n15, 124n19, 131, 136–47, 151–4, 156, 192–3, 202; American Civil 112, 146, 152–3, 191; Clausewitzian 113; climate 138; Cold 6, 113–16, 136–7, 191; Crimean 111; cyber 11; English Civil 123n6; Falklands 21n3, 113; fear of 51; First World (Great War) 62, 69, 82, 111–13, 119, 123n3, 129, 149, 152, 163, 182, 190–1, 198n7; holy 96; ideological 136; Iraq 191; nuclear 51, 111, 113, 123, 123n8, 134, 137–8, 146, 152; Peloponnesian 81, 101n4, 149n10, 188; of religion 60, 111; Second World 62, 69, 82, 92, 99, 110, 112–14, 116, 123, 140, 149, 152, 163, 191; Seven Years 76n5; Spanish Civil 113; Third World 113; Thirty Years' 109; Vietnam 118; Yugoslav 122
warming, global *see* climate, change
weapons 61, 69, 75n1, 109, 113, 141, 161; nuclear 116, 126, 135–7, 144, 154, 191–2
welfare, welfarism 92, 108, 164–5, 168, 178, 184, 188; *see also* state
wellbeing 27, 72, 87, 140, 164, 170, 176, 178
will 5, 10, 33, 37, 66, 89, 91, 111, 115, 120–1, 170; the people's 27, 82, 88
women 5, 7, 61–2, 93, 95, 130, 154, 166, 189, 171, 204